Domestic Programs of the
American Presidents

Acknowledgments

We wish to thank Charles F. Faber for writing the foreword. We acknowledge the help of the librarians of the Des Moines Public Library, both at the main library and the south side library. We appreciate the assistance of Pamela K. Faber, who ordered and checked out books for us.

We wish to thank our secondary school English teachers, Dr. Signi Falk of Coe College, and Dr. Paul Burke of Grandview College, who taught us how to write. Inez McAlister Faber provided inspiration for learning and writing.

Richard B. Faber
Elizabeth A. Bedford

To Pamela Faber, wife and mother.
To Fred Bedford, son-in-law and husband.

Domestic Programs of the American Presidents

A Critical Evaluation

By Richard B. Faber *and*
Elizabeth A. Bedford

Foreword by Charles F. Faber

McFarland & Company, Inc., Publishers
Jefferson, North Carolina, and London

Library of Congress Cataloguing-in-Publication Data

Faber, Richard B., 1932–
    Domestic programs of the American presidents : a critical
evaluation / by Richard B. Faber and Elizabeth A. Bedford ; foreword
by Charles F. Faber.
        p.   cm.
    Includes bibliographical references and index.

    ISBN 978-0-7864-3183-0
    softcover : 50# alkaline paper ∞

    1. United States— Politics and government.   2. United States—
Politics and government — Philosophy.   3. Presidents— United
States— History.   4. Political culture — United States— History.
I. Bedford, Elizabeth A., 1980–   II. Title.
E183.F34   2008
973 — dc22   2008004075

British Library cataloguing data are available

On the cover: foreground Presidential Seal; background ©2008
Shutterstock

Manufactured in the United States of America

McFarland & Company, Inc., Publishers
  Box 611, Jefferson, North Carolina 28640
    www.mcfarlandpub.com

Table of Contents

Foreword

by CHARLES F. FABER

When the Framers of the Constitution met behind closed doors and shuttered windows in Philadelphia that hot summer of 1787, they struggled with many questions. One dilemma they faced was how to create a strong enough central government to hold the nation together without giving the government so much power it could be tyrannical. Among the attempts to deal with this dilemma was an effort to invent a tripartite central government — three equal branches — with a separation of powers among them. This was a new experiment in government — one that had never been tried before.

In their wisdom the Founders wrote the Constitution in general terms whenever possible, being specific only when necessary. They decreed that the executive branch would be headed by a president, elected for a limited term of office and subject to the rule of law. Few specific presidential duties in relation to programs either domestic or foreign are mandated by the Constitution. The most important responsibilities of the president are to see that the laws passed by Congress are faithfully executed, to recommend such for their measures as he deems necessary and expedient, to appoint and hold accountable the principal of the executive departments, and to appoint judges and all other officers of the United States whose appointments are not otherwise provided for in the Constitution.

The young nation was fortunate that in George Washington it had as its first chief executive a man who understood the inherent tension between the need for a strong central government and the necessity of avoiding too much concentration of power in the hands of one man. He wisely eschewed all the trappings of monarchy. As the first president of the fledgling republic, Washington navigated uncharted waters. Every action he took set a new precedent.

One of the major problems facing this new president was the state of the economy: inflation had caused the currency to be depreciated. There was a division of opinion on whether the central government should assume war debts of the states. Under Washington's leadership a compromise was reached, allowing for the assumption of debts and the creation of a national bank. Neither of these actions was specifically authorized by the Constitution, yet Washington was able to accomplish them, thus expanding the power of the presidency. Over the years Americans have come to accept that one of the president's main responsibilities in the domestic area is management of the nation's economy. Andrew Jackson attempted to assert presidential control of the nation's finances. The president's role in the budgetary process was strengthened by presidents Polk, Taft, Wilson and Harding. Franklin D. Roosevelt put the full force of his office behind an effort to pull the nation out of a severe economic depression.

Lyndon Johnson proposed a Great Society program, including Medicare for the elderly, educational assistance for the young, food for the hungry, housing for the homeless, legal protection for African-Americans, poverty grants for the poor, rehabilitation for the disabled, higher benefits for the unemployed, fair labeling for consumers, civil rights and a safer environment for all. None of these presidential initiatives were specifically authorized by the Constitution nor were many promoted by early presidents.

Increases in the power to influence other aspects of American life have perhaps not been so dramatic as those in the economic arena, but they nonetheless exist. Readers of this book will find countless examples of this development. The power of the presidency has increased tremendously since Washington's time. It has not been a steady increase; strong presidents tend to increase the power of the office. Weak presidents sometimes (but not always) let some of that power slip. It is an ebb and flow of peaks and valleys; each peak is higher than the previous peak and each new valley is not as low as the previous valley.

Introduction

The Constitution is not specific about presidential powers and duties in the area of domestic programs. The Constitution says that Congress shall have the power to promote the general welfare of the United States and to make all laws that shall be necessary and proper. The president executes those laws and recommends further acts that he feels are necessary.

Much has been written about U.S. presidents, but our work is the only one that in one volume deals with domestic programs only and includes all the presidents from Washington to George W. Bush. The chapters on some of the early presidents are shorter than later ones. The office of the presidency has grown in the area of domestic programs since 1900.

In this study every topic not considered foreign relations is considered domestic. Even so, there is some overlap, as in treaty ratification and in tariffs.

No ratings or rankings appear in this book. It contains information, analysis, interpretation and commentary about domestic programs.

Emphasis is placed on domestic programs involving meliorative reform. The first presidents, Washington, John Adams, Jefferson and Madison, were revolutionaries throwing off colonial rule and establishing constitutional reform. Jeffersonian democracy and Jacksonian democracy reformed the United States by bringing government to the common man. Abraham Lincoln led the United States through the Civil War and his domestic program brought about the elimination of slavery.

There were presidents who were twentieth-century reformers: both Roosevelts, Wilson, Truman, Kennedy and Lyndon Johnson improved the lives of Americans; particularly Franklin D. Roosevelt, who led our nation through the worst depression in history.

Although the co-authors are both Democrats, Republican presidents like Abraham Lincoln and Theodore Roosevelt are praised for their domestic programs. Our goal is to describe each president's domestic programs factually and to analyze and assess them in terms of their wisdom, effectiveness and benefit (or harm) to the nation's well-being.

George Washington

George Washington, war hero and president of the Constitutional Convention, was sworn in as the first president of the United States on April 30, 1789. He had been elected unanimously by the Electoral College. He was also elected unanimously to his second term in 1792.

"The top priority items during the first presidential term were domestic in nature — organizational matters for the new government and implementation of systems that would impact on the daily lives of citizens in each state. These were topics about which George Washington had exceptional talent and skills; they suited his well-organized, logical, meticulous, judicious, firm mind."[1]

Washington chose the department heads who later became his Cabinet. Alexander Hamilton was the Secretary of Treasury; Thomas Jefferson became Secretary of State; Henry Knox was chosen for Secretary of War; and Edmund Randolph was selected for Attorney General.

Alexander Hamilton, Secretary of Treasury, brilliant in the field of finance, presented to Congress his First Report on Public Credit in 1790. There were three kinds of debt: a foreign debt of $11 million, domestic war debt of $40 million and state war debts of $25 million. Hamilton proposed the federal government assume these debts. At first the proposals were defeated by Southern states that had largely paid off their debts. Then a famous dinner took place at Jefferson's where Hamilton was promised the assumption of state debts in return for the location of the national capital on the Potomac. Washington chose the exact location.

Hamilton's department was the most complex. Appointed and confirmed to manage the nation's finances, credit, banking, accounting and the collection of taxes, he also had under his jurisdiction the customs department, the beginning coast guard, lighthouses and the Post Office. Hamilton asked Congress for the authority to make all purchases for the entire government, but it was such a burdensome job that Congress created a new office, Purveyor of Public Supplies, in 1795. Congress also asked the secretary of the treasury to provide statements of receipts and expenditures of all public money as well as plans for improving federal revenues.

The president had power to appoint new executive department heads but the right to remove them was a critical issue. The president's right of removal passed in the House. In the Senate a tie vote was broken by the vice president to keep centralized control in the executive branch strong.

In his first inaugural address, George Washington said the foundation of his domestic policy would be the "immutable principles of private morality." He sought a balance between agriculture and industry. Even though he was becoming more urban, he clung to the belief that agriculture, represented by the self-sufficient yeoman, was of primary importance to the United States.

Washington was a slave owner. He stopped buying slaves in 1772, but he continued to use them. When he left Philadelphia, his slaves there were left to de facto freedom. In his will Washington provided for the freeing of all the rest of the slaves after his widow's death. The slavery issue was one that could tear the new nation apart. According to Nordham[2] it was intentionally avoided at the national level and left to the states.

George Washington did not have a good record with minorities. Slaves, Indians and women were not considered citizens and were not permitted to vote.

Washington favored Congress avoiding the slavery issue. He believed unity grounded in order was more important for the stability and survival of the nation than liberty and happiness. Justice and equality were not only lesser values than order but dependent upon order. According to Burns and Dunn,[3] the reverse was true and Washington failed to understand the proper balance among three values: life, liberty, and the pursuit of happiness.

The new government considered Indians "independent powers" and dealt with them through treaties. The government also recognized Indian ownership of tribal land and tried to buy it from them. The American policy was negotiation, land purchases, shows of liberality, guarantees of protection from encroaching whites, and assurances of trade and education. Indians saw it differently: a pattern of white advances, Indian defense, and white retaliation. President Washington insisted on moderation, patience and justice, expressing concern for the Indians' plight because the "poor wretches" and "ignorant savages" had no newspapers in which to air grievances. Only one side of the story became known — the white side. Washington wanted to establish a conviction in the minds of the Indians of U.S. love of justice and good faith. "Government agents will not defraud you," he assured the chiefs of Seneca nation, "or to assist in defrauding you of your lands or other things."[4] He insisted treaties be held sacred. But as a last resort, after negations failed, Washington sent a force of 2000 into Ohio Territory in October 1790. General St. Clair led an expedition which met disaster.

He waged war with the Indians until defeating them in the Battle of Fallen Timbers in 1794. This temporarily ended the Indian threat in the Northwest. In the Southwest Indians were pacified by treaties.

Washington left the question of the Bill of Rights to Madison and the House of Representatives. There were no political trials and purges of political adversaries in the United States.

Washington was a hands-on president, but his success depended on the collective leadership of Washington, Hamilton, Jefferson and Madison. Part of the greatness of Washington lay in his understanding how to lead others. Patronage was one area in which he assumed sole responsibility.

Washington, leaving the question of banking and currency to Hamilton, had his own priorities for the nation: unity, security, order and economic development — goals that were interdependent and inseparable.

Hamilton had proposed a national bank in 1790, but the bill creating the bank was not passed until 1791. There was opposition. When Washington signed the bill into law, people showed confidence, buying script (certificates to buy bank shares at a later time). The assumption of debts and the establishment of the national bank curtailed inflation and stimulated the economy, bringing a prosperity that continued throughout Washington's two terms. Peace and prosperity were the key ingredients of his success.

When Hamilton's allies in Congress asked for advice, he had just the opening he craved. He meticulously compiled impressive reports on public credit, the national bank, and manufacturing; he intervened in the framing of bills at the start and all the way in between. Hamilton's policies shaped the country into an economic and industrial giant rather than the self-contained, backwater, agricultural and mercantile nation that it might have otherwise become.

Although he was involved in agriculture, Washington was pleased with the developing industries in the Middle Atlantic and New England states. Taxes were low, permitting growth.

Hamilton wanted capital concentrated in the hands of a small class of men who would develop the American economy and create factories, jobs and a powerful, urbanized nation. Madison, Jefferson and other Republicans believed the government should aid ordinary citizens, farmers and small manufacturers in a democratic republic.

In January 1790 Hamilton made his First Report on Public Credit. Hamilton planned to establish the sound credit of the country as well as provide capital for significant industrial projects. Hamilton demanded government intervention, government regulation and planning, and government stimulation of business. In December 1791 he proposed government aids to business, subsidies, bounties for inventions, internal improvements, and encouragement of immigration of manufacturers and workmen. He approved adding women and children to the labor force in factories. Factories would be in the North and raw materials would come from the South. Congress never voted on Hamilton's plan. It was Hamilton's only defeat. Hamilton presented his Report on Manufactures to Congress on December 5, 1791. Madison sounded the alarm. Madison also attacked Hamilton's economic policies.

Washington drew closer to the Federalists. Neither Washington nor Hamilton wanted an opposition party. Jefferson opposed Hamilton's views in a letter to Washington in 1792 and, after a personal condemnation by Hamilton, Jefferson left the Cabinet at the end of 1793. In 1797, as vice president, Jefferson accepted full leadership in the opposition Republican Party.

Political parties developed in America during Washington's presidency. The first pre-party politics involved the struggle over ratification of the Constitution. Supporters were called Federalists and opponents were called Anti-Federalists.

After the formation of political parties, Washington was insulted by the opposition. He was charged with being "infamously niggardly" in private dealings. His only education, they said, was on horseback. He had been involved in "gambling, reveling, horseracing and horse whipping." He was, they claimed, "a most horrid swearer and blasphemer." He supposedly had taken British bribes when he commanded American troops. His subordinates in the administration were called rascals, liars, jackals, drunks, demagogues, atheists and fops. Washington said nothing back and retained his poise in public but suffered in private.[5]

Radicals in western Pennsylvania, resisting the excise tax on whiskey, engaged in some acts of violence in the summer of 1794. Local officials did not act. Washington called up militia from four states. In September the forces assembled and marched west. Resistance disappeared as several thousand men fled to Kentucky. A few were arrested for treason and two were convicted. Washington pardoned them.[6] This successful military action strengthened the national government and the presidency.

Though Washington's first term was more successful than his second, he failed to establish a national university, a formal defense force, or an effective, realistic Indian policy. Washington's successes in the domestic area were that the U.S. government gained its executive and legislative precedents; added a Bill of Rights to the Constitution; established U.S. credit at home and abroad, fostering manufacturing and encouraging commerce; put down an insurrection; secured the frontier and forged a policy for the disposition of public land.

However, George Washington's place in history is secure. (For unknown motives, some recent historians attack Washington.) Washington was trusted for honesty, integrity and sincerity in his dedication to and devotion for his country. He was impartial and fair-minded and used sound judgment. George Washington was "the father of our country" (Henry Knox in 1786), "first in War, First in Peace and First in the Hearts of His Countrymen" (Henry Lee in 1799). George Washington held a unique position in his own lifetime. He was a rare, unique, gifted individual.[7]

John Adams

John Adams was elected president in 1796 by a margin of three electoral votes over his opponent Thomas Jefferson, who became vice president. Adams kept Washington's Cabinet, which was a mistake; three men were secretly loyal to Hamilton and later openly disloyal to Adams. Timothy Pickering, Secretary of State; James McHenry, Secretary of War; and Oliver Wolcott, Secretary of the Treasury were the three Cabinet members who, with Hamilton, tried to sabotage the Adams Administration.

Finally Adams summoned McHenry on a routine matter affecting the War Department. Suddenly, Adams became angry. His temper flared and he launched into a tirade against McHenry, who resigned the next day. Four days later Adams asked for Pickering's resignation. Pickering refused to resign and Adams fired him. The president did not ask Wolcott to resign. Wolcott resigned on his own late in the Adams Administration. Samuel Dexter became Secretary of War and John Marshall accepted the Secretary of State position.

Adams maintained a strong and growing economy. No panics occurred during his administration. Inflation was not a problem. He kept the fiscal policies of the Washington Administration; prosperity continued. The national debt increased by only two million dollars during the John Adams Administration.

Adams believed slavery was evil and opposed its extension to any more parts of the country. He supported freedom of religion and opposed religious bigotry.

The top priority items in the Adams Administration were in the field of foreign relations and are not considered in this study except when domestic programs are involved with foreign relations. One such exception is the passage of Alien and Sedition Acts by Congress, which Adams signed. On June 18, 1798, an act was passed extending the residence period for citizenship to fourteen years. A week later the Alien Act empowered the president during war or at the threat of war to seize, secure, or remove from the country all resident aliens who were citizens of the enemy nation. The treason and sedition bill provided a fine of not more than five thousand dollars and imprisonment for not more than five years for any persons, aliens or citizens, who should undertake to oppose or defy any law of the United States or threaten any U.S. officer. Similar penalties were reserved for those found guilty of printing or writing against the government of the United States, either house of Congress or the president. Truth was admissible in defense and the duration of the act was two years. Ten printers and editors were imprisoned under the act.

"The Alien and Sedition Acts have been used so persistently to indict the Federalists and the Adams' administration that an effort to put in their proper perspective is warranted. The new nation was in its infancy. Not ten years old, its existence was threatened by faction and dissention within and by the world's most formidable military power from without. The press ... was perhaps the most violent and vituperative that was to appear in ... American History. Under such circumstances it was hardly surprising that the government took steps to protect it and, as it felt, the country, by requiring that the newspapers should tell the truth."[8]

For national defense Adams called for an army and a navy. The Department of Navy was created in 1798. In order to pay the defense expenses, Congress passed an unpopular direct property tax in 1798. The new taxation program resembled the Stamp Act. There were taxes on legal documents used in business transactions, grants, deeds, wills and naturalization certificates. But the most controversial was the House Tax involving private residences. This was the first time the federal government tried to lay a direct levy on the people themselves; in the past only state or local governments had done this. The House Tax was progressive based on the wealth of the owner and the ability to pay. Riots broke out in eastern Pennsylvania led by John Fries. Fries was arrested, convicted and sentenced to hang. Later, Adams granted a general amnesty, freeing Fries and the others who had been arrested. It was a riot, not an act of treason.

In his annual message of 1800, Adams asked for a reform of the national judiciary. In 1801 three circuits were expanded to six. Twenty-three new posts were created. Adams began appointing judges right away, as his term as president ended on March 3, 1801. It took awhile, but the judges were appointed and confirmed before Adams' last day in office. Three commissions were signed on the last evening. All of the new judges were highly qualified. The most important of these positions was that of Chief Justice of the Supreme Court; John Marshall was Adams' appointee. The Republican charge that Adams stayed up late appointing "midnight judges" is false.

John Adams was dignified, except when he lost his temper. He was completely honest and kept his promises. In personal and public morality, Adams was excellent.

Thomas Jefferson

When Thomas Jefferson became president of the United States, he was already the leader of the Republican Party, the author of the Declaration of Independence and the author of the Statute of Virginia for Religious Freedom. He was America's leading writer, its principal architect, one of its foremost historians, one of its respected anthropologists, its pioneer paleontologist and president of the American Philosophical Society.

Sworn in on March 4, 1801, as America's third president, he walked from the boardinghouse where he stayed to his inauguration. Simplicity replaced the pomp and ceremony of the two Washington inaugurations and the Adams inauguration. Jefferson spoke of majority rule and the rights of the minority. His tone was conciliatory toward his opponents. He spoke of the need to encourage agriculture and commerce. Jefferson favored government by the common man.

Jefferson had been elected by the House of Representatives after a tie with Aaron Burr in the Electoral College. The twelfth Amendment to the Constitution remedied this situation by requiring electors to vote for one person as president and the other for vice president. Jefferson was easily elected to a second term and refused to run again for a third term.

Alexander Hamilton, who still led the Federalists, favored government by the privileged class. Hamilton was killed in a duel with Aaron Burr in 1804.

Jefferson saw independence as a prelude to the real revolution: reform in the institutions through which America would work out its destiny. He wrote to a friend, "We can no longer say there is nothing new under the sun. For this whole chapter in the history of man is new. The great extent of our republic is new."[9]

Jefferson selected James Madison as Secretary of State, Albert Gallatin as Secretary of the Treasury, General Henry Dearborn as Secretary of War and Levi Lincoln as Attorney General. Madison and Gallatin were brilliant and the other two were able. President Jefferson was also brilliant. There was harmony in the Jefferson Cabinet. There was none of the bickering and political warfare that took place in the Washington Cabinet or the disloyalty that was in the Adams Cabinet. Jefferson had trouble filling the Secretary of Navy position. Finally, Robert Smith accepted it.

Jefferson was pragmatic in support of his ideals. He wanted to reform waste in spending. He wished for improvement in old routines. He advocated progress in securing new constitutional rights. Jefferson was yielding on the surface but firm underneath. Some thought he would lead a caretaker government. They were wrong. Jefferson had been a strict constructionist in interpretation of the Constitution; however, as president he made many pragmatic decisions, in which he interpreted the Constitution loosely.

Jefferson, a poor public speaker and an excellent writer, wrote his annual speeches to be read. His speeches also appeared in newspapers. Jefferson was guarded in public spoken comment and reckless in private correspondence. Meriwether Lewis, who had been a captain in the United States Army, was appointed private secretary, but he was not really a secretary. Jefferson planned to use Lewis for his Western experience.

Jefferson proposed a new Judicial Act replacing the previous one. The Act passed in the Senate 16 to 15 with Vice President Burr casting the tie-breaking vote. It passed the House 59 to 32.

James Monroe, governor of Virginia, sought Jefferson's advice about sending free African-Americans and convicted slaves to Sierra Leone in Africa. Jefferson referred the matter to Great Britain, who controlled Sierra Leone.

Jefferson planned a great university in Virginia. Later, he founded the University of Virginia. He was very proud of this accomplishment.

Jefferson established separation between church and state, speaking at Danbury, Connecticut, near the end of the first year of his presidency. It was a reiteration of his Statute of Virginia for Religious Freedom in 1777, nine years before it was enacted into law.

Thomas Jefferson was hampered in his work by diarrhea and migraine headaches. He vaccinated himself for smallpox and later vaccinated his family and a Virginia neighborhood. Virginia schoolchildren had scratches on their arms by the man who had scratched out the Declaration of Independence.

A new state, Ohio became the third state west of the Appalachians. Kentucky and Tennessee were already states. The governor of the Northwest

Territory, General Arthur St. Clair, opposed Ohio statehood and deserved removal because of complaints. Jefferson used his "smooth handle" philosophy. He directed Madison to send the old general a reprimand. St. Clair appeared the next day at the Ohio Constitutional Convention to declare null and void the enabling act passed by the United States Congress. Then Jefferson had Madison fire St. Clair.

Journalist James T. Callender fled Scotland to the United States during Adams' presidency to escape a sedition trial. He gained employment and started writing attacks on Federalists. He claimed George Washington was a scandalous hypocrite who for personal gain had authorized the robbery of his own army. He called President John Adams a British spy. He said Alexander Hamilton embezzled public funds. In order to prove the charge false, Hamilton had to reveal a romance with the wife of a Treasury employee. Callender was arrested under the United States Sedition Act. He was fined $200 and sentenced to nine months in jail.

When Jefferson became president he pardoned all persons convicted under the Sedition Act. Callender was promised remission of his $200 fine. When remission was slow Jefferson paid $50 of the fine. Not satisfied, Callender asked for a government job. Jefferson did not answer his letters or give him a job. Callender was hired by a Federalist newspaper in 1802 and he launched a smear campaign against President Jefferson. He reported that Jefferson tried to seduce a neighbor's wife, Betsy Walker, in 1768. He claimed that Jefferson kept at Monticello a "Congo Harem," the queen of which was a slave, Sally Hemings. Callender said Jefferson fathered some of Hemings' children.

When Jefferson first became president, some New England preachers charged that Jefferson was an atheist and would turn churches into temples of prostitution. Church members were advised to hide their Bibles to keep the government from confiscating them.

Jefferson never answered any accusations about his private life or his religion. None of the charges have ever been proved beyond doubt. Jefferson's public life was scandal free. He never talked about his personal, private life. Historical evidence indicates that he had been a person with high moral character.

The Embargo Act was passed. It hurt the economy. Agriculture and commerce suffered. However, manufacturing expanded and flourished.

When Jefferson became president on March 4, 1801, there were fifteen states. The whole United States was east of the Mississippi River. The unorganized Northwest Territory made up the rest of the country. It was near the Great Lakes.

To the west was the Louisiana Territory, which included the Mississippi River and all the land drained by it. Louisiana was first owned and explored by the French. Later it was sold to Spain. There was a rumor that Spain had traded it to France again.

The American settlers on the east bank of the Mississippi River wanted to know who owned this territory. Almost half of the American population lived there. They earned much of their money by shipping goods and produce down the Mississippi River to New Orleans. Almost half the produce of the United States passed through a foreign city. The goods were stored along the river in warehouses. Americans had the right to store goods in New Orleans without paying taxes on them. This was the Right of Deposit.

When Jefferson came into office, he knew Spain controlled the lower Mississippi River and port of New Orleans. Spain threatened American settlements in the lower South by threatening to induce them to leave the Union and become separate states under the sway of Spain. Jefferson decided to assert American power in that region, hoping to pressure Spain to give up its North American colonies. He began to plan an expedition that would explore the heart of the North American continent, both American and foreign territory alike, to be led by his secretary, Meriwether Lewis. He devised this expedition as scientific, seeking to amass knowledge of the natural world. At the same time it would assert the American presence in the continent's interior.

The settlers could not send their produce over the Appalachian Mountains, even though American cities on the Atlantic seacoast needed it. Wagons and packhorses could not carry as much as river flatboats. Traveling by water was easier and faster. Larger oceangoing ships stopped at New Orleans and carried the goods up the Atlantic coast to the eastern American cities. American products were also shipped to European cities. American produce and goods found an eager market overseas.

The people of the United States worried about France controlling the port of New Orleans. They were afraid if Napoleon Bonaparte, the ruler of France, owned New Orleans, he might close the port to American trade. This would stop the American Mississippi trade route and destroy the economy of the western half of the United States.

Jefferson discussed the New Orleans situation with his advisors. One of his first actions as president was to appoint a new minister to France, Robert Livingston. He asked Livingston to find out the truth about the sale, whether France or Spain owned Louisiana. Jefferson told him to buy New Orleans and East and West Florida. The president warned him not to trust Napoleon. Livingston arrived in France on December 3, 1801.

Livingston discovered that Spain had traded Louisiana to France, but had kept Florida. France sent a fleet to take Hispaniola. From this Caribbean island, France could invade the United States by way of the Louisiana Territory.

Suddenly on October 18, 1802, the Right of Deposit by Americans at the port of New Orleans was taken away. The order was given by a Spanish customs officer, Don Juan Ventura Morales. No one knew if he was acting under French or Spanish orders.

Americans arrived at New Orleans in the winter of 1802-1803 as usual. However, they could not put their cargo in the warehouses. They could not sell it or ship it. The produce rotted in their flatboats or on the piers. Eventually it had to be dumped into the river.

This spelled ruin for thousands of farmers who protested to their congressmen. The congressmen demanded that President Jefferson do something about it. In response, Jefferson sent James Monroe, recent governor of Virginia, to France. As a special ambassador, he was supposed to help Livingston negotiate in France. Monroe sailed to France on March 9, 1803.

Jefferson authorized Monroe to do one of two things. One was to insure Americans' right to free passage down the Mississippi with the right to deposit produce in New Orleans. His other option was to buy the port itself and the nearby lands. The two negotiators were authorized by Congress to offer France from $2 million to $10 million. Napoleon considered the offers.

Napoleon Bonaparte had lost most of the troops he had sent to put down a slave rebellion on Hispaniola. Some troops died from yellow fever and others were killed in sudden night raids by rebels hidden in the hills. Napoleon would need even more troops to control Louisiana. The Louisiana Territory would be just too expensive. Napoleon needed troops and money if he were to declare war on Great Britain. He made a quick decision to get rid of his American property, which left him free to concentrate on Europe. Napoleon Bonaparte made a counteroffer.

The United States could not have New Orleans and the small amount of land around it. But, if the price were right, it could purchase all of Louisiana. What price would America offer him? As a dictator, Napoleon could make instant decisions affecting his whole country. However, Livingston and Monroe came from a democratic country and were supposed to get congressional approval for major decisions like this. But Congress was across the ocean and traveling there by ship would take three or four months. Napoleon wanted their decision immediately.

Joseph and Lucien, two of Napoleon's brothers, had not been consulted about the offer to sell Louisiana. They were horrified when told about it. The idea of giving up on a New World empire appalled them, because they both rode on the coattails of Napoleon's successes. Joseph had his own secret reason for trying to stop the sale of Louisiana. He had been offered a bribe by England's Ambassador to France if he could persuade Napoleon to keep Louisiana.

Joseph and Lucien went to the palace on the morning of April 7, 1803. They dared to interrupt Napoleon who was in a bathtub, immersed to his neck in perfumed water. At first they talked about plays and poetry. The brothers reminisced about their childhood and talked about trivial matters. Then, both Joseph and Lucien spoke their minds. They berated Napoleon for considering the sale of Louisiana to the United States. Furious, Napoleon stood up, and then threw himself back in the bath, splashing and drenching Joseph. Napoleon screamed that he could make decisions without anyone's consent. Joseph shouted back that he himself would head a movement to block the sale.

The sight of the heated argument was so upsetting that a bathroom servant fainted. Attendants came to remove the servant, help Napoleon out of the bathtub, and dress him. Napoleon was so angry that he smashed his own snuffbox by hurling it on the floor. Then Joseph and Lucien left. On April 11, Napoleon's foreign minister Charles Talleyrand asked Livingston if the United States would like to buy all of Louisiana. At first Livingston said no; the United States just wanted New Orleans and the Floridas. Then Monroe arrived the next day.

Livingston and Monroe discussed the offer. They examined their directions from the president. Jefferson's orders were to be flexible and get the best deal possible for the United States. The two Americans negotiated with Napoleon and Talleyrand. Finally, they agreed on about $15 million for all of Louisiana.[10] The deal was struck. On April 30 the papers were drawn up. Although they had no authority to spend $15 million or to purchase land other than New Orleans and the Floridas, both Livingston and Monroe signed the treaty.

Americans reacted to the news that their county had doubled in size with shock, delight, astonishment and dismay.[11] Suddenly the United States of America was larger in size than most major powers in Europe.

Many of Jefferson's enemies accused him of loving the French and taking worthless real estate off their hands. Jefferson believed the powers of the government had to be spelled out in the Constitution, which said nothing about the right of the president or Congress to purchase land. This was the first time this problem had been considered. Jefferson suppressed his qualms about constitutionality. He made an executive decision to stand by the action of his ambassadors.

President Jefferson brought the completed treaty to Congress and asked them to approve it. After a long and bitter debate, Congress approved the treaty with Napoleon by a huge majority. The people of the United States approved.

The United States financed the Louisiana Purchase by a loan from a British bank that paid cash to Napoleon. The bank had obtained the Prime Minister's permission to make the loan. The bank turned ownership over to the United States in exchange for American bonds. These bonds were United States government promissory notes that would be paid back at 6 percent interest in 15 years.

It wasn't known exactly how much land was purchased. Not even Napoleon knew. The eastern border was the Mississippi River. To the North it bordered Canada and to the south it bordered the Gulf of Mexico until it reached Texas. The borders with Canada and Texas were vague. The Rocky Mountains separated the Louisiana Purchase from the Pacific Ocean in the west.

Historian Henry Adams thought the purchase of the Louisiana Territory was a major achievement. It "ranked in historical importance next to the Declaration of Independence and the adoption of the Constitution."[12]

Jefferson was curious, as were all Americans, about the new Louisiana Territory. He returned to planning the Lewis and Clark expedition. In a message to Congress in January 1803, Jefferson asked for money for an expedition "to provide an extension of territory which the rapid increase of our numbers would call for."[13] Jefferson only requested $2,500 from Congress to finance a "voyage of Discovery" to the shores of the Pacific. Due to the low budget, his request was approved.

The expedition's first priority would be to find and map the Northwest Passage. After extensive reading and research, Jefferson framed a set of instructions. Then he showed this draft to his Cabinet. Madison had nothing much to say. The shrewd, astute Attorney General Levi Lincoln, a superb politician, warned that there might not be a Northwest Passage for the expedition to find, which would make the expedition a laughingstock.

Lincoln urged Jefferson to list goals that the explorers could meet, even if they failed in their primary purpose. Jefferson agreed and reshaped his draft. Jefferson's confidential letter to Meriwether Lewis, dated June

20, 1803, was the expedition's charter and set the standard for the future explorations. In addition to looking for a Northwest Passage, the group was to map the continent's interior, to assess its plant and animal life and natural resources, and to establish diplomatic and trade relationships with Native American nations.

Jefferson had appointed two men from the Charlottesville area to lead the expedition to explore the territory: Captain Meriwether Lewis, who had been his private secretary, and a seasoned explorer, Lieutenant William Clark. Lewis and Clark hired other hardy explorers. They hired Native American guides, including Sacagawea, from the Snake tribe. She spoke many Native American languages.

Secretary of the Treasury Albert Gallatin located money to outfit and support the Lewis and Clark expedition, and the group left St. Louis, Missouri, in May 1804. It was years before they returned.

As Lewis and Clark traveled west, they discovered the land was rugged, with vast, towering mountain ranges, wide stretches of desert, and turbulent, rushing rivers that even canoes could not travel. They learned that North America was wider than anyone had believed. They finally reached the Pacific Ocean in November 1805, but when they returned in 1806, they had to report to Jefferson that the Northwest Passage did not exist, but that a route mostly via rivers was possible. They had gone up the Missouri River, climbed the Rocky Mountains, and floated down the Columbia River to the ocean. They traveled eight thousand miles in more than two and a half years.[14] President Jefferson was delighted with the explorers' rich reports, travel journals, and plant and animal samples. In many ways he was a western explorer. He was a full partner in the success of the Lewis and Clark expedition.

Jefferson had asked them to see if the land could be settled. They were supposed to treat Native Americans peacefully. He asked for scientific records of the plants and animals. Jefferson was especially interested in rare animals or those thought to be extinct. Lewis and Clark's records were later published.

Jefferson was aware of fossilized bones of the woolly mammoth, which had been found in western Virginia. He didn't think that a whole species of animals could become extinct. He felt if bones were found, no matter how old, then the species must exist somewhere in the world. He asked Lewis and Clark to search for animals not known in the eastern states.

They found no living mammoths. They did bring other types of fossils and samples of Native American crafts. Lewis and Clark returned with extensive maps, reports, plant and animal specimens, along with journals and lists of vocabularies of Native American languages. They persuaded Native American nations to send diplomatic missions to "the Great Father" in Washington, D.C. Jefferson set up rooms in the Executive Mansion and Monticello to display choice items the explorers had collected. He sought to have their findings made available to the world's scientific community.

The Jefferson Administration tried to have friendly relations with Native Americans, but its policy was based on assumptions that were highly troubling. Jefferson urged his countrymen not to be hostile to Native Americans, but he also set out to reshape Native American societies so that they would fit in with his "empire for liberty." Despite his commitment to separation of church and state, Jefferson sent Christian missionaries to establish schools in western territories to educate Native Americans and convert them to Christianity. He tried to persuade Native American people to adopt European and American policies of land ownership and an economy based on individual farming and giving up their cultures based on hunting, gathering, and communal agriculture. Jefferson wanted men to take on the tasks of agriculture which traditionally had been the province of women.

If Native Americans adopted this new way of life, they could join with their white neighbors and build a new society devoted to liberty and peace. If they kept their old ways, Jefferson warned, they would be overwhelmed by the expansion of the white American republic and "disappear from the earth."[15]

By acquiring from France the port of New Orleans and the territory of Louisiana and by planning the Lewis and Clark expedition, Jefferson proved to be a versatile, adaptable chief executive.

Jefferson had been a great leader. He was a man of great vision. He promoted human rights for all people, including slaves and Indians. He supported federal aid to education and for internal improvements. Jefferson's interests covered a wide range. He studied law, diplomacy, architecture, botany, farming, raising animals, meteorology, and science. He was a husband, father and devoted grandfather. He believed that knowledge was better than ignorance and that excellence should be a constant goal. Democracies, he felt, specially need to be reminded of this lesson.

Jefferson was a complete, fully rounded person, fully developed both intellectually and emotionally. Woodrow Wilson said, "Jefferson's principles are sources of light because they are not made up of pure reason, but spring out of aspiration, impulse, vision, sympathy. They burn with fervor of the heart...."[16]

James Madison

James Madison, father of the Constitution, one of the Founding Fathers, one of the founders of the Republican Party, congressman, writer and Secretary of State, was inaugurated as the fourth president of the United States on March 4, 1809. The War of 1812 and the events leading up to it dominated Madison's administrations.

Madison's inaugural address was mostly about foreign relations. He supported the Constitution and civil liberties, especially freedom of religion and the press. He promoted agriculture, manufacturing and commerce. He encouraged science and education.

Madison advocated freedom of conscience, speech and assembly. He believed in respect of all persons regardless of race, religion, economic status or gender. He promoted humane treatment of all including Indians and slaves. Even though he was a slave owner, Madison recognized the evils of slavery and favored its general elimination.

A friend of the Indians, Madison did not know that General William Henry Harrison entered forbidden land belonging to the Indians at the Battle of Tippecanoe. General Andrew Jackson was ordered to drive whites off Indian land in Mississippi. This was not done.

Madison made unsatisfactory initial Cabinet appointments with the exception of the brilliant Albert Gallatin as Secretary of the Treasury, a carryover from the Jefferson Administration. Robert Smith, Jefferson's Secretary of Navy, became Secretary of State, William Eustis became Secretary of War, and Paul Hamilton was chosen for Secretary of Navy. Smith couldn't handle his job and Madison did Smith's work as well as his own until he replaced Smith with the capable James Monroe. Eustis was replaced by John Armstrong, who was replaced by James Monroe, who performed double duty at State and War. Gallatin was Madison's top asset. When Gallatin was sent to the peace conference in Europe, the

Treasury Department was in chaos until the appointment of Alexander Dallas who restored order. Hamilton was replaced by William Jones.

In April 1812 Vice President George Clinton died. His nephew DeWitt Clinton ran for president against Madison, who was up for reelection. Madison won the Republican caucus. Clinton, also a Republican, obtained the backing of the Federalists. Elbridge Gerry of Massachusetts was Madison's vice presidential candidate. Madison was re-elected with 128 electoral votes to 89 for Clinton.

The War of 1812 will be discussed here only as it affected domestic programs. The loss of foreign trade hurt the economy, especially in the New England states. The national debt grew as Congress refused to increase taxes. Most Federalists and most New Englanders opposed the war and refused to support the war effort. Washington, D.C., was burned by the British. Baltimore, where "The Star Spangled Banner" was written, was saved.

He was so preoccupied with foreign affairs that Madison introduced few domestic programs until 1815. He took office during an economic decline. Due to continuing difficulties with England and France, Madison was unable to restore American trade enough to pull the country out of its economic woes. Because the Madison Administration had to depend on loans to finance the war, inflation accompanied the growing deficit. Madison was not strong in the area of fiscal policy. In 1813 Secretary of the Treasury Albert Gallatin went to Europe on a peace mission. Financial chaos existed until Alexander S. Dallas became Secretary of the Treasury.

President Madison gave primary attention to domestic affairs after the war. Internal taxes were continued. The land tax was cut in half. Veterans' pensions were authorized.

After the war, prosperity returned, a national bank was re-chartered in 1816, public credit revived and revenues increased. A low tariff protected manufacturing and promoted trade. Internal improvements passed over Madison's veto.

In his last State of the Union message, Madison talked about the reduced national debt and lower government spending. He spoke of American safety and success in the fortieth year of independence. He said the sole object of government is public good and promoting peace on Earth and good will to men.

James Madison, the United States' shortest and smallest president, spoke with a thin, frail voice. But he was a terrific writer. He was honest, sincere, and dedicated, a man with vision. He had the highest moral values and excellent character.

Madison and Jefferson saw the University of Virginia started in 1819 after they had both left office. Resettlement of free American slaves in Africa was started by Madison and Monroe. In 1833 Madison became president of the American Colonization Society.

A New England congressman claimed that Madison was acting like "an old clucking hen." "As a president he is but little better than a man of straw and has no independence in anything."[17]

Henry Adams described Madison as an inept, confused and bungling man. He claimed that Madison's final months in office ended in political stagnation.

Robert Frost was taken by the dream of the Founding Fathers, which, as he saw it, was "a vision to occupy the land with character." "And lately I've decided the best dreamer of it was Madison.... I think I know ... what Madison's dream was. It was just a dream of new land to fulfill with people in self control."[18]

According to Robert Rutland, Madison's place in history is both high and secure. Madison was the Founding Father.

John Adams said that Madison's administration "has acquired more glory and established more union than all three predecessors put together."[19]

James Monroe

On March 4, 1817, James Monroe was inaugurated as the fifth president of the United States. D. D. Tomkins became vice president. The inauguration ceremony was held outside because Speaker of the House Henry Clay, sore because he was not named Secretary of State, refused to let the House chambers be used.

As Monroe rose to give his speech, people saw a striking resemblance between him and George Washington. Skipping over issues such as the national bank, Monroe spoke of the necessary outcome of the War of 1812. Now, he said, the government once again lay in the hands of the people to whom all credit was due. The states were protected by a government under a mild parental system but still enjoyed their separate spheres, he stated. It had been forty years since the Revolutionary War and twenty-eight years since the Constitution was ratified. The people, he said, had self-government the whole time and were happy. He claimed the nation's prosperity was dependent on our raw materials, soil, industry and capital, not dependent on foreign countries. The army, navy and militia should be moderate but sufficient, stated James Monroe, the last of the Revolutionary War heroes to be president.

Monroe planned a trip to visit forts and posts from Baltimore to Portland and west to Detroit. Daniel Webster urged a New England tour to strengthen patriotism and restore political harmony. The president visited ship building construction sites, inspected docks and visited factories.

Monroe received a thunderous welcome in Baltimore. He became popular in New York by his Republican plainness, ease and simplicity. He received tremendous ovations at Boston and visited Harvard College. He was welcomed all the way to Portland and on to the West. The trip really helped President Monroe and the country. During this trip the expression "Era of Good Feelings" came about.

Monroe selected John Quincy Adams for Secretary of State. Adams had a long diplomatic service record and was from New England. The Secretary of the Treasury position was offered to Henry Clay, who refused it, and then the post was given to William Crawford of Georgia, who had been a rival of Monroe in the election of 1816. For Secretary of War, Monroe appointed John C. Calhoun from South Carolina, a rising congressman. The Attorney General position went to William Wirt, Monroe's close friend and an able lawyer from Virginia. For Secretary of Navy, Jacob Crowninshield was held over from the previous administration. Adams, Calhoun and Wirt remained loyal to Monroe, but Crawford, bitter about losing the presidency, worked against Monroe. Two ex-presidents, Thomas Jefferson and James Madison, offered friendly advice when asked.

In the field of foreign affairs, the Monroe Doctrine and the acquisition of Florida had a positive effect domestically. The United States achieved a national identity, became more secure and expanded its territory.

Monroe's first message to Congress, on December 2, 1817, voiced the spirit of his northern tour. He said established peace left the United States free to turn its attention to domestic programs. He claimed the economy was flourishing with population and resources increasing rapidly. Monroe said the revenue from imposts, tonnage and the sale of public lands met all the government's needs to support civil government, the military and navy, and payment of the interest on the national debt. Monroe said internal taxes were no longer needed and he recommended their repeal by Congress. On December 23, 1817, Congress repealed them, increasing greatly the popularity of the administration, but later events proved that it was a mistake.

The causes of the Panic of 1819 go back to 1811 when the national bank was not re-chartered. Eighty-eight banks were in business in 1811. There were two hundred eight banks in business in 1813. Each bank could issue bills equal to three times its capital. These notes could be redeemed on demand in gold or silver or the bank could refuse to comply without penalty. There was no check to prevent the issue of notes beyond the legal limit. Far more bills were issued than banks were able to redeem. After the news of the burning of Washington reached bank centers, a plunge into irresponsibility occurred. The United States government lost five million dollars. At the end of 1814 the U.S. Treasury was empty.

After the war, the dumping of British goods on American markets hurt American manufacturing. British restraints were renewed on American trade. An accumulation of labor-saving devices, a decline in land values and unemployment in the large cities led to the depression.

A disorderly currency and unsound financial and credit conditions contributed to the Panic of 1819. The war had drained U.S. specie circulation. Demand for gold and silver by Europe and its gravitation to the East Indies added to the problem.

The Second United States Bank was chartered on April 16, 1816. The financial situation carried over to the Monroe Administration. William Jones, the inefficient president of the Second United States Bank, aided and abetted land speculation by granting liberal loans in the West and in the South. The immediate cause of the Panic of 1819 may be attributed to the United States Bank. In the summer of 1818 the Bank instructed all its branches to accept no notes but its own, to demand immediate payment of all state bank notes and to renew no personal loans. The national bank stopped discounts and pressed local banks to redeem their paper; they in turn pressed the people who were involved in reckless land speculation. Disaster ensued. State banks failed. Merchants, farmers and planters were ruined.

Secretary of the Treasury Crawford reported to Adams, "The banking bubbles are breaking. The staple productions of the soil, constituting America's principal articles of export, are falling to half and less than half the prices which they have lately borne, the merchants are crumbling to ruin, the manufactures perishing, agriculture stagnating, and distress universal in every part of the country."[20]

The national bank could not escape the storm which was overwhelming state banks. Debtors blamed the U.S. Bank and became its bitter enemies. Early in 1819, unsuccessful attempts were made to repeal the National Bank Charter. State legislatures who lacked the power were swamped with demands to tax the bank out of existence. In the case of *McCullogh v. Maryland* the U.S. Supreme Court ruled Congress did have the power under the Constitution to incorporate the bank and the power to establish branches in the states. The Court also ruled the state tax unconstitutional.

After the Court's ruling, Congress decided to reform rather than destroy the bank. An examination of the Baltimore branch revealed that the bank supposed to be for the whole United States catered to the interests of a ring of favored stockholders in Baltimore. Bank president Jones and the board of directors were forced to resign. With the bank on the brink of ruin, Monroe appointed Langdon Cheves to take over the bank.

After a run on banks in the South, Monroe decided to make a tour of the South. He left on March 30, 1819, in the midst of the financial depression to tour the South as he had the North at the beginning of his administration. He inspected shipyards and arsenals at Norfolk. He attended public dinners where he was received with respect. At Charleston he was honored with speeches, salutes, dinners and balls as George Washington had received on his tour. At Savannah Monroe arrived at the same time as the steamship *Savannah*. Monroe was given a ride, round trip to Tybee. He was so favorably impressed that he asked his host to bring the ship to Washington, D.C., later and the government might buy it to be used on the China coast. At Athens, Georgia, two important toasts were given; one to the Colonization Society and the other in condemnation of the slave trade.

From Georgia to Nashville, Monroe went through the Cherokee Nation and visited a mission school attended by sixty Indian children. From Nashville he traveled to Louisville and Lexington. At Lexington Monroe was accorded the warmest reception of the tour. John Quincy Adams attributed the heartiness of the demonstration to a desire to counteract an attempt by Clay's friends to slight the president by showing him little attention.[21]

After a visit with Andrew Jackson about internal improvements and a speech in which Monroe expressed his anxiety for a constitutional amendment to empower Congress to provide for canals, roads and bridges, Monroe went back to Washington, D.C. Despite the lavish entertainment accorded him on the trip, he saw the distress of the people. He addressed the panic by asking for an increase in the tariff. He left other possible solutions to Congress.

Congress did nothing much about the financial crisis because Missouri applied for statehood as a slave state. Congress became involved with all the ramifications of the slavery question, which threatened the very existence of the union.

Under the British Crown each colony had slavery; however, in the North and the East where no cotton or rice was grown and where climate or economics made slavery an unprofitable form of labor and where the demand for all types of labor, both skilled and unskilled, was fully supplied by bondservants, menials, apprentices and free workers, moral opinions about slavery were aroused. In 1787 slavery was excluded in the Northwest Territory. Free slaves were a problem. The South feared a slave insurrection and in the North freedmen had poor working conditions. James Monroe approved of the American Colonization Society and signed the 1819 legislation providing the return to Africa of slaves illegally captured. He zealously enforced the law. Monroe appointed two agents and sent a public ship to the territory acquired in Africa in the name of the society. In 1824, in recognition of Monroe's services, the inhabitants of Liberia named their capital Monrovia.[22]

The Constitution permitted slave states to count three-fifths of their slaves for representation in the House. The Senate was made up of two senators from each state. There was equality by admitting a slave state when a free state was admitted to the union. In 1819 there were twenty-two states — eleven slave and eleven free — but the North was growing faster in population and would soon overtake the South in representation.

Missouri was a part of the Louisiana Purchase and no one had expected that area to be settled for one hundred years. Consequently, nothing had been said about slavery in the debate on its purchase. Missouri had been settled largely by slaveholders. The Free Soilers in Congress were determined to prohibit the admission of Missouri as a slave state. The South was just as determined to extend slavery across the Mississippi River. The first debate in Congress about Missouri was fiery — slave versus free. The debate became so heated that Cobb of Georgia prophetically commented, "You have kindled a fire, which all the ocean cannot put out, which seas of blood can only extinguish."[23]

James Tallmadge of New York proposed to amend the bill of admission to the effect that further introduction of slavery be prohibited and that all children of slaves would become free when reaching the age of twenty-five. Clay led the forces of slavery. The bill passed the House with the Tallmadge amendment, but the amendment was struck out by the Senate. The dispute carried over to the next Congress.

In the North, people gathered at public meetings and organized committees of correspondence to forbid the extension of slavery into new states. In the South, an angry spirit prevailed. It was now felt efforts to restrict slavery were leveled at an institution interwoven with their very existence.

The Sixteenth Congress assembled with eighty-six newly elected members who had not served in Congress before. Fifty-six of these were from free states, giving the North a numerical advantage in the House over the South. One of the problems Monroe had in the Sixteenth Congress been with the Speaker of the House, Henry Clay, who immediately brought up the slavery question. A free state, Maine was ready for admission to the union. Angry warfare broke out in the House. Monroe stayed out of the congressional debate.

The Missouri Compromise was signed by President Monroe on March 6, 1820. Missouri was admitted as a slave state, but slavery in the rest of the Louisiana Territory north of 36'30' was prohibited.

Monroe was re-elected without opposition in 1820. He was inaugurated on March 5, 1821. In his inaugural address the president summed up the events of his first term. He spoke of the future optimistically. He stressed his policy of peace and good will reinforced by preparation. He spoke falsely of extraordinary prosperity combined with the repeal of the direct tax and excise. At the end he qualified this a bit by saying the depths of the depression had been reached and the nation was on the way back up to a general prosperity. He mentioned Congress had made two loans to cover deficiencies in revenue.

Spain signed the Florida Treaty in 1821. Monroe persuaded Andrew Jackson to be the territorial governor. Monroe then created three revenue districts in Florida. Jackson had some problems with the former Spanish governor José Callava and quarreled with Judge Elique Fromentin who issued a writ of *habeas corpus*. All three appealed to President Monroe, who met with his Cabinet about the troubling matter. Only Adams strongly upheld Jackson. Monroe, Calhoun and Wirt approved of Jackson in general but Fromentin was a federal judge. The problem was ended by the normal course of events, when Jackson resigned in poor health and temper. Jackson was disgusted because his own friends were not appointed to Florida jobs. In his annual address of 1821, Monroe stated the case mildly, praising Jackson and repeating his confidence in Fromentin. Jackson wrote angry letters to Monroe for a while, stopping when he became a candidate in the 1824 presidential election. The subject of Florida remained quiet for almost twenty-five years, when the territory applied for statehood.

Cheves capably managed the national bank until it retrieved its losses and reputation by regaining its capital in 1820. Cheves retired and was replaced by Nicholas Biddle who carried on constructively. The bank in 1820 declared a dividend.

During the eight years of Monroe's administration, a great western migration took place. Clay and Calhoun were leaders of a rising school of nationalism. Clay's American System was a scheme to promote national ends by creating a self-sufficient nation with a high protective tariff. The revenue from the tariff would pay for internal improvements such as roads, bridges and canals.

In his second inaugural address Monroe had mentioned roads and canals, but at the end of his speech said a constitutional amendment would be required. The House failed to pass an appropriation for internal improvements by a large enough margin to override a veto. The debate revealed a sharp degree of sectionalism. The West and the middle states were opposed by New England and the southern seaboard states. Several proposed bills failed.

The Cumberland Road needed more repairs. A bill was passed appropriating $9000 for repairs of the Cumberland Road and authorizing the president to cause the erection of tollgates and the appointing of toll gatherers. Monroe vetoed the bill as unconstitutional, his only veto. Again he asked for a constitutional amendment in his sixth annual address. Monroe decided Congress could provide a simple appropriation to repair the Cumberland Road. An act was passed on February 28, 1823. The following year he suggested each state collect tolls within its borders. On April 30, 1814, the General Survey Bill was approved, a $30,000 appropriation bill to defray expenses and authorizing the president to use the engineering corps of the army in making surveys, plans and estimates for roads and canals of national importance from a postal, commercial or military view. After stormy debate in both houses of Congress, the bill passed and was signed by Monroe.

Clay proposed extending the Cumberland Road from Canton, Ohio, to Zanesville, Ohio, and a survey for a future extension to the capital of Missouri. The act passed and Monroe signed it on March 3, 1825, in the closing hours of his administration.

During his presidency James Monroe worked to improve the situation of the American Indians. He urged a liberal and humane U.S. policy toward all the tribes.

The public demanded Indian-owned lands without proper compensation and the forcible removal of Indians to the West. Monroe wanted to end tribal ownership of Indian land and to issue individual plots to them. Indian agents, land speculators and territorial governments mistreated Indians. Monroe asked Congress to define the character of Indian rights and to stop breaking treaties.

President Monroe believed in freedom of speech and expression. He believed in freedom of religion. Although a slave owner, Monroe believed in human rights and dignity for all. He worked to end the slave trade and he treated Indians humanely.

Monroe generally made good appointments, but there were some scandals. Theodorick Bland, a judge in Baltimore, and Joseph Skinner, postmaster in Baltimore, were suspected of involvement with pirates.

Monroe acted consistently on a firm set of moral values and principles. He was trustworthy and honest, a man of integrity.

People liked Monroe for his courtesy, lack of condescension, frankness, goodness, and kindheartedness. A good writer and tireless worker, he was not a scholar and did not have a swift nor a rich mind, but he used good judgment.

Monroe refused to endorse a candidate in the hotly contested presidential election of 1824. At age sixty-seven James Monroe returned to his home in Virginia upon completion of his second term. John Quincy Adams wrote admiringly of James Monroe, "...strengthening and consolidating the federative edifice of his country's Union, till he was entitled to say, like Augustus Caesar of his imperial city that he had found her built of brick and left her constructed of marble."[24]

In the letter that Monroe treasured most, John Marshall wrote, "In the momentous and then unlooked for events which have since taken place, you have filled a large space in the public mind, and have been conspicuously instrumental in effecting objects of great interest to our common country. Believe me when I congratulate you on the circumstance under which your political course terminates, and that I feel sincere pleasure in the persuasion that your administration may be viewed with real approval by our wisest statesman."[25]

John Quincy Adams

Son of a president, a former diplomat and Secretary of State, John Quincy Adams was inaugurated as the sixth United States president on March 4, 1825. In his inaugural address he appealed for national unity. He said the Constitution and the confederated representative democracy had proved itself for a nation stretching from sea to sea. The time of trial was in the past, party strife had withered away. Now was the time for individuals to unite to bind the Union together into a government at once federal and national. He reviewed the successes of the Monroe administration. He spoke of exploration of the West and of scientific research and surveys that prepared the way for further application of natural resources to internal improvement working for future posterity.

Adams was elected as a minority president. Of the four candidates — Andrew Jackson, Adams, William H. Crawford and Henry Clay — Jackson received a plurality of popular votes and electoral votes, short of a majority in the Electoral College. The House of Representatives chose among the top three electoral vote getters: Jackson, Adams and Crawford. Clay, with the least number of electoral votes, was dropped. Clay, Speaker of the House, threw his support to Adams and John Quincy Adams was chosen president by the House.

During the Era of Good Feelings the Federalist Party weakened and by 1824 did not nominate a presidential candidate. Sectional candidates were named by their states. There were no party platforms and no issues were discussed. It was largely a contest of personalities. The negative campaign took place in the press. Candidates or their supporters supplied newspapers and local orators with ammunition proper or improper against the record, politics, person, character, religion or morals of a rival. Adams' diplomatic achievements were belittled. His opponents said he was aristocratic, that he was not easy to access, of quick temper, not a real Republican but a renegade Federalist, did not pay his debts and was a Socinian. Some people in Philadelphia claimed he did not dress properly and had attended church barefoot.

The elections of John Quincy Adams were not party victories, not triumphs of political principles and not even personal successes. He had no platform, no program and was not the choice of the people. His only hope as a minority president was to combine his adversaries and their patronage under his own leadership.

John Quincy Adams wished to continue the Era of Good Feelings. He did not believe in political parties or sections. He intended to keep Monroe's Cabinet and only fill vacancies.

John C. Calhoun was elected the new vice president. Calhoun planned to be the power behind the presidency. Before the Cabinet selections were made, George Sullivan, representing the Calhounites, met with President Adams and named men for Cabinet appointment that pleased Calhoun. Sullivan reported that if Clay became Secretary of State, opposition to the administration would be organized at the outset.

In the Monroe Cabinet, Adams had been Secretary of State and Calhoun had been Secretary of War. In addition to these two vacancies Crawford resigned the Secretary of the Treasury position due to ill health. The appointment of Henry Clay as Secretary of State led to charges of a corrupt bargain. Calhoun and Martin Van Buren, each wanting to be president after Jackson, who they thought would be next, formed a coalition of politicians uniting behind Jackson in opposition to Adams. Calhoun misjudged Adams as he later misjudged Jackson. James Barbour was selected to be Secretary of War by Adams, who also appointed Richard Rush Secretary of the Treasury.

Adams wanted to be a man of the whole nation, but the other leaders, except for Clay, would not support the administration, nor would their followers. Even among Clay's followers, some did not support Adams. The administration as constructed did not correspond to Adams' full design for national harmony. It was on a broad base but not broad enough to conciliate, to harmonize, and to unite opposing factions coalescing and tending to become sectional. The supporters of Crawford, Calhoun and Jackson failed to support their president. The South became distrustful of Adams as he spoke more of national issues.

Adams believed liberty had been won in the United States (at least for white persons) and was no longer in danger. The people could prevent absolutism. The Constitution would not permit people to endanger the right of property. Liberty was to be enjoyed with assistance of a strong national government. At this time Adams had little concern for the security of individual liberty, except for the dormant slavery problems. He strengthened property rights by a new bankruptcy law, just for debtor and creditor, continuing a sound banking system and by a national independent judiciary.

"For full enjoyment of both personal liberty and private property the first necessity was union. The second necessity was a strong national government to administer the resources of a continent for improvement of the general welfare. With Union achieved and preserved, the future of the nation would be a republic coterminous with the continent of North America, filled by a mighty people, marching under one flag, speaking one language, living one way of life and liberty, with capabilities of freedom and power such as associated man had never before witnessed on this earth."[26]

Adams believed liberty was power. His nationalism involved cementing sectional interests together by a network of national highways and canals. He felt public benefits would solve Constitutional scruples. He favored a humane policy of transferring Indians to west of the Mississippi, educating and civilizing them, perhaps assimilating them into citizenry eventually. Public lands in the West would increase in value. Scientific administration would settle the Indians carefully. The national debt would be paid off and a stream of internal improvements would reach from the Atlantic to the Pacific. This settlement would afford an unequal home market. Similar statements were part of his annual messages to Congress. In private correspondence he mentioned a cautious tariff which was the duty of Congress, representing the sections and interests of the whole country.

Adams promoted education. He felt someday an enlightened people might bring liberty to African-Americans.[27] It was not safe to talk about yet. At the time of the Missouri Compromise Adams had written in his diary, "If slavery be the destined sword in the hand of the destroying angel which is to sever the ties of this Union, the same sword will cut in sunder the bonds of slavery itself. Dissolution of the Union for cause of slavery would be followed by a servile war between the two severed portions of the Union. It seems to me that its result must be the extirpation of slavery from this continent; and calamitous and desolating as this course of events in its progress must be, so glorious would be its final issue, that, as God shall judge me, I dare not say that it is not to be desired."[28]

President John Quincy Adams spent considerable time working on his first annual message to Congress. By November 22 he had completed a preliminary draft that he read to his Cabinet. In it he proposed a series of internal improvements and the creation of a Department of the Interior to handle the mounting domestic problems. The entire Cabinet opposed presenting it at this time.

Adams sent the message to Congress on December 5, 1825, to be read by a clerk. After foreign affairs he wrote about internal improvements. Then came the main explosion: "The great object of the institution of civil government is the improvement of the condition of those who are parties to the social compact, and no government, in whatever form constituted, can accomplish the lawful ends of its institution but in proportion as it improves the condition of those over whom it is established."[29]

Congress reacted to the speech with hostility. But here was a bold, courageous and statesman-like assertor of what the national government could do to advance the economic, intellectual, and cultural well-being of the nation. He presented to Congress a program of breathtaking scope. He offered a vision of what could be achieved to increase the happiness of the people, and he tired to point out the responsibilities of a country blessed with a freely elected government that no other nation in the world enjoyed.

President Adams only made appointments to fill vacancies. The remainder of the Monroe civil service he kept, except for those involved in criminal activity. Disloyalty in his executive department really harmed the Adams presidency. Too many government officials worked for Jackson and against Adams. The president's supporters urged him to remove his enemies from office and replace them with his friends. Adams stubbornly refused.

Adams needed cooperation to get his domestic program through Congress. He did not get it. To be a man of the whole country, he needed to exercise strong leadership. He did not. As one proposal after another failed to gain approval, including those favoring the country's intellectual and scientific pursuits, which deeply disappointed Adams, he privately renewed his own scientific interests, particularly the study of botany. He asked consular officials, naval officers, and anyone having access to interesting and unusual species of animals, plants, and seeds to inform him of them or arrange their importation.

Opposition to Adams led to the formation of two major political parties. Adams and Clay led the National Republicans and Jackson and Van Buren led the Democrats. After the 1826 election the Adamsites or National Republicans were a minority in Congress.

During the Adams Administration the National Road was extended from Wheeling, Virginia, to Zanesville, Ohio. Construction was begun on the Cleveland and Akron Canal, the Dismal Swamp Canal, the Chesapeake and Ohio Canal, and the Louisville and Portland Canal around the falls of the Ohio River. On July 4, 1828, construction of the first passenger railway, the Baltimore and Ohio Railroad, started, opening up a new form of transportation that ultimately stretched across the nation.

In foreign relations Adams received bi-partisan support, except for the Tariff of Abominations. Adams signed it although it was not the act he wanted because he felt that he could not use the veto unless an act was unconstitutional. Prosperity continued domestically even though world trade was harmed.

John Quincy Adams as president was not respected by the public. Before his presidency he had been a respected diplomat and Secretary of State. After his presidency he won again great respect as a congressman. His presidency had been the least successful part of his career. He would have liked to have been president of all the people, but he didn't cater to public opinion. Many people were under the spell of Andrew Jackson and failed to appreciate Adams' good qualities. He put principle ahead of expediency.

Adams stood for Indian rights and prevented an Indian war over land in Georgia. He averted war with the Winnebago Indians in Michigan.

Adams was a scholar. He was brilliant, the only president to have had poetry published. He was one of only four presidents admitted as an undergraduate to Phi Beta Kappa.

John Quincy Adams is remembered for his views on liberty. He believed in freedom of speech and press and the right of peaceful dissent. He supported freedom of religion. He wished to alleviate poverty. He was for decent treatment of slaves and Indians. After his defeat for re-election in 1828, he served in the House of Representatives where he was respectfully called Old Man Eloquent. He was noted for his outspoken anti-slavery speeches. He died on the floor of the House.

Andrew Jackson

Jackson's presidential candidacy in the 1824 campaign was powered by a little group of Tennesseans, including lawyer John Overton, one of the West's wealthiest men, and Jackson's oldest friend, Senator John Eaton. William B. Lewis was a close friend living on the plantation next to Jackson's Hermitage. A master politician, Lewis knew how to start a movement in such a way to make it look spontaneous and to win for it the prestige or popularity needed to produce the desired effect, at the right time and place. The candidate, meanwhile, would prepare to be caught up by the movement which, from the start, his manager plotted.

Lewis worked like the director of play. He made political action into theater. Many important things were done behind the scenes, concealed from the audience. If necessary, he would have his star performer adjust the way he played the role, with a constant eye on the desired effect. The climax of the performance would be reached when the actor came down to the footlights and bowed to the "will of the people."

William G. Sumner describes Lewis and his function:

> He had the great knowledge required by the wirepuller-knowledge of men, good judgment of the influence which would be potent, if brought to bear on each man or group. He knew the class amongst whom Jackson's popularity was strongest. He knew their notions, prejudices, tastes and instincts. He knew what motives to appeal to. He wrote very well. When he wanted to go straight to the point he could do so. When he wanted to produce effects or suggest adroitly without coming to the point, he could do that too. He knew Jackson well....

The Tennessee legislature nominated Jackson for president in 1828. Jackson resigned from the Senate to devote himself to the presidential campaign. His Nashville backers plotted a strategy for beating Adams in 1828.

General Andrew Jackson, famous Indian fighter, hero of the Battle of New Orleans, former territorial governor of Florida, judge and senator, was inaugurated seventh president of the United States on March 4, 1829.

In Jackson's presidential candidacy in the 1824 campaign, the political issues stressed most often in the newspapers were the tariff, internal improvements, Indian removal, slavery, and territorial expansion. The parties and their candidates were concerned with political issues only insofar as they could attract voters. The fact they often talked out of both sides of the mouth shows it was winning office that counted above all else. But the Jackson people could not make their candidate go against slavery or for Indian rights.

The presidential campaign of 1828 had been dirty, low-down and mean. It was claimed that the John Quincy Adams Administration had been despotic, unconstitutional, dishonest, immoral, corrupt and would imperil the nation if re-elected.

Andrew Jackson was attacked by his opponents who were involved in name calling and spreading lies about him, his mother, and his wife Rachel Jackson. It was claimed that Jackson's mother had been a common prostitute with the British Army, the general an African American, and his wife a bigamist. General Jackson believed these political attacks led to Rachel's death on December 23, 1828. After he was no longer president in July 1838 Andrew Jackson joined the Presbyterian Church. "The hardest thing for Old Hickory to say was that he had forgiven his enemies; and he made it clear that only HIS enemies were absolved. Those who had slandered HER remained for God to deal with."[30]

In the campaign Jackson avoided the issues and ran on his popularity. In his first inaugural address, Old Hickory spoke of a judicious tariff first and turning the rascals out and bringing reform to Washington second. The outcome of the election of 1828 was a Jackson victory. He was re-elected in 1832.

Jackson's backers formed a new party, soon to be called the Democratic Party. It was really the Jackson Party, because its leaders listened to his advice even after he left the White House and until his death. In Congress the party was masterfully organized by Martin Van Buren, a New Yorker 15 years younger than Jackson. Van Buren had built a powerful political machine in upstate New York. Local Jackson committees were organized up and down the country. Their job was to carry on propaganda for Jackson, to make known his services to the nation, to refute charges against him, to attack the Adams Administration, and to stop information, ideas, and reports with one another. They set up a headquarters in Washington. They organized parades, raffles and barbeques and handed out liquor generously. They gave out buttons and hats with hickory leaves attached. The headquarters served as both a command center and a public relations agency.

The city was overrun by thousands of Jackson supporters. Many of them were common men and many of them wanted government jobs. In his Cabinet, President Jackson named Martin Van Buren as Secretary of State and Samuel Ingham as Secretary of the Treasury. He selected his steadfast and confidential friend, Senator John Henry Eaton of Tennessee, for the Secretary of War post. John MacPherson Berrien was Jackson's choice for Attorney General. John Branch filled the Secretary of Navy position. A holdover from the previous administration, John McLean stayed as Postmaster General and Jackson announced his intention to raise the position to Cabinet rank.

Eaton's appointment raised a storm of controversy concerning his wife, Margaret "Peggy" O'Neale Timberlake Eaton. Peggy, a young widow and daughter of a tavern-keeper, was not accepted into the Washington society because of her bad reputation. The Cabinet wives refused to call upon the Eatons and the White House hostess Mrs. Emily Donelson, Rachel Jackson's niece, who disagreed with the president about Peggy Eaton. Old Hickory stuck by the Eatons and was hurt by Donelson's attitude. All Jackson's Cabinet members but one resigned over the Eaton disagreement in April 1831.

Jackson replaced many government employees with men loyal to him. Old Hickory was credited with starting "the spoils system." It was not a clean sweep. The number of removals is greatly exaggerated. More than nine thousand jobs out of eleven thousand were left undisturbed.[31]

Jackson formed a "kitchen cabinet" of advisors in addition to the department heads. He was the first president to use friendly advisors in this way.

Jackson, a champion of the people, believed in the people. He felt a common man could do a government job. He made some good appointments and some bad ones. His worst appointment was that of Samuel Swarthout as collector of customs at the Port of New York. In 1838 Swarthout sailed for Europe. "An examination of his accounts disclosed that Colonel Swarthout was entitled to the distinction of being the first American to steal a million dollars."[32]

Andrew Jackson believed in freedom of speech and the press and the right to dissent for all white males, except for when it came to abolitionist publications sent through the U.S. mail. A slaveholder himself, Jackson denied civil rights to slaves and Indians. Old Hickory may have said "The only good injun is a dead injun," and whether he actually made this statement or not is unknown, but it reflects the old Indian fighter's attitude. Jackson had a poor attitude toward the judiciary. It is claimed that President Jackson said, "John Marshall has made his decision, now let him enforce it."[33] Jackson went ahead and illegally and unconstitutionally drove the Southwest and Georgia Indians across the Mississippi River.

The Tariff Act of 1828 led to rebellion in South Carolina, where the state openly threatened to "nullify" the law and not pay the duties. Following the Hayne-Webster debate about not only the tariff but about the question of nullification, South Carolina, under the leadership of Calhoun and Hayne, declared a new federal tariff law passed in 1832 as null and void. Jackson's position was not known. When the president at a dinner gave a toast which settled the issue, he looked straight at Calhoun and said, "Our union; it must be preserved."[34] Afterwards, one word was added, making it "federal union."

Andrew Jackson was an enemy of the national bank and of its president, Nicholas Biddle. Jackson vetoed the charter of the bank because he considered it an elitist bank favoring business over the common people. Jackson put government funds in certain state banks called "pet banks." For doing this the Senate censured Jackson. The censure was erased from the record three years later. Jackson, in order to restore the money market, issued the Specie Circular, which required payment in gold or silver in the sale of public lands. The Panic of 1837 was brought about by Jackson's Specie Circular and other factors, but the next president, Martin Van Buren, received the blame for the depression.

An assassination attempt took place on January 30, 1835, when Jackson attended a funeral for a member of Congress. Two shots at close range misfired. Jackson was unhurt.

Andrew Jackson and Thomas Jefferson are considered the founders of the Democratic Party of today. Jackson, a strong leader who brought power to the office of president, had the backing of the people. His popularity with the common man and with the population as a whole had never been greater. He expanded the democratic revolution started by Thomas Jefferson.

Martin Van Buren

Martin Van Buren, former state senator, state attorney, governor of New York, Secretary of State and vice president, was inaugurated president of the United States on March 4, 1837. He was the political "boss" of upstate New York. He considered himself an advocate of Thomas Jefferson and his political philosophy, but Van Buren was more pragmatic than Jefferson. Van Buren followed a very popular president, Andrew Jackson, who chose Van Buren to run in the presidential election of 1836.

Van Buren was more concerned about the economy than his Cabinet selections. The evidence of a coming panic was everywhere. Van Buren could not foresee when it would come and he did not know what to do about it. It worried him. He was troubled more with dyspepsia than he had ever been, a sure sign of stress; and he was taking a concoction of water, soot and powdered charcoal, something a friend had suggested that actually gave him some relief.[35]

Since Van Buren and Jackson were both Democrats, Van Buren did not think it advisable to remove and replace public officers. Van Buren kept most of Jackson's Cabinet. Lewis Cass had resigned as Secretary of War. Benjamin Butler became temporarily both Secretary of War and Attorney General. Butler, anxious to quit, was the only outstanding Cabinet member. Levi Woodbury was Secretary of the Treasury, a capable and experienced man who had previously been Secretary of Navy. John Forsyth served as Secretary of State. Forsyth, from Georgia, represented the Deep South in the Cabinet. He was dependable but lacked creativity. The weakest member, who was the oldest and the richest man, was Secretary of Navy Mahon Dickerson. Van Buren offered Dickerson the mission to Austria, but he refused. Amos Kendall, Postmaster General, had a keen mind but he was in poor health. Joel Poinsett filled the War Department vacancy. Poinsett was the most sophisticated member of the Cabinet.

In his inaugural address, Van Buren spoke of the great experiment of democracy, the current state of domestic tranquility, and the federal balance between state and national power with notable exceptions. Van Buren spoke of the Founding Fathers; he said he felt he was in a later age and, while following tradition, he would respond to change. He spoke of a bright future but with perils. The greatest of these was the problem of slavery. Van Buren opposed abolition of slavery in the District of Columbia. He also opposed abolition of slavery in any slave-holding state.

Van Buren had been in office only a short time when the Panic of 1837 struck the nation. On March 17, 1837, I. and L. Joseph of New York City went broke. The immediate cause had been the collapse of the cotton market in New Orleans. The Josephs, one of the largest dealers in domestic exchange, had been so involved with banks, merchants and jobbers that their failure affected commercial centers all along the Eastern seaboard. Until May 1 failures occurred almost daily.

Despite pressure, on May 4, 1937, Van Buren refused to cancel the Specie Circular. In one day, panicked depositors withdrew well over $2 million. On May 10, 1837, all New York City banks suspended all specie payment. Following New York's lead, all states stopped specie payment.

The New York State legislature passed the Safety Fund Law which was signed by Governor William L. Marcy. The Deposit Banking Act had to be repealed. Van Buren issued a call on May 16 for a special session of Congress on the first Monday of September. At various times during the summer of 1837 President Van Buren sent out letters to the best financial minds among Democrats, asking for advice for congressional action. They came up with the idea of an independent treasury and independent subtreasuries scattered about the nation. The Independent Treasury Bill passed in the Senate on October 3, 1837, but failed in the House by thirteen votes. Not until 1840 was the Subtreasury Act passed.

Van Buren was blamed for the Panic of 1837 because he was president when it took place. The causes go back to the previous administration: speculation in sales of public land, too many bank loans and Jackson's Specie Circular. By September 1837 most of the factories had closed and there were over 600 bank failures. For the next few years the United States suffered through one of the worst panics (or depressions) in history.

Van Buren believed that the federal government should not interfere with business and that it had no duty to help those who suffered from the depression. He thought the president's responsibility was limited to keeping the government's finances in order. Twice Van Buren issued treasury notes stimulating the economy. He declared a moratorium on bond payments. Van Buren's depression measures were considered radical and destructive by businesses, but he accomplished his primary goal of rescuing the public credit. A recovery brought prosperity temporarily in the winter of 1839-1840; then a European depression brought hard times until 1845.

Van Buren was not the tool of slave-holding planters nor of northern bankers, industrialists, and merchants. His special interest was in small, independent farmers. Van Buren reduced working hours for government employees to a ten hours a day. Although Van Buren supported the continuation of slavery in the states where it already existed, he was opposed to its spread.

Van Buren had bipartisan support in foreign relations and a lower tariff helped our domestic economy. Also, a foreign relations issue involved the slavery question when the *Amistad* was permitted to return to Africa. On domestic programs Van Buren faced opposition from Whigs and some Democrats.

Andrew Jackson was responsible for ordering the removal of the Cherokee and Seminole Indians. The army with much cruelty forcibly moved the Indians from their ancestral lands to the wilderness across the Mississippi River. John Ross, a successful merchant and planter, led the Cherokees to halt removal twice and gained support in the North. James Fenimore Cooper's early "Leather-Stocking Tales" portrayed the Indian as a romantic symbol with qualities Americans cherished. Van Buren inherited the Indian removal from the Jefferson Administration. Van Buren thought he should continue the policy. The Seminoles under Osceola fought the army until he was captured in a deceitful and flagrant violation of a flag of truce. Osceola died in prison. Van Buren had ordered the army to make the removal humane. Instead, the army tortured the Indians. Many of them died.

Van Buren appointed one midnight judge, Peter V. Daniel, whose confirmation by the Senate was late on March 2, 1841. In the election of 1840 Van Buren, running as a Democrat, lost to the Whig candidate William Henry Harrison.

Van Buren's enemies called him effete, a fop and a dandy. He was accused of trickery and deceit. The Whigs in the election of 1840 said, "Little Van is a Used Up Man."

As leader of the Democratic Party, Van Buren was clever and skillful, maneuvering candidates and elections. His nicknames were "The Little Magician" and "The Red Fox of Kinderhook."

In 1848 Van Buren ran for president as the losing Free Soil candidate.

He voted for Douglas in 1860, but when the Civil War broke out he supported Lincoln. On July 24, 1862, Van Buren died. Abraham Lincoln wrote about Van Buren, "the grief of his friends will measurably be assuaged by the consciousness that while suffering with disease and seeing his end approaching his prayers were for the restoration of the authority of the government of which he had been head, and for peace and good will among his fellow citizens."[36]

William Henry Harrison

General Harrison, Indian fighter, territorial governor of the Northwest Territory, territorial governor of Indiana and war hero in the War of 1812, was the first Whig to become president of the United States on March 4, 1841. Following the inaugural ceremonies, nominations for Cabinet positions were received from President Harrison and all were unanimously confirmed.[37]

Harrison was elected on the slogan "Tippecanoe and Tyler, too." The facts are that Harrison was not a hero at the Battle of Tippecanoe. There were more Americans killed than Indians. When the Indians ran out of ammunition, they withdrew to the woods. Harrison rode into the Indian camp, stole their utensils and tools, and set fire to their dwellings and their granary, destroying the Indian food supply for the winter.

Harrison's Cabinet consisted of Secretary of State Daniel Webster, Secretary of the Treasury Thomas Ewing, Secretary of War John Bell, Attorney General John Crittenden, Postmaster General Francis Granger, and Secretary of Navy George Badger. John Tyler was vice president.

President William Henry Harrison became ill with pneumonia on March 24 and died on April 4, 1841, only one month after his inauguration. As he was dying, he spoke to his doctor, whom he probably mistook for his successor, saying, "Sir, I wish you to understand the true principles of the government. I wish them carried out. I ask nothing more."[38]

John Tyler

For the first time in American history, a president died in office. John Tyler was vice president. There was some question as to whether Tyler should be a president or an acting president. Tyler claimed the title and the office, strengthening the office of vice president and setting a precedent for the future. Congress passed a resolution on May 31, 1841, recognizing John Tyler as president of the United States.

On April 9, 1841, Tyler issued an address to the American people, which was considered his inaugural address. He favored strengthening the army and navy. He promised to recommend to Congress measures to reform the spoils system. He advocated changes in the government's financial system, provided they would be constitutional. He reasserted his states' rights doctrine.

John Tyler, a Virginian, had been a Democrat until he split with President Jackson over states' rights issues. In 1834 Tyler joined the new Whig Party. When he became president in 1841, he still championed states' rights and was in opposition to the nationalism of many of the Whigs. For this reason and others he clashed with Congress over domestic programs.

He kept the Cabinet he inherited from Harrison. This was a mistake. Most of these men were loyal to Henry Clay, a Whig leader and enemy of Tyler. Clay wanted to win the next presidential election in 1844 and was determined to make Tyler look bad. Tyler needed to get rid of Harrison's Cabinet, but to avoid a row over dismissing the Cabinet, he formed a Kitchen Cabinet of his friends whose views were in accord with his. This Kitchen Cabinet included Thomas R. Dew, president of William and Mary College; Judge N. Beverly Tucker, of Williamsburg; Duff Green; representatives Wise, Gilmer, Marrory and Cushing; and Senator William C. Rives.

There were problems between the president and his Clay-dominated,

Harrison-inherited Cabinet. Finally, after Tyler's veto of a bank bill Clay wanted, the whole Cabinet resigned except Daniel Webster. Tyler wanted to keep Webster, but he was glad to get rid of the rest of them. More people served as Cabinet members in the Tyler Administration than in any other in American history. Two of them, Abel P. Upshaw and Thomas Gilmer, were killed in a gunboat explosion.

The United States in 1841 still had not recovered from the Panic of 1837. The estimated revenues for 1841 were less than disbursements. The deficit needed to be met. At first Tyler was unable to improve the nation's economy and his enemies in Congress deliberately made the problems worse. However, prosperity gradually returned, although neither the president nor Congress is entitled to credit for the improvement.

Tyler did not want the tariff rates in the Compromise Act of 1833 changed. He felt the subtreasury system was unsatisfactory. He called for Congress to devise a plan reserving to him the power of rejection of any measure, which in his view would not be unconstitutional or endanger the prosperity of the country. Tyler did not, by suggesting a fiscal agent to manage government funds, surrender his lifelong position on states' rights. Congress, controlled by Whigs in both houses, ignored six resolutions made by Tyler on June 7, 1841, calling for fiscal reform. Congress instead looked to Henry Clay for leadership.

Tyler vetoed two national bank bills. His Exchequer plan was tabled by Congress in 1842. President Tyler approved a bill providing for the distribution among the states of the proceeds from the sale of public lands. He opposed internal improvements paid for by federal funds. The budget deficit during the Tyler Administration was less than the deficit during Van Buren or Polk administrations. Tyler vetoed two tariff bills in 1842. Congress then passed one he could sign.

The Whig Party opposed President Tyler, as did the Democratic Party. His only supporters were a small group in the House of Representatives called "the Corporal's Guard" and one senator, William C. Rives. Tyler's worst enemy was Representative John Minor Botts who tried unsuccessfully to have Tyler impeached.

President Tyler was treated harshly by the press. Tyler was deeply hurt by attacks and insults in newspaper editorials. *The Richmond Whig* was very abusive. Its rival, *The Enquirer*, reported: "The Richmond Whig calls Mr. Tyler the Accident of an Accident ... whom Nature never intended to elevate above the trial of ten dollar warrants upon plain cases, a man destitute of intellect and integrity ... if so miserable a thing can be called a man — base, selfish and perfidious — a vast nightmare over the Republic."[39]

James K. Polk

A former state legislator, U.S. congressman, Speaker of the House and governor of Tennessee, James K. Polk became the first darkhorse candidate to be elected president of the United States.

Polk was inaugurated in March 1845, and his administration was dominated by foreign relations, including the Mexican War. The tariff, a foreign relations matter, was also an important domestic program.

In Polk's Cabinet James Buchanan served as Secretary of State. The Secretary of the Treasury was Robert J. Walker. William L. Marcy was selected for the Secretary of War position. Three men served as Attorney General: John Y. Mason, Nathan Clifford and Isaac Touncey. The Postmaster General was Cave Johnson. George Bancroft and then John Y. Mason served as Secretary of Navy. George M. Dallas had been elected vice president.

Polk completely dominated his Cabinet. He dominated the whole executive branch. He had things his way and permitted no opposition. James K. Polk increased the power of the presidency in a Jacksonian manner. A Democrat, Polk had been a supporter of Jackson and was nicknamed "Little Hickory." However, he lacked the charisma and popularity of Andrew Jackson.

Of his domestic measures, the most important to Polk was a low tariff act. The Walker Tariff of 1846 benefited all segments of the economy. Increased trade brought prosperity even to the manufacturing interests that had wanted protection. The revenue increased because the amount of imports increased. Polk ordered imports stored in warehouses until duties were collected. Those duties were paid by those who probably were most able to pay.

Polk was successful in the restoration of the independent treasury. No federal taxes were levied. Polk kept government spending down. Revenue from the tariff climbed. Polk established an office similar to that of Director of the Budget. Polk did not have to raise taxes to support the Mexican War, but the war caused the national debt to go up instead of down, as the president had planned. Polk's fiscal policies were conducive to stability. He ordered department heads to avoid waste. Although the national debt went up, inflation was not a problem due to Polk's policies.

Because of constitutional scruples, Polk opposed spending federal funds for internal improvements and for helping poor people. He did not distribute the surplus to the states. He vetoed rivers and harbors bills because he considered them to be pork-barrel projects and possibly unconstitutional. He should have used the surplus in constructive ways.

Polk believed in the freedom of speech and press. He supported freedom of religion and spoke out against bigotry. However, he did not have a good record with Mormons, failing to protect them from mobs in Nauvoo, Illinois. He did nothing for the women's suffrage movement, or to improve the lot of the poor. He did nothing about the hardships of children working in factories. He ignored the poverty of immigrants. On his last day in office, Polk signed the bill creating the Department of Interior.

"Polk was a slaveholder and a plantation owner in Mississippi and his sympathies were with the South, yet he was first and foremost a Union Man.... [H]e saw the approaching division over slavery a danger to the Union, and that his whole policy was to find and enact a compromise that would avoid the establishment of geographical parties which he felt would destroy the Union."[40] Polk opposed the Wilmot proviso. He sent Attorney General Nathan Clifford from Maine to see if his friends in Congress from the North could modify their position.

In his fourth annual message to Congress on December 5, 1848, after the election was over and it was known that the Whigs had won, Polk delivered a plea for reason by outlining three modes of settlement which would be acceptable to him: (1) pass no legislation on the slavery question, leaving the problem to be settled by the territories when they applied for admission as states, (2) extend the Missouri Compromise line to the Pacific, or (3) provide for the settlement of the issue by a judicial tribunal. He also advised the Congress that if none of these modes was adopted then Congress should find a solution. He concluded his remarks on the new territories by pointing out that evidence of an abundance of gold and silver had been found in these territories."[41]

James K. Polk as president succeeded in obtaining a lower tariff, the independent Treasury bill and his foreign relations efforts. He failed to help the lower classes and the immigrants. He failed to solve the slavery question. In 1860 it was too late for Senator Stephen A. Douglas to bring about a compromise with his doctrine of "squatter sovereignty." In 1848 President Polk, who saw the danger clearly, failed to use more dynamic leadership to bring about a compromise.

Zachary Taylor

General Zachary Taylor, hero of the Mexican War, was inaugurated president of the United States on March 5, 1849. General Taylor, nicknamed "Old Rough and Ready," had spent years on the frontier, causing him to disdain pomp and circumstance. Taylor was a Westerner like Andrew Jackson, Davy Crockett and William Henry Harrison. Later, Abraham Lincoln would profit from the same stereotype. Taylor, a slaveholder, always treated his slaves well. Old Rough and Ready was poorly educated, a career military man; he had no political experience and had never even voted.

After the election of 1848 and before Taylor's inauguration, James K. Polk, the outgoing president, wrote that "without political information and without experience in civil life," Taylor was "wholly unqualified for the station ... having no opinions or judgment on his own upon any one political subject, foreign or domestic; he will be compelled to rely upon the designs of the Federal party who will cluster around him and will be made to reverse ... the whole policy of my administration.... The country will be the loser by his election, and account it as an event which I shall deeply regret."[42]

In Taylor's inaugural address he avoided specifics but stated principles he took seriously. He faced fearful responsibilities but would be assisted by men well known for talents, integrity and purity of character. His guide would be the Constitution, and for its interpretation he would look to judicial decisions and the example of previous presidents.

Taylor was successful and had support in foreign relations. More important in Taylor's administration were domestic programs. The most important domestic issue was slavery, especially in the new territories. Should there be slavery in the new territories? Taylor's party, the Whigs, were in the minority in both houses of Congress. Taylor had won the presidency with plurality of popular votes. By carrying New York Taylor was elected by the Electoral College.

Alexander H. Stephens had predicted that because Taylor had "been elected by the people without the aid of schemes and intrigues and without any pledge to serve the country faithfully, having no friends to reward and no enemies to punish," he would face a "bitter hostility by a set of leeches who look upon the public office as nothing but spoils for political hacks to revel on."[43]

Old Rough and Ready was handicapped in selecting his Cabinet because he knew so few politicians personally. Senator John W. Clayton of Delaware became Secretary of State. A successful Pennsylvania lawyer, William M. Meredith, was appointed to the position of Secretary of the Treasury. Thomas Ewing of Ohio became Secretary of Interior. Ewing replaced many Democrats with Whigs and soon gained a reputation as the administration's hatchet man, but he ran his department well.

Old Rough and Ready made one bad appointment. At the request of Robert Toombs and Alexander Stephens, Taylor selected George W. Crawford as Secretary of War. A scandal later involved Crawford, Meredith and Attorney General Reverdy Johnson. Nothing was proven but reputations were damaged in a conflict-of-interest claim against the U.S government.

William Preston in the Navy Department and Postmaster General Jacob Collamer rounded out the Cabinet selections. The two leading Whigs, Henry Clay and Daniel Webster, were not appointed to Taylor's Cabinet. Both were elected to the U.S. Senate. Millard Fillmore of New York was Taylor's vice president.

Taylor, a slaveholder, had always supported the right of non-slaveholders to oppose the expansion of slavery. He believed that nature and previous laws and customs had already settled this issue of slavery in the new territories and did not want to stir up problems with the North about slavery. Thomas Hart Benton and Sam Houston agreed with Taylor. William H. Seward from New York made friends with Taylor, but allowing Seward to appear as an adviser was a mistake. Seward angered the South and Taylor received attacks from Southern Whigs and from Democrats in both the North and the South.

Taylor's annual message was delivered on December 24, 1849. He reported that agriculture should be more prosperous; tariff rates should be revised to benefit farmers and laborers. He recommended a branch mint in California. He suggested a geological and mineralogical exploration followed by a division of California into small lots for gold mining. He asked Congress to reduce postage to five cents per letter regardless of the distance involved. He advocated statehood for California and New Mexico.

Taylor served in a time of prosperity. He kept taxes low and reduced the national debt. He favored federal financing of internal improvements. Taylor supported civil liberties. He supported the rights of immigrants and opposed the Know-Nothings. He treated Indians better than most American presidents. Taylor insisted on humane treatment of all the American people.

A crisis occurred in Congress over slavery. Taylor stated clearly that preservation of the Union was his top priority. The South was divided over the slavery issue, as was the North. The Whigs were divided and the Democrats were divided.

Taylor had a plan called "The President's Plan" in which California and New Mexico would be admitted to the Union and the boundary between Texas and New Mexico would be determined by the courts. Congress proposed the Omnibus Bill. Taylor indicated he would veto it. Had Taylor lived and vetoed the Compromise of 1850 and had the South accepted this veto, the Civil War might have been averted, but if any states seceded, the war might have started sooner.

Taylor suddenly became ill on July 4 and died July 9, 1850. Horace Greeley announced that Taylor's immense popularity with the American people lay in "the great goodness of his heart, the exceeding sincerity of his transparent common sense, so broad and strong as to amount to wisdom, in a firmness that faced every danger and shunned no responsibility, and in a patriotism and sense of honor which threw an almost chivalrous halo over the sturdy elements of his nature.... A Southern man and a slaveholder, his mind was above the narrow prejudice of district and class and steadily aimed at the good of the nation as a whole."[44]

Millard Fillmore

Born into poverty, Millard Fillmore, by self-education and hard work, climbed the political ladder. A former state assemblyman, U.S. congressman, comptroller of New York and vice president, Millard Fillmore became president of the United States on July 10, 1850, after the death of Zachary Taylor the previous night.

Fillmore favored a high protective tariff and as chairman of the Ways and Means Committee had pushed a higher tariff through during Tyler's administration, but he did not raise the tariff significantly while he was president.

He strengthened the defenses at Fort Sumter when South Carolina threatened secession. Fillmore was willing to take strong action to protect the national interest.

Due to increased industrialization, development of railroads, and settlement of new agricultural areas in the Midwest, America enjoyed a period of prosperity under Fillmore. The Treasury had a surplus. Although his economic policies favored business and commercial interests, wages of labor kept up with inflation and agriculture prospered during his administration. Fillmore was on the side of capital, but he was not anti-union and labor unions grew stronger. He believed government should help business. He advocated granting federal lands to subsidize railroad building and thought both state and federal governments should help build and improve canals, rivers and harbors for the benefit of the commercial class. Fillmore did not use government powers to promote the general welfare except insofar as the public was helped by internal improvements. He kept taxes low and reduced the national debt.[45]

Millard Fillmore regarded African-Americans as inferior to white people. He signed a Fugitive Slave Law and favored its vigorous enforcement. He supported the Compromise of 1850. President Fillmore believed slavery was wrong and when in the future it disappeared, the freed slaves should be sent back to Africa. Meanwhile, slavery was permitted by the Constitution and he felt it was the duty of the president to uphold the Constitution.

He was for restricting the rights of immigrants to vote and hold office. He supported freedom of speech and the press. He favored separation of church and state. He opposed government support of Catholic schools. By his strict enforcement of the Fugitive Slave Act he put property rights above human rights.

Fillmore served in a time of economic prosperity. The Treasury had a surplus.

The most important events of the Fillmore Administration were the signing into law by the president of the five measures making up the Compromise of 1850. Congress worked out the compromises designed to preserve the Union and Fillmore was sympathetic. The five provisions of the Act were:

1. California was admitted as a free state;
2. New Mexico and Utah territories were to be determined to be slave or free by their state legislatures when achieving statehood (popular sovereignty);
3. Texas was compensated by assuming old Texas Republic debt;
4. Slave trade was abolished in the District of Columbia; and
5. A new and drastic Fugitive Slave Law was instated.

In July 1850 Congress debated the Texas–New Mexico boundary dispute. Fillmore sent more troops and a strong letter to the governor of Texas that led to a settlement reached in August.

Fillmore's most important Cabinet member was Daniel Webster, his Secretary of State. Webster brought prestige and political support from everywhere except abolitionist New England. John Greenleaf Whittier attacked Webster in a popular poem full of righteous scorn called "Ichabod," following Webster's speech on March 7, 1850, supporting the Compromise of 1850. Other New England writers who denounced Webster were Ralph Waldo Emerson, James Russell Lowell and Henry Wadsworth Longfellow. George S. Boutwell, an anti-slavery Democrat, was elected governor of Massachusetts. Robert Rantoul ran for Congress denouncing the law and won election. Later, he was chosen to finish Webster's Senate seat, which became vacant when Webster left to become Secretary of State. Charles Sumner, a fanatic and eloquent speaker, served as Massachusetts' other senator. Sumner was anti-slavery.

The new Fugitive Slave Law, a part of the Compromise of 1850, caused problems. In October 1850 the first challenge came. In Pennsylvania a marshal tried to invoke the new law by raising a citizen's posse. Instead, the crowd broke into the jail and rescued the fugitives. Two Pennsylvania judges, Robert C. Grier and John Kane, asked the president to issue a general order authorizing the use of federal troops in all such crises. The president was reluctant to use federal troops, but he recognized anything less might prove totally ineffective. He was not concerned for the slaveholders, but he did fear that any failure to enforce the law would strengthen Southern secessionists. He would, as he wrote Webster, "admit no right of nullification North or South."[46] Attorney General Crittenden and Webster were absent from Washington, but the remainder of Fillmore's Cabinet agreed unanimously that he had both the power and the duty to use military force in support of civil authority to enforce the law.

After painful soul searching, Fillmore instructed the marine commander at Philadelphia to assist the marshal or deputy if he were supported by a federal judge. Hoping that it would prevent rather than cause trouble, he announced that all marshals and commissioners would have the same support, when needed.

"God knows," he wrote Webster, "that I detest slavery but it is an existing evil, for which we are not responsible, and we must endure it, and give it such protection as is guaranteed by the Constitution, till we can get rid of it without destroying the last hope of free government in the world."[47] He would use "force only as a last resort, but if necessary," he "would bring the whole force of the government to sustain the law."[48]

The slavery issue was not dead. Harriet Beecher Stowe published *Uncle Tom's Cabin* in March 1852 and by election day was a bestseller. The success of the book angered people in the South.

Millard Fillmore was the last Whig president. In the presidential race of 1852 Fillmore received many cards and letters of support. Fillmore, slow to enter the contest, lost his party nomination for president to Winfield Scott. A Democrat, Franklin Pierce, was elected to the presidency.

Franklin Pierce

After Pierce's victory in the 1852 presidential election, there was much speculation as to how this comparatively unknown and inexperienced man could handle the problems of the presidency. Opinions varied. Nathaniel Hawthorne, who had just written Pierce's biography, summed it up to their mutual friend Horatio Bridge.

"I have come seriously to the conclusion that he has in him many of the chief elements of a great ruler. His talents are administrative; he has a subtle faculty of making affairs roll onward, according to his will, and of influencing their course without any trace of his action. There are scores of men in the country that seem brighter than he is, but [he] has the directing mind, and will move them about like pawns on a chess-board, and turn all their abilities to better purpose than they themselves could do.... He is deep, deep, deep. But what luck with all! Nothing can ruin him." So spoke his friend. In Boston, R. H. Dana, Jr., wrote in his diary the day after election, "The country 'gone with a rush' [for Pierce]. A New Hampshire Democratic, dough face, militia colonel, a kind rate country, or at most, state politician, President of the United States!" So spake State Street, the Democratic political machine in Boston. Would he measure up to expectations of Hawthorne or was he cast in the mold described by Dana?[49]

Franklin Pierce, a former Vermont state legislator, state speaker of the house, U.S. representative, U.S. senator and Mexican War veteran, was inaugurated president of the United States on March 4, 1853. In his inaugural address Pierce pledged "devoted integrity in the public service ... rigid economy in all departments," and protection of state rights. "If the Federal Government will confine itself to the exercise of powers clearly granted by the Constitution," he said, "it can hardly happen that its action upon any question should the institutions of the States or interfere with their right to manage their own people." Having promised no interference with slavery, Pierce extolled the Union, on which he had fastened his "best and dearest hopes."[50]

Moreover, the laws of the Compromise of 1850 were strictly constitutional and should be enforced, especially the Fugitive Slave Act. The Constitution, he proclaimed, recognized involuntary servitude as an "admitted right." His own total ignorance of the moral and religious dimensions of the controversy over slavery soon dampened the enthusiasm of even his most ardent followers.[51]

Pierce was a very handsome man. He appeared presidential, but he was an inept leader and seemed to be overwhelmed by the position. A Northern man with Southern sympathies, he was called a "doughface." His Executive Branch was run by department heads. His administration was dominated by Congress.

The three most important Cabinet members in the Pierce Administration were Secretary of State William Marcy, Secretary of War Jefferson Davis and Attorney General Caleb Cushing. Pierce tried to appoint all factions of Democrats to office. The fundamental proposition he adopted in his Cabinet appointments was harmony. He aimed to conciliate as many factions as possible. He determined to forget past heresies, especially the bolt of 1848, to question the loyalty of none who had accepted the Baltimore platform and voted for him. For this reason he chose to head his Cabinet with a prominent "barnburner" and a leading southern rights advocate. Prominent Democrats not selected for the Cabinet were James Buchanan and Stephen A. Douglas. Some were his enemies.

Pierce negotiated 52 Indian treaties at gunpoint, taking 174 million acres from tribes, paying them less than ten cents an acre. Previous administrations had forced the Native Americans west of the Mississippi. Now that land was wanted by white settlers, too. Pierce decided on two involuntary reservations for the Indians. One was in Dakota, the other in Oklahoma. The Native Americans' rights and interests were never considered and their traditional way of life was destroyed.

The president vetoed the Dorothea Dix Bill to provide institutional care for the indigent mentally ill because he said it cost too much. This same Franklin Pierce authorized huge funds to chase and capture fugitive slaves.

Pierce served during a time of economic prosperity. The tariff was lowered. Taxes were low. Spending was reduced in every department except the War Department. Constitutional scruples slowed progress in Pierce's domestic programs. Several administration bills were enacted: regulation of steamship travel for the safety of passengers, safeguarding coasts from shipwreck; four new regiments with camels and dromedaries for army transportation; four new revenue cutters, two acts reorganizing the navy, providing a retired list and better discipline; increased salaries for federal judges; a registered mail system and a postage stamp requirement; and $300,000 to enlarge the Postmaster General's building.

On its own initiative Congress established a court of claims, authorized construction of a telegraph line to the Pacific by providing a right of way and promising protection, and voted to give 160 acres of land to all veterans, their widows or minor children, a blanket grant which Pierce signed in spite of its size; he had a tender spot for old soldiers.

A number of administration bills failed, including tariff revision and a Pacific railroad bill that failed by one vote in the House. Reorganization of the judicial system and law department failed. There was little increase in the Navy. Pierce vetoed a mail steamer bill. He used a pocket veto on an internal improvements bill in Michigan. He had signed one improving a river in Georgia.

In his first annual message to Congress in December 1853, President Pierce advocated reduction of the national debt, revision of the tariff and placement of Indians on reservations to make more room for white settlers, and grants to railroads. Pierce displayed a fundamental attitude with strict adherence to precedent rather than creative leadership, which was a dangerous violation, he thought, of tried doctrines and was advocated by unstable, unprincipled men or dangerous fanatics. He favored a laissez-faire policy by the central government toward states.

The message was optimistic and indecisive. Pierce drew on precedent and deference to Congress and demonstrated his great weakness as a leader. He did not understand the Union, nor realize incompatibility between sections or intensity of rivalry. The president lacked friends in Congress. He had the support of faction. After the election of 1852, the party leaders did not need him, but Pierce did not understand this; he was under an illusion. He considered himself his party's leader. He was not. He tried to impose upon it a program of party policy for which he had neither the authority or backing. He ignored party chiefs, especially the senators.

In the spring of 1854 the Gadsden Treaty was signed, by which Mexico ceded territory south of New Mexico for a railroad. The United States made this purchase for a payment of $10 million.

Pierce supported the Kansas-Nebraska Act passed in 1854. The slavery issue in Kansas and Nebraska was now to be decided by popular sovereignty. Fighting broke out in "Bleeding Kansas." Sectionalism increased. The Republican Party was born.

President Pierce convinced himself by the enactment of the Kansas-Nebraska Bill that he and his party had laid the slavery question away permanently. His initial mistake was appointing Andrew H. Reeder as territorial governor of Kansas. Next was fraud in connection with Indian lands. The Kansas-Nebraska Act led to speculation in Indian lands under the Preemption Act of 1841, in which much desirable land the United States held in trust for Delaware Indians was to be sold at auction to speculators for the Indians' benefit. Another very desirable area was occupied by mixed-race Kansas Indians as a perpetual reservation under the Kansas Treaty of 1825. Many of the hopeful land hunters were ignorant or careless of these restrictions and began speculations which the authorities of the Indian office held to be unlawful. Backed by an opinion of Attorney General Cushing, the Indian agents were ordered to drive the squatters from the Delaware lands, and then the trouble began. The Indian agents, especially B. F. Robinson for the Delaware, began to protest the activities of the army, engaging in speculation and encouraging squatters who were planning an association to prevent any competitive bidding at auction. Worse still, Robinson and others began to complain of Governor Reeder, who had a scheme to get Indian lands for himself and locate the capital on his land, increasing its value. Reeder did not go through Indian agents and dealt directly with the occupants of the reserves. By November 6, 1854, protests from Indian agents against Reeder's deals were sent to Washington, charging Reeder and his associates, including two judges, with unlawful conduct and with cheating the Indians. Similar charges were made against military authorities at Fort Leavenworth.

No action was taken until January 10, 1855, when Reeder's contracts came to Indian Commissioner George W. Maypenny for an opinion. The commissioner denounced Reeder to the president and disapproved his contracts. Reeder was robbing the Indians by offering such a low price and the papers were carelessly drawn. Pierce sent Reeder's papers back without approval. An Ohio congressman moved that the documents be called for and on February 3 the president sent them in. The papers aimed to show that the president and Interior Department were trying to protect the Indians and contained the full story of Reeder's deals, accompanied by the charges against him and Maypenny's denunciation of his conduct. In order to justify himself, Reeder forwarded charges against Agent George W. Clarke.

Then came March 30, election day in the territory; up to that time the trouble, in Pierce's eyes, had just been an unsavory real estate scheme in which his own appointees had participated. After the election, however, rumors and reports of disorder and fraud began to appear in the press. Missourians had crossed the border on election day and, according to the free-state people, cast enough votes to elect a pro-slavery legislature. Reeder, under threats of personal violence, accepted the situation, certified the election and issued a call for the legislature to meet in July in Pawnee, where Reeder owned property. He realized his position was precarious. To protect himself, he challenged Maypenny to prove his charges or resign.

Reeder made a trip to Washington to defend himself. His opponent, Senator David R. Atkinson of Missouri, came too, demanding Reeder's resignation. Pressure for Reeder's removal increased. Pierce offered Reeder a different position if he would resign. Reeder refused to resign and returned to Kansas only to enter into a bitter quarrel with the legislature about Reeder's location of the capital. Pierce fired Reeder on July 28, 1855. Wilson Shannon replaced him.

In his 1855 annual address, Pierce attacked Republicans. He said there was danger that the constitutional principle of state rights could be overthrown.

On December 3 the president received a request by telegram for troops to support the law in Kansas. Pierce promised to send soldiers; however, the crisis quickly passed, for in a few days Shannon advised that had made a truce. Troops were not sent, not yet.

The U.S. House of Representatives failed to organize. Day after day went by. Finally Alexander H. Stephens grew impatient and suggested to Howell Cobb that the president send in his message about England even though the House was not organized. Pierce then, without waiting, sent in his message.

Shortly after the first of the year, news from Kansas again became alarming. Free-state sympathizers were about to set up an organization of their own and disregard the lawful territorial government. To Pierce, such action was treason. Pierce decided to send in a message on Kansas, although Congress was still unorganized. He set forth the gravity of the situation. On January 24 the president's message was received. He listed Reeder's misconduct. He said the Topeka constitution was in defiance of lawful government and this was revolution. Pierce made two recommendations: (1) provide a constitutional convention and the speedy admission as a state and (2) appropriate expenses to maintain order. The Know-Nothings refused to organize under the Democratic caucus. Nothing was accomplished. Nathaniel P. Banks, a Republican, was elected Speaker of the House.

Republicans organized on February 22, 1856, on a free soil basis.

Kansas difficulties were used by Republicans as propaganda. They found every act of the Pierce Administration wanting. They said Pierce was a weakling who had sold out to the South in hopes of re-nomination. They said he was the creature of a dangerous and callous oligarchy which demanded the spread of slavery, a cruel and barbarous institution. William H. Seward called him a tyrant and likened his policies toward the oppressed Kansas to the despotism of George III.

Pierce was having difficulty seeking re-nomination in 1856. Democrats had been campaigning on the Kansas-Nebraska Act as a measure for freedom. The doctrines of state rights and slave protection appealed to the Southern Democrats. In the North Pierce was unpopular. Even in his home state of New Hampshire, voters were unappreciative. The Connecticut election was a disaster. The shame of the repeal of the Missouri Compromise was bitterly felt and Pierce was held responsible for the difficulties in Kansas. Southern supporters had reservations. Alexander H. Stephens blamed Pierce for sending Reeder to Kansas. This regime had been marked by personal feuds. The chief trouble was the realization by many practical leaders that Pierce, a weak candidate, could not be elected. Many were looking for someone else. James Buchanan loomed as the figure of unity.

On May 14, 1856, a new outbreak occurred. Pierce blamed free-state men. On May 24 Lawrence was sacked. Just before the convention the Pottawatomie Creek massacre took place.

Pierce vetoed two internal improvements bills. Pierce sent troops to Kansas on June 10. He removed Col. Edwin V. Sumner and replaced him with General Persitor F. Smith on June 27.

The Republicans nominated John C. Fremont on June 19. "Bleeding Kansas" was a valuable issue on a platform of Pierce mistakes. Robert Toombs' bill was a last chance for Kansas to become a slave state. The scheme appealed to Douglas and Pierce. The bill was reported back from committee on June 30 by Douglas. Lewis Cass and Toombs came to the president's defense. Toombs' bill passed the Senate on July 2, but the House didn't even consider it.

Pierce removed Shannon, the governor of Kansas, on July 28. He had removed J. B. Donaldson as marshal because Col. Sumner dispersed the Topeka legislature by force. The Senate made a call on July 21 for papers which enabled Pierce to make public a report by Davis that no orders were given. Pierce replaced Shannon with John W. Geary. The Senate and House were deadlocked on the army bill.

A report came from Smith calling for more troops; free men were in arms and were expected to destroy the capital. Pierce called for a special session of Congress to meet in three days. Daniel Woodson was acting governor while Geary was waiting for Congress. After a week, Pierce signed the army bill. Geary left for Kansas. Pierce assured him of support and sent more troops to Smith. Pierce sent orders to Geary to organize the militia. Davis ordered Smith to suppress insurrection against civil authority. Davis further ordered the governors of Illinois and Kentucky each to have two militia regiments ready to send into Kansas territory upon General Smith's requisition. Having dispatched a messenger with all these orders, the administration gave them to the press on September 6. Several thousand Missourians invaded on September 27.

The Democrats in 1856 did not re-nominate Pierce for president. His failure to lead, his mistakes, his poor speaking ability, his drunkenness, his lack of respect for non-whites, his enforcement of the Fugitive Slave Act and, most of all, his support of the Kansas-Nebraska Act led Americans to look upon the Pierce Administration unkindly.

Gideon Welles described Pierce as "a vain, showy, and pliant man ... [who] by his errors and weakness broke down his administration and his party throughout the country."[52] Eighty years later, Allan Nevins described him as "one of the quickest, most gracefully attractive, and withal weakest, of the men who have held his high office ... on the whole a man of shallow nature."[53] Biographer Roy Franklin Nichols wrote in 1993, "Pierce's greatest misfortune was that, disorganized and numbed by personal tragedy, he seemed to understand little of the forces outside himself which were combining with his inward insecurity to make him one of democracy's most unfortunate victims. It is only his due that the stereotype created in his lifetime be replaced by a more realistic portrait. Reconsideration of his complex life experience reveals not mere weakness, but a difficult combination of inner conflict, tragedy and national confusion which prevented him from meeting the challenge of his great responsibility."[54]

James Buchanan

A Democrat, Buchanan was inaugurated on March 4, 1857. A former state legislator, U.S. congressman, U.S. senator, minister to Russia and to Great Britain and Secretary of State, Buchanan had been overseas when the controversial and divisive Kansas-Nebraska Act had been passed in 1854. In the election of 1856, Buchanan, the favorite of the four candidates for the Democratic nomination, had not taken a position on the Kansas-Nebraska Act. The other candidates for Democratic nomination were President Franklin Pierce, Stephen Douglas and Lewis Cass. The Whig Party had disintegrated and most of them joined the new Republican Party, whose candidate was John C. Fremont. The Know-Nothing Party and the remaining Whigs supported ex-president Millard Fillmore. Although he received less than half the popular vote, Buchanan won easily in the Electoral College.

In his inaugural address, Buchanan said he would serve only one term, weakening his presidency. Lewis Cass, senile and lazy, was a mere figurehead as Secretary of State. Buchanan ran the State Department himself. Two good Cabinet members were Secretary of the Treasury Howell Cobb and Attorney General Aaron V. Brown. Jacob Thompson, Secretary of Interior, and John B. Floyd, Secretary of War, were involved in a scandal in which bonds held for Native Americans were stolen and cashed.

Buchanan was not noted for domestic programs but for the lack of them. He believed Congress, not the president, should be responsible for domestic programs. The president then would execute them. The Panic of 1857 damaged Buchanan's administration. It began in the late spring of 1857 when the New York branch of an Ohio corporation suspended payment after trying to call in unrecoverable loans. Cobb concentrated government gold in New York City, which helped business. But Buchanan refused to help thousands of common people who had become miserable.

Fourteen hundred state banks and five thousand businesses, including railroads and factories, were bankrupt by the fall of 1857. Land values plummeted and jobs disappeared. In cities in the North, men and women took to the streets, searching for employment and begging for food. In the agricultural South, people were not in a recession. Buchanan attributed the panic to the speculations and borrowings of greedy Northern capitalists.

Buchanan did nothing about the Panic of 1857. He announced in his first annual message that the government was "without the power to extend relief." Instead, he urged more use of specie, the redemption of the public debt in gold rather than paper money, more restrictions on state banks' freedom to issue paper currency, and no new public works projects by a federal government that was broke. The president announced reform, not relief. He asked Congress to pass new bankruptcy, banking, and credit laws to prevent future panics. Buchanan's so-called reforms actually hurt rather than helped the economy. Recovery came slowly after much suffering.

The nation was torn apart by the slavery issue, especially by the question of slavery in the territories. Buchanan, striving for peace, supported the Crittenden Compromise and Lecompton Constitution. Pro-slavery forces approved the Lecompton Constitution, but the U.S. Congress rejected it. Northern voters were so angered at Buchanan for his support of the Lecompton Constitution that the Democrats lost control of both houses of Congress in the election of 1858. After the Republican win in the election, the federal government reached a stalemate. Republican bills were defeated by Southern senators or vetoed by the president.

Tall, stately, and stiffly formal, presiding over a rapidly dividing nation, Buchanan grasped inadequately the political realities of the time. Relying on constitutional doctrines to close the widening rift over slavery, he failed to understand that the North would not accept constitutional arguments which favored the South. Nor did he realize how sectionalism had realigned political parties. The Democrats split, the Whigs were destroyed, giving rise to the Republicans.

Popular sovereignty, Pierce's responsibility, had not worked in "Bleeding Kansas." Sectional rivalry became more heated after the pro-slavery Dred Scott decision, in which the Missouri Compromise was declared unconstitutional.

Buchanan had written a letter to Supreme Court Justice Robert Grier, influencing his vote on the Dred Scott decision. Don Fehrenbacher wrote, "Buchanan's intervention contributed significantly to the change in the substance of the Dred Scott decision." Again, as with his choices for the Cabinet, Buchanan extended the prerogatives of the presidency to promote

Southern interests and to grasp for the final solution of a problem he believed was caused solely by interfering Northerners. But rather than acknowledge that the Dred Scott decision destroyed their main platform, the Republicans, whom Buchanan felt should immediately "yield obedience," denounced and repudiated such an iniquitous judicial determination. Buchanan believed the disruption of the Union that followed was their fault, not his.[55]

John Brown, a fanatical abolitionist, led a raid at Harper's Ferry in 1859 to get guns and munitions for a war to free slaves. The raid failed and John Brown was hanged.

Buchanan was attacked in the press by Northerners, Southerners, Democrats and Republicans. After Lincoln's election, South Carolina seceded from the Union, followed by six other states of the Deep South: Georgia, Florida, Alabama, Louisiana, Texas and North Carolina. After the secession, Cabinet officers and congressmen from those states resigned. Buchanan then had less opposition. To Buchanan's credit, no state seceded until after Lincoln was elected. The Civil War did not start while Buchanan was in office.

As a strict constructionist, Buchanan condoned slavery, as did the U.S. Constitution. Buchanan never married. He is the only bachelor president in American history. He died in 1868 of old age. He was 77.

Buchanan supported freedom of speech and the press and the right of peaceful dissent. He supported freedom of religion and opposed bigotry. He opposed political parties that were prejudiced against non–Protestants, foreigners and immigrants. He respected all white people, but condoned slavery and allowed mistreatment of slaves and Native Americans. Buchanan's record of religious tolerance was challenged by the Utah War, or Mormon War. Troops were sent but the dispute was settled peacefully. Buchanan vetoed a popular Homestead Act which would have given 110 acres of free land to settlers.

Abraham Lincoln

A Black Hawk War veteran, state legislator, U.S. congressman and leader in Illinois of the opposition to the Kansas-Nebraska Act, Lincoln ran for U.S. Senate against Stephen A. Douglas. Although he ultimately lost the election, Lincoln won national attention with his nomination acceptance speech in which he said, "A house divided against itself cannot stand. I believe this government cannot endure permanently half slave and half free."[56] Lincoln challenged Douglas to a series of debates. The debates made Lincoln a national leader of his party.

Elected in 1860, Lincoln became the first Republican president. Following Lincoln's election, seven Southern states seceded from the Union and formed the Confederate States of America. This meant war! The first shot of the Civil War was fired by the South at Fort Sumter.

The first Battle of Bull Run took place on July 21, 1861. Thirty-thousand Northern troops commanded by General Irvin McDowell attacked an equal force of Confederates commanded by General P.G. T. Beauregard. McDowell swept back the Confederate left flank. Victory seemed sure. The Virginia brigade led by Stonewall Jackson arrived by rail and checked the Union advance. The Southerners then counterattacked, driving the Union soldiers back. Retreat turned to rout. McDowell's men ran toward Washington, D.C., abandoning their weapons and trampling sightseers who had come to watch the battle. Panic engulfed Washington. Richmond, the Southern capital, exulted. Both sides expected Washington to fall within hours. But the inexperienced Southern troops were too disorganized to follow up their victory.

Southern confidence soared, while the North realized how difficult it would be to subdue the Confederacy. After the defeat at the Battle of Bull Run, Lincoln devised a broader, more systematic strategy for winning the war. The navy would blockade all Southern ports. In the West operations designed to control the Mississippi would be undertaken. A new army would be mustered at Washington to invade Virginia. Congress authorized the enlistment of 500,000 three-year volunteers. After Commanding General Scott's retirement in November 1861, he was replaced by 34-year-old Major General George B. McClellan.

McClellan was the North's first military hero. He drove the Confederates from the pro–Union counties of Virginia, clearing the way for the admission of West Virginia as a state in 1863. McClellan, a braggart, inflated its importance. He defeated only 250 Confederates.

After Bull Run, no heavy fighting took place until early 1862. General Ulysses S. Grant captured forts Henry and Donelson. Grant then moved his forces toward Corinth, Mississippi. Southern General Albert Sidney Johnson surprised Grant by attacking at Shiloh. Grant, with reinforcement, turned the tide the second day. Grant was so shaken by the unexpected attack and appalled by his losses that he allowed the enemy to escape. He was relieved of his command. Although Corinth eventually fell and New Orleans was captured by a naval force under the command of Captain David Farragut, Vicksburg, key to the control of the Mississippi, remained in Southern hands. A great opportunity had been lost.

Lincoln said, "Voorhees, don't it seem strange to you that I, who could never so much as cut off the head of a chicken, should be elected, into the midst of all this blood?"[57]

At Shiloh, Union losses exceeded 13,000 and the Confederates lost 10,699. The South lost General Johnston.

In Virginia, General McClellan moved his army by water to the tip of the peninsula formed by the York and James rivers in order to attack Richmond from the southeast. After the battle between the *Monitor* and the *Merrimack* on March 9, 1862, the North controlled these waters. McClellan's plan alarmed many congressmen because it seemed to leave Washington unprotected. McClellan now displayed the weaknesses that eventually ruined his career. He considered war a kind of gentlemanly contest (like chess) in which maneuver, guile, and positive strategy determined victory. McClellan began the peninsular campaign. Proceeding deliberately with 112,000 men by May 14, he established a base only a few miles from Richmond. A swift thrust might have ended the war quickly but McClellan delayed. As he pushed forward, the Confederates caught part of his force separate and attacked at the Battle of Seven Pines. There were 10,000 casualties but the battle was indecisive. The Confederate commander, General Joseph E. Johnston, was severely wounded; leadership of the Army of Northern Virginia passed to Robert E. Lee. Lee was far superior to McClellan. Where McClellan was complex, egotistical, and perhaps unbalanced, Lee was courtly, tactful and without McClellan's vainglorious belief that he was a man of destiny. Yet on the battlefield Lee's boldness skirted the edge of foolhardiness.

To relieve pressure on Richmond, Lee sent General Stonewall Jackson, soon to be his most trusted lieutenant, on a diversionary raid in the Shenandoah Valley, west of Richmond and Washington. Jackson struck hard and scattered Union forces in the region, winning a number of battles and capturing vast stores of equipment. Lincoln sent 20,000 reserves to check him — much to the dismay of McClellan who wanted the troops to attack Richmond from the North. After Seven Pines, Lee ordered Jackson back to Richmond. While Union armies streamed toward the valley, Jackson slipped stealthily between them. On June 25 he reached Ashland, directly north of Richmond, the Confederate capital.

Before then McClellan had possessed clear numerical superiority but he had only inched ahead. Now, the advantage lay with Lee and the very next day Lee attacked. For seven days the battle raged. McClellan fell back to a new base on the James River where the guns of the navy protected his position. The loss of life was terrible. The Northern casualties were 15,800 and those of the South nearly 20,000.

Lincoln, exasperated with McClellan, reduced his authority and placed him under General Henry W. Halleck. Halleck called off the peninsular campaign and ordered McClellan to move his army to the Potomac, near Washington. He was to join General John Pope, who was gathering a new army between Washington and Richmond. Had McClellan captured Richmond when he had a chance, the war could have ended.

It is understandable for the president to have lost confidence in McClellan, but it was a bad mistake to allow Halleck to pull back the troops. When they withdrew, Lee seized the initiative. With decisiveness and daring he marched rapidly north. In late August, he defeated General Pope and his confused troops at the Second Battle of Bull Run. Lincoln replaced the incompetent Pope. Lincoln in desperation turned back to McClellan even though McClellan had expressed contempt for the president.

Lee again took the offensive. Acting with boldness, he divided his forces and invaded the North. Stonewall Jackson took Harper's Ferry, capturing more than 11,000 prisoners. Another force pressed as far north as Hagerstown, Maryland. McClellan proceeded with his usual slowness until a captured dispatch revealed Lee's plans. Then McClellan moved more swiftly, forcing Lee to fight on September 17 at Antietam.

On a field that offered no room to maneuver, 70,000 Union solders fought 40,000 Confederates. When darkness fell, more than 22,000 lay dead or wounded. Casualties were evenly divided and Confederates lines remained intact. Lee's position was perilous. His men were exhausted. McClellan had not used his reserves and new federal units were arriving hourly. A bold Northern general would have continued the fight through the night or attacked at daybreak. Lee could not retreat without inviting disaster. McClellan, however, did nothing for an entire day while Lee scanned the field in futile search of some weakness in the Union lines; he held his fire. That night the Confederates slipped back across the Potomac into Virginia.

Lee's invasion had failed; his army had been badly mauled; the gravest threat to the Union in the war had been checked. But McClellan had let victory slip through his fingers. Soon Lee was back behind the defenses of Richmond, rebuilding his army. Once again Lincoln dismissed McClellan from his command. This was the final time.

Lincoln said, "As a nation we began by declaring that all men are created equal. We now practically read it all men are created equal, except Negroes. When the Know Nothings get control it will read all men are created equal except Negroes and Foreigners and Catholics."[58]

After the victory at Antietam on September 22, Lincoln made public the Emancipation Proclamation. It said after January 1, 1863, all slaves in areas in rebellion against the United States shall be then, thenceforward, and forever free. Abraham Lincoln determined that "we must free the slaves or be ourselves subdued." In 1862, he finally got his chance.[59]

Lincoln's impetus for issuing the Emancipation Proclamation was military, not moral, necessity. But after taking pen in hand on January 1, 1863, he said, "I never in my life felt more certain that I was doing right than I do in signing this paper."[60] He stated, "If my name ever goes into history it will be for this act, and my whole soul in is it."[61]

The slaves of the South after January 1, 1863, whenever the Northern Army approached, laid down their plows and hoes and flocked to the Union lines in droves. Many became soldiers. The Emancipation Proclamation did not eliminate racism, but it was a step forward. Lincoln also helped end slavery by proposing the Thirteenth Amendment to the Constitution. He approved a congressional bill for the desegregation of the horse-drawn streetcars in Washington and for the acceptance of African-American witnesses in federal courts. He accepted a black ambassador from Haiti. Lincoln urged, in his last address, immediate suffrage for educated African-Americans and for African-American soldiers. This was a small first step leading to universal suffrage. He established the Freedman's Bureau to promote the welfare of ex-slaves.

Lincoln put down a Sioux uprising in Minnesota. Of 303 Indians sentenced to die, Lincoln commuted the sentences of all but 39, one of whom he pardoned.

Using his war powers, Lincoln by decree authorized the suspension of *habeas corpus*. Freedom of speech was preserved, and no espionage or sedition law was passed. There was no real censorship. The Constitution was stretched but not subverted. Lincoln's war powers were softened by his humane sympathy, his humor, his lawyer-like caution, his fairness toward his opponents and his overall character. He grieved for the war dead on both sides. Lincoln granted many commutations and pardons for soldiers who had received the death penalty for sleeping on guard duty or desertion. He felt there was too much killing in the war and soldiers should not be executed.

McClellan was replaced by General Ambrose E. Burnside. Burnside lacked the necessary self-confidence. He was too aggressive. He sent wave after wave of troops to be mowed down by Lee at Fredericksburg. The next day, December 14, General Burnside, tears streaming down his face, ordered the evacuation of Fredericksburg.

Burnside was soon replaced by General Joseph Hooker. "Fighting Joe" Hooker was ill tempered, vindictive and devious. Hooker was no better than Burnside. He was more like McClellan. In April 1863 Hooker had 125,000 men concentrated at Chancellorsville. He outnumbered the Confederates 2 to 1. He should have forced a battle at once. Instead he delayed. Lee sent Jackson to a position on Hooker's unsuspecting flank. Jackson attacked on May 2 at 6 P.M.

Completely surprised, the Union forces crumbled, brigade after brigade overrun before they could wheel to meet Jackson's charge. At the first sound of firing, Lee had struck along the entire front to impede Union movements. If the battle had started earlier in the day, the Confederates might have won a decisive victory; as it happened, nightfall brought a lull, and the next day the Union troops rallied and held their ground. Heavy fighting continued until May 5, when Hooker retreated in good order. At Chancellorsville the Confederates lost 12,000 men, including Stonewall Jackson, killed by a bullet from his own men while returning from reconnaissance. The Confederate Army had suffered another fearful blow to its morale.

On July 1 in Gettysburg, Pennsylvania, a Confederate division clashed with two brigades of the Union cavalry. Both sides sent for reinforcements.

The Confederates won control of the town. The Union army, commanded by General George G. Meade, took a strong position on Cemetery Ridge. Lee's men occupied Seminary Ridge, a parallel position. By nightfall on July 3, the Confederate army was spent and bleeding, the Union lines unbroken. On July 4 the armies rested. On July 5 Meade let opportunity pass and, like McClellan at Antietam, permitted Lee retreat to safety.

On the same July 4 in the West, where General Halleck had been called east and Ulysses S. Grant had reassumed command of the Union troops, the North won a great victory, capturing Vicksburg and gaining control of the Mississippi River. Lincoln made Grant commander of all federal troops west of the Appalachians. Grant won the Battle of Chicamaugua and the Battle of Chattanoaga. In March 1864 Lincoln summoned Grant to Washington and named him Supreme Commander of the armies of the United States.

In the meantime, Abraham Lincoln gave his greatest speech at Gettysburg in which he said, "government of the people, by the people, for the people, shall not perish from the earth."[62]

Grant decided to strike Lee around Richmond and send Sherman from Chattanooga to Atlanta. Grant could not defeat Lee at Cold Harbor. He put Petersburg under siege.

In 1864, a draft call for 500,000 men by Lincoln did not sit well with the public. After losses at Kennesaw Mountain, the situation improved for the North. On September 2, Sherman entered Atlanta. Instead of following the Confederates, he marched unopposed from Atlanta to the sea.

To pay for the war, the North raised taxes, sold bonds and printed paper money called "greenbacks." For the first time, an income tax was leveled. The National Banking Act was passed, establishing a national currency and a network of national banks.

Lincoln supported farmers and laborers. He supported the right to strike and favored broad immigration. The Homestead Act was passed. The Morrill Land Grant Act was passed.

Lincoln was re-elected in 1864. Lee could no longer withstand the federal pressure around Petersburg and Sherman's march through Georgia, into South Carolina, and then into North Carolina had been a disaster for the South. Further resistance would be futile. On April 9, 1865, Lee surrendered to Grant at Appomattox Court House.

Abraham Lincoln was shot by an assassin, John Wilkes Booth, on April 14, 1865. President Lincoln died the next day.

"Not often in the story of mankind does a man arrive on earth who is both steel and velvet, who holds in his heart and mind the paradox of terrible storm and peace unspeakable and perfect. Here and there across centuries come reports of men alleged to have these contrasts. And the incomparable Abraham Lincoln, born [in 1809] is an approach, if not a perfect realization, of this character."[63]

Abraham Lincoln really deserved his nickname, "Honest Abe." He held himself to the highest standard in both his public and personal life. Lincoln wrote, "Others have been made fools of by the girls, but this can never with truth be said of me. I most emphatically, in this instance, made a fool of myself. I have now come to the conclusion never again to think of marrying, and for this reason I can never be satisfied with anyone who would be blockhead enough to have me."[64]

Later, he wrote, "Nothing new here, except my marrying, which is a matter of profound wonder."[65]

Historian Mark Van Doren said, "To me, Lincoln seems, in some ways, the most interesting man who ever lived. He was gentle but this gentleness was combined with a terrific toughness, and iron strength."[66]

Andrew Johnson

President Abraham Lincoln, a Republican, decided he wanted a wartime Union ticket for his re-election in 1864. He selected Andrew Johnson, a Tennessee Democrat who had remained loyal to the Union, for his vice-presidential running mate. They won easily. On the day of the inauguration, March 4, 1865, Johnson spoke first and became involved in a scandal. It appeared that he was ill or intoxicated or both. He spoke incoherently and in poor taste. His speech ran overtime and two senators stopped him. He was soundly criticized in Congress and called disgraceful by some of the newspapers. Lincoln said, "I have known Andrew Johnson for many years. He made a bad slip the other day, but you need not be scared; Andy ain't a drunkard."[67] "Parson" Brownlow wrote, "Nobody in Tennessee ever regarded him as being addicted to the excessive use of whiskey."[68] After this Johnson was accused of speaking while drunk only once, on Washington's birthday in 1866. Johnson spoke well from a written copy but poorly in a "stump" speech.

Lincoln was shot on April 14, 1865, and died the next day. Andrew Johnson was sworn in as president of the United States. The new president said, "I have long labored to ameliorate and elevate the condition of the great mass of the American people. Toil and an honest advocacy of the great principal of free government have been mine — the consequences of God. This has been the foundation of my political *creed*.... I want your encouragement and countenance. I shall ask and rely upon you and others in carrying the government through its present perils."[69]

Johnson made a mistake by keeping Lincoln's Cabinet, men who were loyal not to Johnson but to his enemies, the Radical Republicans in Congress. Johnson wanted to implement Lincoln's policies for Southern Reconstruction but he was blocked. The Radical Republicans wanted to punish the South by continuing military rule, avoiding *habeas corpus* and trial by jury into peacetime. Congress passed the Tenure of Office Act. Secretary of War Edwin A. Stanton pigeonholed a request for orders from the governor of Louisiana and two hundred people were killed. When the death penalties for the Lincoln assassination were carried out, Stanton tore out a page containing the clemency recommendation of the court on Mrs. Surratt's sentence. After her death Stanton replaced the torn-out page. When Johnson discovered this he asked for Stanton's resignation. Stanton refused and continued to issue orders without the president's knowledge. Johnson fired Stanton, but under the Tenure of Office Act, Johnson couldn't fire Stanton. Congress impeached Johnson. Johnson was acquitted. Then Stanton resigned.

Johnson's domestic programs were devoted to the welfare of all the people, including former slaves. He supported family farms and wanted free land for poor Southern whites. His tax policies favored the poor at the expense of the rich. He gradually called in paper money in order to keep inflation under control. He encouraged economy in government spending. His tax program passed because Congress concentrated on defeating his tariff proposals.

Johnson opposed federal aid for internal improvements as he thought it should be left to the states. He opposed federal aid to education because of his state rights views. In 1867 President Johnson appointed as the first U.S. Commissioner of Education Henry Barnard, one of the nation's best educational leaders of the nineteenth century.

In 1866 an Indian uprising over a railroad being constructed over their land led to an attack on Fort Kearmy and terrified whites. A peace commission moved the railroad and the army fort. Johnson treated Native Americans fairly.

Johnson was a former slave owner but the Civil War and the ratification of the Thirteenth Amendment ended slavery. Johnson treated ex-slaves and Indians well. In his first State of the Union message, the president said African-American suffrage should be left to the states; former slaves should be protected in all their liberties, in the right to work, to own property, and to receive just pay for their work. He opposed compulsory colonization but favored assisting those who wanted to emigrate. He believed the two races should try to live side by side in a state of mutual benefit and good will.

He supported freedom of speech and the press and the right of peaceful dissent. He supported freedom of religion and opposed bigotry. He vigorously opposed the Know-Nothing movement and its prejudices against Catholics and foreigners. Johnson opposed injustices of the

Reconstruction era and the denial of *habeas corpus* and trial by jury. He opposed abuses under military rule. His vetoes of the Freedman's Bureau Bill and the Civil Rights Bill were not based on bias but on a desire for reconciliation with the South.

After the war there was a breakdown in public morality and corruption was widespread. Commissioner of Internal Revenue E. A. Rollins was involved with Whiskey Ring. Johnson asked for and received Rollins' resignation. Rollins was indicted, but acquitted because the Whiskey Ring controlled the judge and jury. Johnson himself was honest, dedicated and moral.

Ulysses S. Grant

Grant received an appointment in 1839 to the United States Military Academy at West Point. He graduated twenty-first in a class of 39 in 1843. Grant served in the Mexican War with diligence and bravery, twice being cited for gallantry under fire.

After the Mexican War, Grant was stationed at various places, including the West Coast. Unhappy and lonely, separated from his family, Grant drank too much. He received a reprimand and resigned from the army in 1854 to rejoin his wife and children.

When the Civil War broke out, Grant returned to the army. The war gave Grant a second chance. This shabby, cigar-smoking West Pointer became the hero of the Civil War. In 1866, he was honored by Congress as General of the Army, the first time this title had been awarded. In 1867-1868, he served briefly as acting Secretary of War.

General Grant, a Republican, was elected president in 1868 and re-elected in 1872. In the campaign of 1868, the Democratic newspapers searched Grant's military record and announced the general was lacking in "real ability or real character." He was a "butcher," a "liar," a "drunkard," a "weathercock" and a "puppet."[70] His order removing Jews from his department in 1862 was flaunted before Jewish citizens.[71] On the other side, the Democratic candidate, Horatio Seymour, it was claimed, had a "disloyal" war record and the danger involved in his election constituted the main burden of polemic orations.[72]

When Grant was elected, the American people hoped for an end to turmoil. Grant provided neither vigor nor reform. Looking to Congress for direction, he seemed bewildered. One unidentified visitor to the White House noted "a puzzled pathos, as of a man with a problem before him of which he does not understand the terms."

The Union Pacific Railroad was headed by the Credit Mobiler, who hired themselves for tremendous profit. They built the track from Omaha to Utah. Schyler Colfax, Grant's vice president, had been implicated in the Credit Mobiler scandal.

During his campaign for re-election in 1872, Grant was attacked by liberal Republican reformers. Grant called them narrow-headed men with eyes so close together that they could look out of the same gimlet hole without winking. Grant's friends in the Republican Party came to be known proudly as the Old Guard. Grant allowed Radical Reconstruction to run its course in the South, bolstering it at times with military force.

Grant's domestic program was a failure. He did not deal effectively with the Panic of 1873. His fiscal policies were counterproductive. Grant urged economy in government spending. He stopped appropriations on buildings not yet started. Public works were postponed. A return to specie payment was postponed. Congress passed a bill that would increase currency, but President Grant vetoed it. Grant favored big business over farmers, workers and the common people. He was more interested in aid to business than in helping the poor. Even during the depression, he had no poverty programs except those to help ex-slaves and Native Americans.

He promoted repressive tax policies, favoring tax breaks for the wealthy and opposing a tax on high incomes. Congress pressured state legislatures to regulate high passenger and freight rates that were charged by the corrupt railroads. Then, Congress opposed the manufacturers and jobbers who sold farm machinery at inflated prices. Congress received no help from Grant in these endeavors. He sent a message to Congress about the exploitation of newly arrived immigrants, but nothing was done. Grant supported the right of ex-slaves to vote and hold office.

After gold was discovered in the Black Hills in 1874, miners poured into the area, disregarding a treaty and violating the Indians' rights. Skirmishes broke out, and the army tried to round up the Sioux and place them on reservations. Under Crazy Horse and Sitting Bull, the Indians resisted, leading to the battles of Rosebud and Little Big Horn.

Congress created Yellowstone National Park. The president proposed a constitutional amendment requiring each state to establish and maintain free public schools for all children irrespective of sex, color, birthplace, or residence. The amendment would forbid the teaching of religious tenets in the schools, and no funds could be allocated for schools of religious denominations. This progressive and far-sighted proposal was ignored by Congress.

Corruption tarred the Grant Administration. Personally honest, Grant appointed crooks to office that took advantage of him. He was unable to restore confidence during the depression after the scandals were revealed. Grant was so intent on rewarding his friends that his administration was riddled with corruption. His private secretary, Orville Babcock, and two Cabinet members, W. W. Belknap and W. A. Richardson, were caught and had to resign. Many of his other appointees in sub-cabinet level positions were involved in corruption as were many leading businessmen and some members of Congress. The president was a victim, more than an instigator, of the dishonesty and unethical behavior with which his administration is tarred. However, he stopped James Fisk, Jr., and Jay Gould from cornering the gold market even though they had been among the principal fundraisers for his presidential campaign. Grant was not proven personally guilty of any of the scandals of his administration. Grant never accepted bribes but he accepted expensive gifts he shouldn't have. Grant was accused of not keeping his word and abandoning his moral principals in situations involving his friends. Public opinion of Grant plummeted. At the end of Grant's second term, "historians aghast at the lack of public virtue revealed in these four years, have labeled them, 'The Nadir of National Disgrace.'"[73]

Rutherford B. Hayes

A Republican, Hayes won the disputed election of 1876. Samuel J. Tilden, a Democrat, received a majority of popular votes and appeared to have won the majority of the electoral votes giving him the election. However, journalists at the *New York Times* devised a plan to dispute some electoral votes and steal the election from Tilden. In the popular vote Tilden received 250,000 more votes than Hayes. A commission was established to settle the disputed votes. The commission voted 8 to 7 in favor of Hayes on all the disputed votes. Hayes was declared the winner by electoral vote. Nothing like this ever happened until George W. Bush won the 2000 election over Al Gore.

The Democrats had been cheated and were very angry in 1876 and for a time it looked like war. Tilden did not want another Civil War and accepted the result. While other presidential candidates have received a plurality of popular votes and lost, Tilden has been the only presidential candidate to receive a majority of the popular vote and lose. It was indeed a stolen election.

A visionary and reformer, Hayes surprised the Conkling faction of the Republican Party. He even enacted some of the reforms advocated by his presidential reformer opponent, Tilden.

Hayes, a sound money man, opposed greenback and silver advocates. The Bland-Allison Act, which required the federal government to purchase two to four million dollars of silver to coinage, was passed. Hayes vetoed it and Congress overrode his veto. It was intended to help farmers and debtors by inflating the currency. The Panic of 1873 ended and prosperity returned. The administration's fiscal policies did not bring the return of prosperity, which came in spite of them. Hayes resumed payment of specie for greenbacks in 1879. This policy helped restore business confidence and helped business improve. Hayes favored business interests over farmers and laborers. He ordered federal troops to four states to suppress strikes by railroad workers. He issued proclamations against domestic violence. During the Hayes Administration, the nation completed the change from an agrarian society to an industrial one. He did nothing to prevent the development of trusts and monopolies. He did not help the poor.

Hayes was a man of peace. He ended the military occupation of the South by recalling the troops in 1877. During the late 1870s, cattlemen and other groups fought for control of Lincoln County, New Mexico. Hayes ordered a stop to the fighting and appointed Lew Wallace territorial governor. Wallace declared martial law and used troops to bring the Lincoln County War to an end. He ended, temporarily, a number of Indian wars. The Nez Percé War ended with the surrender of Chief Joseph only 40 miles short of the Canadian border after retreating more than 1000 miles.

Hayes had a better record in dealing with Native Americans than most presidents from 1810 to 1900. Secretary of Interior Carl Schurz encouraged better treatment of Native Americans and initiated a number of reforms. In the Grant Administration, the Indian Commissioner had awarded contracts and purchased supplies with a disregard for business principles and honesty. Everywhere manipulation and fraud occurred. Indian agents put their unqualified relatives on the payroll. During the previous administration, Native Americans starved while contractors and agents divided profits. Schurz fired the Indian Commissioner, the chief clerk and the worst employees. Schurz completely reorganized the Indian Bureau and restored honesty to the Indian service. Hayes' Indian policy included fair compensation for lands taken from the tribes, ownership of land by individual Native Americans, and industrial and general education leading to eventual citizenship. Hayes ordered by proclamation the removal of squatters from Indian Territory.

Hayes supported freedom of speech and press and the right of peaceful dissent, but used the military against strikers. He supported freedom of religion and opposed bigotry, but he opposed polygamy by the Mormons. He was not prejudiced against any racial or ethnic group. He vetoed a Chinese Exclusion Act, but the Treaty of 1880 restricted but did not ban Chinese immigration. He favored the Fifteenth Amendment, but did not enforce it.

Hayes found out that 200 politicians were paid by the New York City Custom House and performed no work. Hayes fired them and the top officials, including the collector, future president Chester A. Arthur.[74]

President Hayes eliminated corruption in the executive branch. He stood up to Congress and restored presidential power.

Hayes was actually more of a Democrat than a Republican.[75] He paved the way for Grover Cleveland and for a reorganization of government on honest foundations. After the hate of the Civil War and the corruption of the Reconstruction, he came as a healer to a better future.[76]

James A. Garfield

In 1880 the Republican Party was split between Stalwarts led by Roscoe Conkling and the Half-Breeds led by James G. Blaine. The Stalwarts wanted a third term for U.S. Grant. Blaine and Grant were deadlocked in the convention. Garfield, a compromise candidate, was nominated on the thirty-sixth ballot. Chester A. Arthur was Garfield's running mate. Garfield defeated General Hancock, the Democratic candidate, in the fall election.

Garfield never really took a stand in the election. He lacked political convictions and tried to appeal to all factions. He was a party regular, a pragmatist and tried to make no enemies.

Before President Garfield could develop domestic programs, he was shot by assassin Charles J. Guiteau on July 2, 1881. Doctors repeatedly probed the wound near the pancreas with bare fingers and un-sterilized instruments trying to find the bullet. Garfield died on September 19, 1881. Guiteau, though obviously mentally ill, was hanged on June 30, 1882.

Chester Alan Arthur

Chester A. Arthur, a Republican, was vice president when Garfield was assassinated. He declined to take over during Garfield's disability. After Garfield died, Arthur was sworn in as president the next day.

During the Arthur Administration, the country drifted slowly into an economic depression. Arthur didn't know what to do. Arthur proposed early retirement of silver certificates and abandoning the compulsory coinage of a fixed amount of specie.

Arthur favored business over labor and big landowners over small farmers. Arthur urged revision of homestead laws to protect ranchers from homesteaders. He opposed the fencing of public land. A national Bureau of Labor and a Bureau of Animal Industry were established. Arthur vetoed a bill enacting safety and health standards for steamships bringing large numbers of immigrants to the United States. He objected to the wording. Congress revised the bill and the president signed it. His conservative views on the role of government prevented him from taking other actions to preserve the general welfare.

Arthur proposed the repeal of all internal taxes except on tobacco and liquor. Congress took no action. Even though there was a surplus, neither President Arthur nor Congress wanted to spend the surplus on internal improvements. Congress refused to lower taxes.

Arthur created a territorial government for Alaska. He vetoed a pork-barrel rivers and harbors bill, but Congress overrode the veto. Arthur wanted to preserve forests on the public domain but was unsuccessful.

President Arthur treated African-Americans kindly. He appointed several African-Americans to government positions and called for federal aid to African-American education. He proposed measures to help Native Americans become full citizens and with their gradual assimilation into society. He also proposed legislation to prevent intrusion on land set aside for Native Americans. Arthur kept Garfield's Cabinet and replaced them one by one with stalwarts as they resigned.

Arthur signed a new ten-year Chinese Exclusion Act. Arthur asked Congress to suppress polygamy. He urged caution in granting veterans pensions.

Historians don't know much about President Chester Alan Arthur, as his papers were burned before his death. He had an aristocratic disdain for the public and the public did not like him.

Grover Cleveland

Cleveland, a Democrat, was the only president to serve split terms. He was president from 1885 to 1889 and from 1893 to 1897. Cleveland was the first Democratic president to serve since Andrew Johnson and the first Democrat to win a presidential election since James Buchanan.

An honest reformer in a time of crooked politicians, Cleveland's 1884 campaign slogan was "Public Office is a Public Trust."[77] Cleveland's opponent in the election of 1884 was Republican James G. Blaine, nicknamed the Plumed Knight. Republican reformers called Mugwumps could not support Blaine and decided to back Cleveland.

A Republican newspaper reported that Cleveland, a bachelor, had fathered a child out of wedlock. Cleveland admitted that the accusation was true and said he was paying child support. The scandal nearly cost him the election. In the campaign of 1884, the Democratic Party was called the party of "Rum, Romanism and Rebellion,"[78] which infuriated New York Catholic voters and may have cost Blaine the New York electoral vote and the election.

A conscientious president, Cleveland wiped out corruption in the departments of Interior, Navy and the Treasury. In addition to running an honest government, Cleveland favored lowering the tariff and maintaining the gold standard. He promoted education, including public schools.

President Cleveland showed a paternalistic attitude toward African-Americans, Native Americans and Chinese immigrants. He signed the Dawes Act, which he thought would improve the lot of Native Americans. Unfortunately, the act in the long run had a harmful effect on those he was trying to help. Cleveland was a reformer of Indian policy, except for trouble with the Apaches. In retaliation for raids by Apaches who had left the reservation, the government embarked on a campaign to wipe out the non-reservation Apaches. Soldiers were ordered to kill the men and return the women and children to the reservation. With this one exception, Cleveland supported the rights of Native Americans. When he first became president, Cleveland issued proclamations warning against attempts to settle on Oklahoma lands, closing reservations on the east bank of the Missouri River in Dakota Territory to settlement, and ordering cattlemen to vacate Indian lands and Arapaho reservations. He favored legislation for the education and civilization of Native Americans with a view toward future citizenship. He opposed the Force Bill, aimed at protecting the suffrage of southern African-Americans. Cleveland thought it would be a dangerous expansion of the power of the central government.

The president suppressed the Pullman strike; strikebreakers were hired, installed as federal officials, and given the strikers' jobs. Newspapers falsely reported revolution and anarchy. Attorney General Richard Olney wanted to suppress the strike. Cleveland was reluctant to send troops, so Olney had federal judges issue restraining orders. The army was called out and violence erupted in Chicago. Cleveland then sided with the railroads and assumed power as commander-in-chief. Soldiers enlisted by the Department of Justice as deputies were paid by the General Managers Association, but were certified as federal representatives. Later an official, fully-documented investigation rebuked Cleveland and Olney for failing to protect the rights of labor. The Interstate Commerce Act placed federal controls on business. The Department of Labor was created. Cleveland conserved national resources and protected the environment by protecting the public domain and Indian lands.

While he was in the White House, Cleveland married Frances Folsum on June 2, 1886. A baby, Ruth, was born to this union. A candy bar was named after her.

Cleveland ran for re-election in 1888 against Republican Benjamin Harrison. During the campaign, an interfering British minister said Cleveland was not hostile to British interests and it would be all right to vote for him. This interference hurt Cleveland and he lost the election.[79]

Cleveland recognized that trouble was coming. He said, "The rich were getting rich and the poor poorer."[80] In 1892 Cleveland won the presidency back from Harrison.

The Panic of 1893 had already started before Cleveland's second inauguration. It was a terrible depression. People actually starved. The president failed to deal effectively with the economy. The gold standard was counterproductive. His lower tariff would have helped, but it did not pass Congress.

Opposed to using federal money for internal improvements, Cleveland vetoed a rivers and harbors bill. Cleveland vigorously pursued a policy barring special favors to any economic group. Vetoing a bill to appropriate $10,000 to distribute seed grain among drought-stricken farmers in Texas, he wrote, "Federal aid in such cases encourages the expectation of paternal care on the part of the Government and weakens the sturdiness of our national character...."[81]

He also vetoed many private pension bills to Civil War veterans whose claims were fraudulent. When Congress, pressed by the Grand Army of the Republic, passed a bill that granted pensions for disabilities not caused by military service, Cleveland vetoed it, too. As the depression deepened, he still refused to help poor people.

Benjamin Harrison

A Republican, Benjamin Harrison, a grandson of President William Henry Harrison, served as president from 1889 to 1893, between Cleveland's split terms. In the election of 1888 Cleveland received the most popular votes but Harrison won in the Electoral College.

A leader of the Republican Party, James G. Blaine, the Plumed Knight, was chosen for Secretary of State. William Windom became Secretary of the Treasury. Benjamin F. Tracy was chosen Secretary of Navy. Redfield Proctor was selected for the Secretary of War position. William H. Miller became Attorney General. John Wanamaker was chosen Postmaster General. The Secretary of Agriculture was Jeremiah Ruck.

Harrison's Cabinet choices disappointed and offended several of the most powerful party leaders: Thomas C. (Boss) Platt, Matthew S. (Boss) Quay, and James S. Clarkson. These were men who thought they had made Harrison president. Harrison was willing to acknowledge their contributions to his victory in 1888. He also had a strong belief in his own role. Four years later, only half the states from which the original Cabinet hailed gave Harrison a majority of their convention votes for re-nomination.

Elijah Hatford was Harrison's private secretary. Hatford worked so hard he had a three-week physical collapse in the fall of 1889. Harrison's staff included an assistant secretary, two stenographers, a telephone operator, a purchasing and disbursing clerk, two other clerks, two doorkeepers and four messengers. Harrison had no speechwriters and prepared his state papers himself.[82]

Harrison, in his inaugural address, spoke of progress. Invoking the sanctions of the Founding Fathers for the Republican economic program, he noted that a nationist drive for economic and self sufficiency had fueled the formation of the Constitution in the 1780s. Now, 100 years later, tariff protection represented the same patriotic interest.

He made proposals concerning the Treasury surplus; a stronger navy, subsidies to American steamship lines, and more generous veterans' pensions for Union veterans and their wives and orphans. He spoke of the patronage question and civil service and trusts, and closed by reminding Americans to preserve republican liberty.

Harrison performed the tasks of Cabinet secretaries when they were ill. In January 1891 Windom died. He was replaced by Charles Foster.

Harrison handled a large number of patronage requests personally. How he handled them offended many of the Republican Party bosses. Harrison refused to accept the bosses' patronage recommendations with no questions asked. Matthew Quay, Republican national chairman, handed the president a list of men whom he and a fellow senator from Pennsylvania wanted appointed. When Harrison asked for information about the proposed officials, Quay said that it was not necessary; the two senators vouched for them. Harrison told Quay that he "could not consent to the surrender of the personal responsibility for appointments which the Constitution enjoyed, and he would have proper inquiries initiated on his own behalf, and he hoped the result would be to corroborate the judgment of the senators." This did not sit well with party leaders.

The president and Mrs. Harrison sat through a sermon by Episcopal bishop Henry Potter at the commemoration of George Washington's inauguration. Potter said the course of the American public had declined from the Founders' republican aspirations to a "conception of the National Government as a huge machine, existing mainly for the purpose of rewarding partisan service ... [and] nothing good or true since Washington lived & all goodness in the government had departed." Sharing her husband's discomfort, Caroline Harrison was quite crushed. A few days later, President Harrison appointed the young reformer Theodore Roosevelt to the Civil Service Commission. But Harrison had neither the power nor the inclination to totally wipe out the spoils system. He and his aides continued to replace Cleveland Democrats with Republicans. Patronage power was less a blessing than a curse. With bosses disaffected, office seekers disappointed, reformers alienated, and Democrats alleging sportsmanship, Harrison's reelection proposals were undermined.[83]

James Tanner, Commissioner of Pensions, became a political liability by stretching the rules. Tanner clashed with his boss, Interior Secretary John W. Noble. After a Cabinet meeting in September 1889, Harrison asked for Tanner's resignation. Harrison replaced Tanner with Green B. Raum, a popular and more judicious veteran. The president called for legislation granting a pension to every veteran of the Union forces who could no longer support himself, whether or not his incapacity derived from his service.[84]

Congressional clerks read Harrison's annual message on December 3, 1889. Harrison recommended to Congress tariff revision with preservation of protection, silver legislation that would not inflate the currency, anti-trust legislation, regulatory measures to ensure the safety of railroad workers, and protection of the right to vote, especially for African-Americans in the South. Harrison believed that wise tariff revision could reduce the federal budget surplus, but he also promoted measures that would put the revenue to good use; he increased veterans' pensions, aid to education, aid to internal improvements, and subsidies to the American merchant marine and construction of navel vessels. Harrison took his legislature role seriously. Speaker of the House Thomas Brackett Reed supported Harrison strongly. He blocked obstructionist efforts by the Democrats and earned the name "Czar Reed."

In an era when the use of gold or silver was a main political issue, Harrison favored bimetallism. The Sherman Silver Purchase Act passed, increasing the amount of silver the Treasury was required to purchase each month, with the payment to be paid in Treasury notes, thus increasing the supply of paper money. This helped farmers, laborers, debtors, and the West. However, as most people redeemed their notes in gold, the fear of a drain on the Treasury's gold reserves helped cause the Panic of 1893. Another cause of the depression was the McKinley Tariff Act, which hurt the economy. The worst effects of the depression were not felt until Cleveland's second administration, but it began in Harrison's term. The Sherman Anti-trust Act was the first legislation passed regulating big business, but it was ineffective.

Harrison used the power of government to weaken organized labor and break strikes. Fighting broke out over labor disputes, resulting in twenty deaths at a steel company and thirty miners being killed. During a switchmen's strike, arson, train wrecks and murder occurred.

Farm income was low, but prices for supplies were high. Indebtedness contributed to their distress. Democrats claimed the McKinley Tariff of 1890 caused prices to go so high that farmers and workers would be unable to afford the necessities of life. Harrison did not believe that government programs to help poor people were constitutional.

Harrison's Indian policy led to small wars between Native Americans and white settlers. President Harrison opened Indian lands to white settlement and did nothing to help Native Americans.

President Harrison appointed some African-Americans to government jobs. The Dependent Pension Act was passed by Congress, which granted an invalid veteran a pension of up to $12 per month or, in the event of his death, pensions to his widow and children or parents. Before the end of Harrison's term, pension spending reached $144 million annually, more than 40 percent of the federal government's receipts. Later scholars of the origins of government welfare policy have called the Dependent Pension Act "watershed legislation."[85]

In September 1890, the money market tightened. Harrison and Treasury officials acted swiftly, injecting more than fifty million dollars into the economy through bond purchases, early payment of interest on bonds and increased pension disbursements. Within a week, Halford was able to report to the Cabinet that "the financial situation has been very considerably, if not entirely, relieved."

Harrison visited Johnstown, Pennsylvania, the scene of a devastating flood soon after he had taken office. In the wake of the disaster, the president offered federal assistance to the governor and personally spearheaded an effort to raise a relief fund. Now the entire population of the recovering town, with bells ringing and whistles blowing, came out to show their gratitude to Harrison.

In late July 1890, Harrison sent an anti-lottery message to Congress. Seven weeks later President Harrison signed an act banning the notorious Louisiana Lottery and similar companies from using the mail. In August Congress passed the Meat Inspection Act. The administration secured an end to European meat restrictions by the end of 1891. Congress authorized six new ships, including three coastline battleships. Congress adjourned on October 1, 1890, after one of the most productive sessions in history.

When Harrison became president, the Republicans controlled both houses of Congress. However, he lost the support of his own party, which split. The Democrats won Congress by a landslide in 1890.

Harrison successfully pushed for two measures in the second session. Congress passed a postal subsidy whereby the government paid steamship lines to carry overseas naval goods. Congress also passed a Forest Reserve Act, empowering the president to set aside public lands as national forests. Sequoa and Yosemite National Parks were established. By proclamation he created many forest preserves.

The Fifty-first Congress passed 531 public laws, representing an unprecedented level of legislative accomplishment, unequaled until Theodore Roosevelt's second term.

In the election of 1892, Cleveland received 277 electoral votes to 145 for Harrison and 22 for Weaver. The Democrats won majorities in both houses of Congress.

Harrison was a praying churchman. He was a member of the Presbyterian Church. He was never in a scandal in his personal life.

William McKinley

McKinley, a Republican, defeated Democrat William Jennings Bryan in the election of 1896. The McKinley Administration was mainly concerned with foreign relations, including the Spanish American War.

By about the time of his inauguration the Panic of 1893 ended and prosperity returned to stay through his administration. The Dingley Tariff, with the highest rates ever, passed and included reciprocity. The Gold Standard Act of 1900 was passed. The Republicans took credit for the prosperity. In 1900 McKinley won re-election with the slogan, "The Full Dinner Pail." Prosperity was based on full production and an excess of exports over imports. McKinley changed from a bimetallist to an advocate of the gold standard. He financed the war by raising taxes and selling bonds.

After the war, McKinley undertook a rehabilitation program in Cuba. The starving people were fed and the sick were cared for. Sanitary projects were carried out. Plantations were reclaimed, machinery reconstructed and roads rebuilt. Supplies were sent to the poverty-stricken people of Puerto Rico. Free trade was obtained for Puerto Rico. President McKinley pursued policies providing internal improvements in the newly acquired dependencies. He paved the way for the building of the Panama Canal.

McKinley favored businessmen and industrialists over farmers and laborers. The president treated Native Americans and African-Americans well. He had only an average Cabinet until he strengthened it by adding Elihu Root and John Hay. The Cabinet member closest to the president was James Wilson. Mark Hanna, Republican Party "boss" of McKinley's home state of Ohio, wanted to be a U.S. senator, so McKinley appointed an incumbent U.S. senator, John Sherman, to Secretary of State in the McKinley Cabinet. This was a mistake. Sherman was in poor health. His hearing and memory were so bad he could hardly work.

McKinley had a paternalistic attitude toward Filipinos, Puerto Ricans and Cubans. As a youth he had opposed slavery. He condemned injustices to African-Americans in the South after Reconstruction. McKinley's Secretary of Interior, Ethan Allen Hitchcock, guarded Native Americans from exploitation and injustice. McKinley's most important veto was of a bill opening the Navajo reservation to exploitation. After the Spanish American War was over, McKinley insisted on humane treatment for people in the dependencies, but he did not want citizenship for them.

McKinley supported freedom of speech and rights of dissent. He supported freedom of religion. He was pleased by the great reforms and advances and reforms made in America in the late 1890s. He established a national monument in Vicksburg in 1899. Later it became a national military park. In 1898 he established a national park at Mount Rainier.

McKinley was kind and a gentleman, but a poor leader. He is remembered for the kindness with which he treated Ida, his invalid wife. McKinley started his professional career as a teacher. It is unfortunate that William McKinley left teaching and went into politics.

In McKinley's inaugural address he advocated tariff revision, international bimetallism. He favored arbitration and would work for domestic prosperity. Financial reform would be postponed and the tariff would be raised.[86]

In the friendly atmosphere of the McKinley Administration, industrial combinations developed at an unprecedented pace. Newspapers caricatured McKinley as a little boy led around by "Nursie" Hanna, the representative of the trusts. However, McKinley was not dominated by Hanna; he condemned the trusts as "dangerous conspiracies against the public good."

Public interest reflected McKinley's popularity with the people. "It is clearly apparent that Mr. McKinley assumes the office of president with the goodwill of the country," a Chicago newspaper noted.[87] "Uncle Joe" Cannon, later Speaker of the House, once said that McKinley kept his ear so close to the ground that it was full of grasshoppers.

The president was very well liked and respected. More than once his informal dinners and afternoon smokers which the president attended freely won doubtful votes.

McKinley vetoed a mere fourteen bills in his entire administration; he vetoed the rest in his office and garden before they were introduced.[88]

Senator Chandler wrote a note to McKinley: "Your kind treatment of me has drawn my affection to you as no other President...."[89]

McKinley's chief weakness as an administrator was procrastination and delay in making crucial decisions and his soft-heartedness in facing facts. "He cared nothing about the credit but McKinley always had his way."[90]

McKinley did not hesitate to extract promises of support in return for patronage. "In my judgment, formed after a personal conversation with Major McKinley, there will be no appointments until after the Tariff Bill or at least very few," one politician wrote.[91]

McKinley was re-elected to a second term in 1900 but he was shot on September 6, 1901, by Leon Czolgosz, an anarchist. McKinley died on September 14, 1901.

Theodore Roosevelt

After the Civil War the power of the presidency declined as a corrupt Congress took over until the era of twentieth-century reform. Increased presidential power dovetailed with domestic reform. Theodore Roosevelt was the first Progressive president. He called his reform program the "Square Deal."

In 1885 Woodrow Wilson wrote, "The presidency has fallen from its first estate of dignity because its power has waned; and its power has waned because the power of Congress has become predominant."[92]

For Congress, Theodore Roosevelt felt an increasing disdain. "If this country," Roosevelt wrote in 1897, "could be ruled by a benevolent czar we would doubtless make a good many changes for the better."[93] A former member of the New York State Assembly, U.S. Civil Service commissioner, New York City police commissioner, Assistant Secretary of Navy, war hero and governor of New York, Roosevelt was chosen as a Republican candidate for vice president and elected in 1900. New York Republican boss Thomas Platt wanted Roosevelt to be McKinley's running mate to get the reform-minded governor out of the state. Following McKinley's assassination, Theodore Roosevelt became President of the United States.

Always a reformer, as president, Theodore Roosevelt set out to deal with the whole complex political and social agency of modern industrial society. He had the will to govern. "It is," he wrote about the McKinley assassination, "a dreadful thing to come into presidency this way; but it would be far worse to be morbid about it. Here is the task and I have got to do it to the best of my ability: and that is all there is about it."[94]

Only the federal government, as Roosevelt saw it, once organized to his ideas, could subdue the potentialities for turbulence in American life: clashes of rich and poor, capital and labor, farm and city in the 1890s.

Only the president, he believed, could provide the direction to create and maintain equilibrium. Roosevelt delighted in power. He intended to manage government and society. He assumed responsibilities which his immediate predecessors had not even contemplated.

Roosevelt wrote later, "I did and caused to be done many things not previously done by the President and the heads of the departments. I did not usurp power but I did greatly broaden the use of executive power.... I acted for the common well-being of all our people whenever and in whatever manner was necessary, unless prevented by direct constitutional or legislative prohibition."[95]

Theodore Roosevelt used what he called his "bully pulpit" to appeal directly to the people, going over the heads of Congress and other national leaders. Roosevelt was decisive. Congress could not make up his mind for him. He was a master at compromise. He felt "half a loaf is better than none."

One of the most learned modern presidents, Roosevelt had the historian's sense of the past, especially the American past. He was an authority on military and naval matters, familiar with many languages, a student of biology, and a critic of scientific writing. He knew how to solicit and accept advice. He invited to the White House poets and authors, inventors, explorers, economists, sociologists, ministers, lawyers, business executives, labor leaders, generals and journalists. All were probed for ideas. Theodore Roosevelt, nicknamed "Teddy," read many books. He knew more about domestic affairs than previous presidents did. Theodore Roosevelt was not profound or systematic. He was curious, educable and reflective. He was an intellectual, but a man of action. He was more of a pragmatist than a visionary.

Roosevelt's dominant issue was government's relationship with business. He fought consolidations of industrial wealth and power that were called "trusts." He borrowed ideas from political economists. These competition problems and Roosevelt's recommendations were not new to academic authorities. Theodore Roosevelt was not as radical as the Populists or Knights of Labor in the 1890s. He broke with laissez-faire economics, but he did not want to abolish corporate capitalism. He opposed socialism. He felt through presidential leadership the federal government must have the authority, the will, and the capability to regulate corporate behavior; to prevent unfair pricing, shabby goods, and discrimination in competition; and to prevent dominating activities properly the responsibility of the whole people and their government. Roosevelt felt it was up to the president to create investigative and supervisory bodies within the executive branch and to staff them with competent officers to write and enforce necessary social and economic legislation. It was up to the president to get public support and shepherd legislation through Congress. The president had to challenge the courts, including the Supreme Court.

The Sherman Anti-trust Act of 1890 declared illegal combinations and conspiracies in restraint of interstate or foreign commerce. The E. C. Knight case in 1895 ruled that manufacturing was not interstate commerce. Roosevelt tested the Supreme Court ruling on it. He forced the court to annul this decision by the Sherman Act. The Northern Securities Company controlled several western railroads. Courts earlier had blocked strikes and due process.

The Supreme Court asserted judicial supremacy by judicial review. The court favored business over labor and the rich over poor. In 1895 the Court held the income tax unconstitutional. It ruled against labor on maximum hours and minimum wages.

Advocates of social reform were frustrated. Roosevelt became involved in efforts to use non-judicial instruments of government to undo what the courts had done. Roosevelt appointed judges and prosecutors sympathetic to reform and through them got courts to overrule their bad decisions and sponsor laws to restrict the range over which courts could rule. Roosevelt's first and unexpected assault was the important Northern Securities case, which shocked the lords of American finance. Roosevelt refused to negotiate with J. P. Morgan as a private citizen. Roosevelt's attorney general told Morgan the federal government would not prosecute him, but would proceed against the Northern Securities Company. The Supreme Court ruled in Roosevelt's favor by a five-to-four vote, proving the federal government did have some control over the trusts.

Roosevelt had an opportunity to appoint a new associate justice. On the advice of Lodge, he appointed Oliver Wendell Holmes, Jr. The president thought Holmes was a reformer. He miscalculated. Holmes dissented on the Northern Securities case; Roosevelt told Lodge he was disappointed with Holmes.

President Roosevelt undertook forty-four anti-trust prosecutions, including Dupont, American Tobacco and Standard Oil. The Court broke the tobacco and oil trusts in 1911 after Roosevelt had left office. The Interstate Commerce Act and the Sherman Anti-Trust Act were the bases for trust-busting. To accomplish trust-busting, Roosevelt had to first strengthen the presidency. No incumbent since Lincoln had used his full powers and none since Jackson in peacetime. In Congress, the Republicans followed the leadership of Speaker of the House Joe Cannon and senators Hanna, Aldrich and Spooner, who were defenders of the status quo. The federal bureaucracy had grown, but McKinley had appointed scoundrels in the Post Office Department and time-servers in Interior to sub-cabinet positions.

Roosevelt compromised with powerful senators, conceding them their preferences about the tariff and public finance issues, which were less important to Roosevelt, to get their support for his programs. Theodore Roosevelt reached out to veterans, Catholics, Germans, Methodists, blacks, Hungarians, union leaders and Jews. His delicate distribution of patronage — to a former opponent ready to be converted or to a loyal friend eager to help — gradually wrested party control from Hanna. When Hanna, in 1903, continued to decline an early declaration for Roosevelt's nomination in 1904, President Roosevelt forced his hand by making the issue public when Hanna needed Roosevelt's assistance for his re-election to the Senate. Hanna withdrew his opposition to Roosevelt. Theodore Roosevelt became, in 1903, the master of his own party, indispensable for a president. Roosevelt made his own appointments of his kind of men to senior federal posts and he could press Congress for needed legislation.

In his message to Congress in December 1901, Roosevelt referred to the "grave evils" of big business and asked for "practical efforts" to remove them. He called for legislation banning rebates on freight, expediting anti-trust prosecutions and creating a new Department of Commerce, which would include a Bureau of Corporations to collect and publicize information about industrial conditions. In 1902 President Roosevelt went on a speaking tour, attacking corporate privilege. The staff of the Bureau of Corporations and the staff of the Bureau of Labor provided the information about business structure and operations and about conditions that armed Roosevelt for the initiatives he took after he had won the election in his own right in 1904.

In 1902 Roosevelt interceded to settle the anthracite coal strike. He relied on findings of the Commissioner of Labor and sided with the United Mine Workers, an extraordinary departure from protection of management that presidents had long afforded to management. In 1905, similarly briefed, he approached the problem of railroad regulation. Roosevelt's speeches countered railway propaganda. Midwestern Republican senators were reminded of the growing sentiment for reform among voters. Roosevelt worked out congressional support with the Old Guard Republicans. In the Senate, Roosevelt played back and forth among Progressives, moderates, and Democrats and got exactly what he recommended.

The Hepburn Act of 1906 empowered the Interstate Commerce

Commission to prescribe upon a complaint of a shipper and, after a full hearing, the maximum allowable railroad rate for the service in question. This was only a start, as Roosevelt knew, toward his larger objective: a system in which continuing, informed and disinterested administrative action would supplant lawsuits and legislation as the source for the regulation of transportation and industry. LaFollette and other Progressives wanted Roosevelt to go further for rapid and comprehensive reform. They complained about the president's compromise policy of only getting half a loaf. Roosevelt said he believed in men who took the next step and not those who theorized the two-hundredth step. He spoke of the need to go slow in securing railroad legislation. The highway of commerce had to be open to all on equal terms. It was better to be managed by individuals than by government, but such management worked only on the condition that justice is done the public. He concluded what America needed was to develop an orderly system, and such a system could come only through the gradually increased exercise of the right of official government control.

A bill was introduced to authorize the Department of Agriculture to inspect meat packed for interstate or foreign shipment. Upton Sinclair's book *The Jungle*, about the filth and vile conditions in the Chicago packinghouses, caused an uproar. Senator Albert J. Beveridge, encouraged by Roosevelt, drafted a meat inspection bill in cooperation with the Department of Agriculture. The measure was introduced as an amendment to the pending Agricultural Appropriation Bill. There was opposition but again the president settled for half a loaf and the bill passed. He took the half that affected the relationship between the executive and judicial branches of government.

This meat inspection and the railroad legislation both passed in 1906. Both related to questions under consideration for some years. Both passed because data compiled by the federal government documented the need for remedy, in part because of growing public agitation, to which Roosevelt contributed, and in part by his skillful leadership. Both increased the power of the federal government, but gently because of Roosevelt's compromises. Both acts also spoke to the scope of judicial review.

In 1906 the Democrats won control of Congress, making things difficult for President Roosevelt, as did the Panic of 1907. Roosevelt was blamed for the depression instead of the real reason, undisciplined speculation. The president was able to move ahead by appointing his people to public office and by using his "bully pulpit." President Roosevelt brought many good, young people to federal service by his own youth and vigor, zest, experiences and people.

His Cabinet included only a few weak men who presided over departments for which the president set policy himself. The others, as Roosevelt knew, could do their jobs themselves. One was Elihu Root, Secretary of War, who was replaced by William Howard Taft. The Secretary of Interior, James A. Garfield, was a capable conservationist. Attorney General William W. Moody reorganized the Justice Department.

Below Cabinet level, Gifford Pinchot, Chief Forester, and the most eminent of Progressive conservationists assisted Roosevelt by creating new forests, withdrawing natural timber and mineral lands from private exploitation and preventing the categorical alienation of hydroelective sites.

Charles Prouty, Franklin K. Lane and Herbert Smith served as superior federal commissioners. Henry L. Stimson was appointed District Attorney in Lower Manhattan. Fines of over half a million dollars were obtained from two corporations for violations of the Elkins Act involving a combination in restraint of trade, which were dissolved. Eight officials from three corporations were fined or imprisoned for violations of the law. The government recovered $3,000,000 due to fraud. Yet, for Roosevelt, things were moving too slowly. He was still disappointed in Holmes. He urged recall.

Roosevelt wrote before he left office, "While President I have *been* President, emphatically, I have used every ounce of power there was in the office and I have not cared a rap for the criticisms of those who spoke of my 'usurpation of power'; for I knew that this talk was all nonsense.... I believe that the efficiency of this government depends upon its possessing a strong central executive, and wherever I could establish a precedent for strength in the executive, I did ... bringing big corporations to book — why, in all these cases, I have felt not merely that my action was right in itself, but that in showing the strength of ... the executive establish[ed] a precedent of value. I believe in a strong executive; I believe in power...."[96]

Theodore Roosevelt was a model for strong presidents of the future. He made a case for gradual and moderate reform. Roosevelt had much support in the opposition party. Later Democrats took over the domestic reform movement started by Roosevelt. He started twentieth-century domestic reforms continued by Wilson, Franklin Roosevelt, Truman and Lyndon Johnson.

Far ahead of integration standards of the time, Roosevelt and his family dined with Booker T. Washington at the White House. However, his reputation for racial fairness was blemished by an affair in Brownsville, Texas, when African-American soldiers were accused of shooting up the community. He ordered dishonorable discharges of 160 soldiers who had not been provided with legal representation or given the presumption of innocence. Roosevelt pressured the San Francisco school board to reverse a decision to keep Japanese-American children from attending the city's public schools, but he made a gentlemen's agreement with Japan, severely restricting immigration. Roosevelt opposed Asian laborers working for lower wages and taking white men's jobs. The Dawes Severalty Act was amended in 1906 challenging the Native American reservation system. The president was authorized to parcel allotments to individual Native Americans, making it possible for whites to take over more Indian land by purchasing it from allottees. Many Native Americans sold their land, spent the money, and lived in poverty.

Roosevelt supported freedom of speech, press and religion. He appointed Oscar S. Straus as Secretary of Commerce and Labor; Straus was the first Jewish Cabinet member in America. Roosevelt, after his presidency, supported women's suffrage. Dignity for all was a part of Roosevelt's Square Deal program.

Roosevelt was a great conservationist. The Reclamation Act of 1902 provided for the reclamation and irrigation of arid western lands. He started irrigation or reclamation projects, reserved 125 million acres in national forests, 68 million acres of coal lands, and 1500 waste power sites. He established the first national wildlife refuge at Pelican Island and designated Devil's Tower as the first national monument.

Roosevelt had good cooperation from the courts. He restored public confidence after the Panic of 1907.

William Howard Taft

Taft, a Republican, served as assistant prosecuting attorney for Hamilton County, Ohio, collector of internal revenue for the Cincinnati district, assistant county solicitor, judge on the Cincinnati Superior Court, solicitor general of the United States, federal judge on the Sixth Circuit Court of Appeals, governor of the Philippines, and Secretary of War in the Cabinet of Theodore Roosevelt. Taft became the most popular member of the Cabinet.

Since Roosevelt had served out McKinley's term and then his own term, he felt he should not break the two-term tradition. Taft was Roosevelt's choice to become his successor. In 1906 Taft declared that since the passage of the Dingley Bill there had, in his opinion, been "such changes in the business conditions of the country as to make it wise and just to revise certain schedules of the tariff."[97] This speech was popularly regarded as the opening of his campaign for the presidency.

Taft was not eager for the honor. He had said, "I am not a politician and I dislike politics. I do want to go on the bench, and my ambition is to be Chief Justice of the United States. I would be of more service there to the United States than I could be as President."[98]

When Taft returned to the United States from a tour around the world, in late December 1907, he found Roosevelt impatiently awaiting him. The Panic of 1907 enabled President Roosevelt's critics to charge that the financial chaos was directly attributable to the administration's meddling in business affairs. Theodore Roosevelt was eager that Taft, by answering these charges on behalf of the Roosevelt Administration, should at once open his campaign for the presidency. Roosevelt prevailed upon him to fire the opening gun of his campaign by speaking on the financial situations.

This Taft did and quite outspokenly riddled the claims of the standpatters by saying, "The economic and political history of the past four years is that of a great struggle between the national administration and certain powerful combinations in the financial world.... If the abuse of monopoly and discriminations cannot be restrained, if the concentration of power made possible by such abuses continue and increase, and it is manifest that under the system of individualism and private property the tyranny and oppression of an oligarchy of wealth cannot be avoided, then socialism will triumph, and the institution of private property will perish."[99]

Senator Crane approached Foraker with the suggestion that Foraker support Taft for the presidency in return for Taft's promotion of Foraker's re-election to the Senate. Taft replied: "You ask for a compact between Foraker and myself— that if Foraker supports me I shall ask my friends to support Foraker. Personally I have no objection to Foraker. I have kindly feelings toward him. If it was individual support I could do it. But my individual support isn't requested. Many of my friends in Ohio are opposed to Foraker's return to the Senate. They have determined to oppose him. If I make a pledge with you, it is for them. I will be expected to control them. In other words, to help myself, I must limit their freedom of action, induce them to do something which they do not wish to do, something against their convictions. In plain English, to secure harmony, I must sell out my friends. I refuse to do that. A man might pay too high a price for the Presidency."[100]

Military elements of the party complained that Taft had criticized General Grant for his weakness for strong drink. Taft explained that opponents were deliberately distorting his words and said, "In my Memorial Day address I attributed his resignation from the army in 1854 to his weakness for strong drink because from ... histories I supposed it was undoubtedly true. I referred to the matter only because it seemed to me that it was one of the great victories of his life that he subsequently overcame the weakness."[101]

Taft was nominated on the first ballot at the Republican National Convention in 1908. The Democrats nominated William Jennings Bryan again. Taft was running well ahead when the election was decided for sure by an endorsement, released posthumously, by former Democratic president Grover Cleveland.

Taft lost the support of Progressives in his own party. The Republicans split between Progressives and conservatives. In 1910 President William Howard Taft lost the support of ex-president Theodore Roosevelt.

Taft served in a time of prosperity. He was blamed for high prices and the Republicans lost the congressional elections of 1910. Taft did not deserve his anti-labor reputation. He believed in the right of labor to organize and strike. He recommended a bill limiting injunctions in strikes. Under Taft millions of acres were set aside for preservation, including over a million acres of forest reserves in the Appalachian Mountains. He reserved the mineral wealth beneath the surface of public lands offered for sale. He improved the public land laws and established a Bureau of Mines — charged, among other things, with the duty of studying the welfare of miners — a postal savings system, the parcel post system, and the requirement of safety appliances on railroads.

The Taft Administration prosecuted anti-trust suits. He added the Secretary of Labor to his Cabinet. He created a separate Children's Bureau in the new Labor Department. He called for workman's compensation for railway workers and for workers in interstate commerce. The Pure Food and Drug Act was amended to prohibit the use of misleading labels. He started an amendment authorizing an income tax. It was ratified in 1913 after Taft left office. Congress passed a corporate income tax. The Mann-Elkins Act of 1910 passed, which gave the Interstate Commerce Commission jurisdiction over terminals and services of communication by telegraph, telephone and cable. It placed upon the carriers the proving of contemplated changes. Congress enacted Taft's plan to create a special Commerce Court, composed of experts in commercial law, to which appeals of the ICC could be made.

Taft supported freedom of religion. He did not oppose civil liberties.

He signed the Payne Aldrich Act, removed Chief Forester Gifford Pinchot and did not support curbing the powers of the Speaker of the House, "Uncle Joe" Cannon. However, Taft does not deserve his poor reputation as a president. In 1921 William Howard Taft became the only ex-president to serve as Chief Justice of the United States.

Woodrow Wilson

A brilliant scholar and former professor, Wilson was the only president to have earned a Ph.D. degree. He obtained his doctorate in political science at Johns Hopkins University. He was a professor at Bryn Mawr, Wesleyan and Princeton. He served as a reform president of Princeton. In 1910 he was elected governor of New Jersey and moved into the Progressive camp.

Wilson won the presidential election of 1912, defeating William Howard Taft and Theodore Roosevelt. A Democrat, Woodrow Wilson is still after ninety years identified with American liberalism and meliorative reform of progressivism. Wilson's domestic program was called the New Freedom.

Wilson was a strict moralist. Irish politicians who knew him called him the "Presbyterian priest." He was uneasy with disreputable Democratic machines.

In his inaugural address in March 1913, Wilson summoned "all honest men, all patriots, all forward-looking men" to his side. He called for reduction of tariff, banking and currency reform and restrictions on trusts. He convened a special session of Congress. Wilson addressed Congress in person for the first time since Jefferson. He did so, he said, to demonstrate that the president was "not a mere department of the government hailing Congress from some island of jealous power." He then urged elimination of the protective tariff behind which the crudest American industrial combinations could organize monopoly.

As president, Wilson decided to govern through his party. The Democrats won both houses of Congress in the election of 1912. Wilson relied on the Democrats to put his domestic program through and, in the process, to broaden his party's base and strengthen it for the future. Wilson believed in a strong president leading his party in Congress like a British prime minister in Parliament.

Wilson, still a reformer, had to adjust to congressional policies not wholly in favor of reform. He was skillful working with his party and with his Congress. Respecting Congress, he persuaded Democrats, in private conferences as well as in official speeches, of the merit of his objectives. The lack of a dominating figure among congressional Democrats made Wilson's task easier.

Wilson kept all the factions of the Democratic Party in line; the Southern Bourbons, the city machines and the Southern and Western agrarians. Wilson's Cabinet, especially Secretary of State William Jennings Bryan, helped him win over these agrarians who often were disposed to move beyond the president's goal. But Wilson's attitude and manner served him well. Wilson wrote, "Congress is made up of thinking men who want the party to succeed as much as I do, and who wish to serve the country effectively and intelligently. They have found out that I am honest ... and accept my guidance because they see that I am attempting only to mediate their own thoughts and purposes.... I am not driving them."[102]

According to a Progressive magazine, Wilson restored the prestige of the presidency, which had slumped under Taft. "He has not only expressly acknowledged and acted on the obligation of leadership, as did Mr. Roosevelt, but he has sought to embody it in constitutional form."[103]

Tariff reduction was attempted in 1913. Various consumer goods were added to the free list and protection was removed from iron, steel and other products of the trusts. A modest graduated income tax was levied in the bill to compensate for the loss in revenue. The ratification of the Sixteenth Amendment made the income tax constitutional.

Involved in framing the bill, Wilson set out to guide it through Congress. It passed the House but it ran into trouble in the Senate. Three Democratic senators from states that produced sugar and wool tried to remove those commodities from the free list. Woodrow Wilson, in a speech to the nation, went over the heads of Congress, directly to the people, and the senators relented. The bill passed and the Underwood Tariff Act became Wilson's first reform measure. The president, in 1913, made tariff reduction — an important but traditional objective, not social reform — his target and he won. "I have," he wrote, "had the accomplishment of something like this at heart ever since I was a boy."[104]

Next was the banking system, on which Congress was already working. Wilson accepted two changes: making the appointments to the Federal Reserve Board the right of government rather than the bankers and making bank notes the obligation of the United States government. Wilson conceded enough points to obtain passage of the Federal Reserve Act of 1913 signed in December 1913, only nine months after his inauguration. The Federal Reserve Act was the best ever banking legislation. Wilson and the Progressives acclaimed the act as a major reform.

The Federal Reserve Act was the most significant domestic legislation of Wilson's administration. The law evoked almost universal praise. It established an efficient banking system, a provision for greater flexibility of currency and credit, and creation of more opportunity for equitable business loans and loans to farmers and hopeful enterprises. Wilson also received praise for his performance in helping devise the measure and seeing it through Congress.

Contrary to Wilson's description of purpose in his address to Congress proposing the act, it did not prevent consolidation of money in the hands of a few nor did it place control of the system of banking in the government itself. The Federal Reserve Board had some control, but the regional banks — especially the Federal Reserve Bank of New York, the richest bank — exercised as much and sometimes more control, especially over interest rates. Although the act eased credit for small business, it did not decrease the advantages of big business. The reform was structural, not social. Wilson interpreted those different ambiguous effects as two meanings of the word "reform."

President Wilson referred to Congress the issue of government regulation of business and industry, the remaining item on the agenda of New Freedom. In his opening address to the new session of Congress in 1914, Wilson condemned monopoly. He proposed preventing interrelated banking or managed groups from controlling the major firms within an industry. Congress should, he said, specifically forbid unfair business practices. He asked that the definition of the Sherman Anti-Trust Act then guide business activity and encourage healthy competition. He also noted the need for administrative as well as legislative participation in the process of regulation. He called for the creation of a commission to assist in dissolving corporations found to be in restraint of trade and to advise businessmen about the interest of the anti-trust law.

Congress passed the Clayton Anti-Trust Act in 1914, which expressly forbade interlocking directories and other unfair practices. It was stronger and more effective than the Sherman Act. A separate bill set up an administrative commission to replace the Bureau of Corporations, but with little more authority.

Wilson in 1914 supported a measure drafted by Louis D. Brandies to establish the Federal Trade Commission to prevent the unlawful suppression of competition. Brandies, a brilliant lawyer and reformer, had been an advisor to Wilson in 1912. The bill passed Congress, but the Supreme Court, by judicial review of the orders of the Federal Trade Commission, denied the FTC any regulatory function.

Yet with the enactment of the anti-trust laws, Wilson considered his initial mission accomplished. Those laws, along with the tariff and the banking acts, fulfilled, he said, his "single purpose ... to destroy private control and set business free." He respected both judges and the law.

The Supreme Court interpretations by judicial review did nothing to act against unfair business practices and issued more injunctions against labor unions than in all previous United States administrations combined. When a Supreme Court vacancy occurred, Wilson appointed James C. McReynolds, his Attorney General, to fill it. He made a mistake because McReynolds resisted progress for 13 years. In 1916 Woodrow Wilson appointed Louis D. Brandies to the Supreme Court. Brandies, the first Jew appointed to the Supreme Court, met resistance for his confirmation in the Senate.

Brandies had attacked big business, befriended labor, exposed former president Taft as a liar and revealed J. P. Morgan's New Haven Railroad as inefficient and corrupt. He rejected judicial precedent as a basis for decisions about social policy. Instead his brief mastered statistics about wages, hours and working conditions.

After five months' of debate, the president, at the right time, published a letter about the importance of the position and praising the qualities of Brandies, who was then confirmed. Later in 1916 Wilson appointed to the Supreme Court U.S. district judge John H. Clarke, who could be relied upon for an enlightened reading of the law.

In 1916 Wilson, following the Brandies' appointment, approved additional domestic reform measures, which he had previously opposed. The Federal Farm Loan Act of 1916 was passed which helped maintain national prosperity by providing inexpensive loans to farmers. The Child Labor Act prevented the employment of children. The Adamson Act passed in 1916 established the eight-hour day. The Smith-Hughes Act appropriated funds on a matching basis for agricultural, commercial, industrial, home economics and vocational education in public high schools. The Smith-Lever Act provided funds for a program of agricultural extension. These acts contributed greatly to the general welfare, as did the Federal Highways Act of 1916, which carried the matching funds principle into the area of road building. President Wilson reduced hours of work by railroad laborers and then permitted an increase in rates to cover the costs. The Department of Labor was created. William D. Wilson was appointed the first Secretary of Labor.

The Seaman's Act had passed in 1914 to provide greater safety for sailors and greater freedom for them in their relations with ship owners. The president prevented inflation from becoming excessive during wartime. Prosperity was maintained. Wilson favored union labor; however, he did not support the revolutionary Industrial Workers of the World, known as Wobblies. Wilson did not use federal force against a great wave of strikers in 1919.

President Wilson promoted the welfare of the people through his regulation of big business, his labor policies, his fiscal policies, and his farm bills. The people benefited from the economic aspects of his New Freedom. Wilson's tax policies placed the burden of taxation on those most able to pay. Wilson supported freedom of religion and refused to use a religious test in his appointments.

Twice President Wilson vetoed restrictive and discriminatory immigration bills. The Women's Suffrage Amendment passed during his presidency. He appointed Annette Abbott Adams as assistant attorney general, making her the first woman appointed to a high government position. A strong supporter of human rights, Wilson treated all persons with respect, both at home and abroad. Regardless of status, he tried to improve the lot of all persons.

Wilson's planning of domestic reform was excellent. His long-term goals were of the highest order. He made strong appointments. To the two independent agencies he created — the Federal Reserve Board and the Federal Trade Commission — he made bipartisan appointments. For the most part he selected capable Cabinet officers.

Wilson was an excellent communicator. He was accessible to the press and many reporters and editors liked him. He was the first president to have regular press conferences. He permitted people to come in and talk to him every afternoon. They did not have to have an appointment.

Wilson controlled expenditures appropriately. He vetoed a bill establishing a bureau of the budget not under control of the president.

Woodrow Wilson won re-election in a close contest in 1916. In Wilson's second term, domestic reform was halted as foreign relations took over and the United States became involved in World War I. On the home front powerful agencies were created: War Industries Board, Food Administration, War Labor Administration, Railroad Administration and Fuel Administration. The last two led to inflation. The Committee on Public Information generated propaganda.

The Espionage Act of 1917 and the Sedition Act of 1918 were passed although the United States was never in danger of invasion or even attack.

These were punishments for opinions, which were considered disloyal. Freedom of speech was denied to those opposing the war. Eugene V. Debs, the head of the Socialist Party, was imprisoned for opposing the war, and labor radicals were persecuted during and in the immediate aftermath of the war. Immigrants were harassed because of their foreign birth. Public passions, private vigilante groups, congressional recklessness and judicial timidity contributed to violations of civil liberties and President Wilson did nothing to prevent it.

Doing what he thought was best for the country was Wilson's highest priority. He tried to act in the best interest of all people, including those sometimes overlooked: factory workers, miners, and poor farmers. He fought special interests. He was not hostile to African-Americans or Native Americans. People respected him and supported his reforms. He inspired executive branch personnel to a high level of focused, productive effort. Success in accomplishing domestic goals during his first term has been surpassed by few, if any, presidents either before or after him. He got people to follow him because of his ideas and ideals. Through writings and speeches, he inspired people in an all-out effort to accomplish national goals. He persuaded Congress to pass important domestic reforms. A great speaker and writer, he was able to win over opponents by convincing them he was right. He adhered to a strict moral code. He was completely honest. After the war and after two strokes his support deteriorated.

Warren G. Harding

Harding, a reactionary Republican from Ohio and lifetime newspaper editor and publisher, served as state senator, majority floor leader and lieutenant governor. He lost his bid for governor in 1910. He was elected as a United States senator from Ohio.

Harding's backers were excited by the news of Theodore Roosevelt's death. Daugherty wrote, "I have some ideas about this thing now which I will talk over with you."[105] Scobey wrote, "It looks to me like if you want to be President now, here is your opportunity. Ohio is a pivotal state and they know that you can carry it. If you are going to be a candidate you ought to start soon."[106]

At the Republican National Convention of 1920, Harding was a dark-horse candidate. Three leading candidates — General Leonard Wood, Governor Frank O. Lowden of Illinois and Senator Hiram Johnson of California — were deadlocked. Harding's candidacy was promoted vigorously by his wife and Harry Daugherty. As balloting continued through the day it appeared that none of the frontrunners would get a majority. The convention adjourned for the night. According to legend, a group of party leaders met in a smoke-filled room and selected Harding to break the deadlock just as Daugherty said they would. Harding was nominated the next day.

Harding defeated Governor James E. Cox, a Democrat, in the presidential election of 1920. Harding invented a word in his campaign slogan of "return to normalcy."

President Harding appointed three good, honest men to his cabinet: Charles Evans Hughes, Herbert Hoover and Henry C. Wallace. Some of the other appointees were dishonest, fleeced the government and brought shame and disgrace to the Harding Administration.

The Fordney-McCumber Act was passed. Harding cut taxes on the wealthy. He inherited a depression from the previous administration. Recovery was underway when the president died. The extent to which his policies were helpful is debatable. His approach was primarily the trickle-down theory — cut taxes on the wealthy to encourage investment and thus stimulate the economy. The Farm Loan Act passed and the Packers and Stockyards Act became law. Harding was pro-business and anti-union; however, he pressured the steel industry to end the 12-hour day. The Wilkerson Injunction was unfair to striking railroad workers. Hoover and others attacked the injunction in a full Cabinet meeting with Harding present. In the turbulent meeting, Secretary of Interior Albert Fall shouted at Daugherty, "You don't know any law and you can't learn any.... If the Attorney General is going to do such high-handed ... things, my resignation is in."[107]

Judge Wilkerson's injunction had broken the back of the railroad strike. By mid–November the strike was over and lost.[108]

Harding favored improving labor conditions by the voluntary actions of management rather than by collective bargaining, especially if it involved threat of force by labor unions. He thought unemployment could be eased by voluntary means, cooperation among business leaders and state and local governments, rather than by a federal employment program.

Harding supported the Sheppard-Towner Bill. He created the Bureau of the Budget. He supported the Per Centum Act. Harding supported women's suffrage. He chided Southerners for not allowing African-Americans to vote and called for an end to educational, economic, and political discrimination.

A supporter of free speech, he released political prisoners who had been jailed under the Sedition Act, including Debs and Wobblies. Harding did not go along with the extremists during the Red Scare. He supported freedom of religion.

Harding's great failures were in not setting high performance standards and in not insisting that his subordinates conduct themselves ethically with a high degree of professionalism.

Secretary of Interior Albert B. Fall was involved in the Elk Hills and Teapot Dome scandals. Fall wrote in his own defense, "My borrowing the money may have been unethical [he admitted in 1929 just after his bribery conviction]. I certainly did realize it at the time, and my employing a falsehood to prevent a volcano of political abuse pouring upon the administration that had honored me deserves condemnation; but neither one nor the other justifies the charge that I was disloyal or dishonest as Secretary of Interior and as a member of Harding's Cabinet."[109]

Harding was responsible for the scandal-ridden Veterans' Bureau, headed by Charles Forbes. A visitor entering the White House saw Harding in the Red Room, his voice hoarse with anger, throttling Forbes against the wall. Harding, with a voice hoarse with anger, shouted, "You yellow rat! You double-crossing ... if you ever...."[110] Forbes resigned on February 15.

Harding nominated former president William Howard Taft as Chief Justice of the Supreme Court. Harding took Taft's advice on judicial appointments. Secretary of Commerce Herbert Hoover wrote of Daugherty, "From this man's character, he should never have been in any government."[111]

In March 1923, Charles F. Cramer, the attorney for the Veterans' Bureau, committed suicide. On May 29, another close friend of Harding, Jesse Smith, shot himself to death in Attorney General Daugherty's apartment.

On August 2, 1923, Harding died. The cause of death was food poisoning. His widow, in an effort to protect her husband's memory, burned all of his correspondence she could find. Harding was a man whose friends betrayed his trust.

Calvin Coolidge

A conservative Republican, Coolidge served on the city council in Northampton, Massachusetts. He became city solicitor and then chairman of the local Republican Party. He was elected to the Massachusetts state legislature and mayor of Northampton. Next, he served four terms in the state senate with two terms as president of the state senate. He was elected lieutenant governor and then governor of Massachusetts. He attained national fame by calling out state troops to restore order in the Boston police strike. Coolidge issued a statement: "There is no right to strike against the public safety by anybody, anywhere, anytime."[112] In the election of 1920, Coolidge was elected vice president.

When President Warren G. Harding suddenly and unexpectedly died on August 2, 1923, Calvin Coolidge became the president of the United States. Coolidge was vacationing at his father's home in Vermont at the time. Because the house had no phone, messengers awakened Coolidge's father in person after midnight and told him. The father woke his son and as a justice of the peace administered the oath of office to his son. The new president then went back to bed and back to sleep.

Coolidge won the presidency in his own right in the election of 1924 by defeating Democratic candidate John W. Davis and third-party candidate Robert M. LaFollette. The Republican campaign slogan was "Keep Cool and Keep Coolidge."

Coolidge favored business. He said, "The chief business of the American people is business."[113] He was not anti-labor but he was anti-agriculture. President Coolidge served in a time of prosperity in urban America, but the farmers did not share in the general prosperity. The McNary-Haugen Bill, which would have helped agriculture, passed Congress but was vetoed by Coolidge. The president objected; he said, "Its attempted price fixing fallacy; the tax characteristics of the equalization fee; the widespread bureaucracy it would set up; how it encourages profiteering and wasteful distribution by middlemen; its stimulation of overproduction; and its aid to our foreign competitors ... this taxation or fee would not be for the purposes of revenue in the accepted sense but would simple yield a subsidy ... bureaucracy gone mad ... preposterous economic and commercial fallacy."[114] Congress was unable to overturn the veto. Secretary of Agriculture Henry C. Wallace of Iowa favored the bill.

Coolidge consistently supported high protective tariffs intended to benefit United States manufacturers. His policies harmed the world economy and agriculture in the United States (and in the long run harmed the industries they were intended to protect).

During his administration Coolidge reduced government expenditures. A substitute for McNary-Haugen, the Curtis-Crisp Bill, did not pass. The Division of Cooperative Marketing was created in the Agriculture Department and was provided with a token sum of $250,000 to encourage farm cooperatives.

Coolidge gave a "Government and Business" speech before the New York Chamber of Commerce in which he said, "New York is an imperial city, but it is not a seat of government. The empire over which it rules is not political but commercial ... we can better appreciate the wisdom of the fathers in their wise dispensation which made Washington the political center of the country and left New York to develop into its business centers. They wrought mightily for freedom."[115]

Coolidge vetoed a veterans' bonus bill and Congress passed it over president's veto. He refused to lower tariff rates. He lowered taxes on the wealthy as had Harding, shifting the burden to the middle class. George W. Bush has done the same thing. Coolidge vetoed a soldiers' pension bill. He seemed to think the function of government was to protect business. He agreed with the position of the United States Chamber of Commerce on everything. He was not concerned about enforcing anti-trust laws, even nominating for attorney general Charles Warren, who had been involved in the sugar trust scandal of 1910. The Senate rejected Warren. William Allen White said the business leaders who advised Coolidge did more harm than the scoundrels who scandalized the Harding Administration. Coolidge said the government could do more to remedy the economic ills of the people by a reduction in public expenditures than by anything else. He vetoed a raise for postal employees. He showed little interest in protecting the environment or using the powers of government to improve the health, safety, or welfare of the people.

Coolidge gave lip service to better treatment of racial minorities and freedom of religion, but did nothing. He signed a restrictive immigration bill. He pardoned all prisoners convicted under the Espionage Act. He did little to advance civil liberties. He supported women's suffrage, but had a low opinion of women's qualifications for public affairs. He did nothing to try to improve the lot of the less fortunate, because he believed that hard work would bring the rewards they deserved.

Coolidge made two excellent Cabinet appointments, Frank B. Kellogg and Harlan Fiske Stone. Stone was later appointed to the Supreme Court.

On August 2, 1927, while vacationing in the Black Hills, Coolidge surprised the nation by handing reporters a note: "I do not choose to run for President in 1928."[116]

Walter Lippman wrote, "The politicians in Washington do not like Mr. Coolidge very much, for they thrive on issues, and he destroys their business. But the people like him, not only because they like present prosperity, and because at the moment they like political do-nothingism, but also because they trust and like the plainness and nearness of Calvin Coolidge himself. This is one of the most interesting conjectures of our age."[117]

The Pepper-McFadder Act, authorizing branch banks by national banks, passed. Coolidge signed it.

On hearing of Harding's death, Coolidge's first thought was "I believe I can swing it."[118] Coolidge did not have a telephone on his desk; there was one in a little booth outside his office but he never used it. He told Bruce Barton, "The president should not talk on the phone, you can't be sure it is private, and besides, it isn't keeping with the dignity of the office."[119]

President Coolidge was nicknamed "Silent Cal" because he usually did not have much to say. Coolidge wanted to save time and he found silence was the best way to do this. However, Calvin Coolidge is remembered for his jokes. A leading humorist of the time appreciated Coolidge wit and wrote, "Mr. Coolidge had more humor than almost any public man I ever met. I have often said I would like to have been hidden in his desk somewhere and just heard sly 'digs' that he pulled on various people that never got 'em at all. I bet he wasted more humor on folks than almost anybody."[120]

In an interview Coolidge said, "A lot of people in Plymouth can't understand how I got to be president, least of all my father."[121] The interviewer observed, "I noticed that President Coolidge never grinned after his jokes to punctuate them. This misled people. They sometimes thought his remarks were dumb. Whatever may be said of Calvin Coolidge, he was not dumb."[122]

Coolidge held 520 press conferences. The questions were submitted in advance, Coolidge would answer the ones he wanted and would discard the others. No direct quotations were allowed.

Coolidge kept Harding's Cabinet. But by the end of his presidency all but four had been replaced. The last to go was Hoover, who resigned to run for president in 1928. Hoover's replacement was William Whiting. Coolidge's most trusted advisor was Treasury Secretary Andrew Mellon.

Coolidge's domestic program was called the preservation of stability. He supposedly told reporters that he stood for "stability, confidence and reassurance." Coolidge was fortunate in coming to office when he did.

A magazine reported, "And now the presidency sinks low indeed. We doubt if ever before it has fallen into the hands of a man so cold, so narrow, so reactionary, so uninspiring, and so unenlightened, or one who has done less to earn it, than Calvin Coolidge.... Every reactionary may today rejoice; in Calvin Coolidge he realizes his ideal, and every liberal may be correspondingly down cast."[123]

Coolidge spoke many times about the rights of African-Americans. He deplored lynchings. Gifford Pinchot, at the request of the president, settled the coal strike. Just before the 1924 election, the scandals of the Harding Administration broke but the outcome of the election did not change.

As a result of the Harding Administration scandals, Albert B. Fall, Harry Sinclair and Edward Doheny were indicted. Harry Daugherty and others were forced to resign.

Coolidge signed the Revenue Act of 1924. It was not the bill he wanted. Two problems facing Coolidge were Prohibition and the Ku Klux Klan.

In the 1924 election, Calvin Coolidge stated his own credo: "Many principles exist which I have tried to represent and propose to support. I believe in the American Constitution. I favor the American system of individual enterprise, and I am opposed to any general extension of government ownership and control. I believe not only in advocating economy in public expenditure, but also in its practical application. I believe in a reduction and reform of taxation.... I shall continue to strive for economic, moral, and spiritual welfare of my country."[124]

In his inaugural address, Coolidge spoke of prosperity. He asked that Muscle Shoals be sold.

More than anything else, Calvin Coolidge brought a unique style to the White House. Although known for his public discomfort with chitchat and for his philosophic dislike of excessive leadership, Coolidge was a highly visible leader. "Let well enough alone" was his policy. He believed in predestination and inevitability. His approach was to wait for situations to resolve themselves and act only when absolutely necessary. Coolidge approved the Immigration Discriminatory Act of 1924. He supported the Revenue Acts of 1924 and 1926. The tax cuts for the rich led to the stock market crash of 1929. Coolidge killed the farm relief bills which could have prevented the Great Depression.

Herbert Hoover

Hoover, a Republican born in West Branch, Iowa, became a mining engineer. In 1908 he established his engineering firm with headquarters in London. By 1914 he had become a millionaire. During World War I, Hoover organized food relief for Belgium and headed the United States Food Administration. During the administrations of Harding and Coolidge, Hoover served as Secretary of Commerce.

In the election of 1928, Hoover was elected president of the United States, defeating New York governor Alfred Smith. A Democrat and a Catholic, Smith favored the repeal of Prohibition. Hoover was inaugurated on March 4, 1929.

He added two million acres to the national parks, called the first White House conference on child health and protection, championed prison reform, and modified tax cuts to favor lower-income Americans.

Hoover was blamed for the Great Depression, which he did not cause. Before he became president he had frequently warned against speculation in stocks. Hoover warned against "real estate and stock speculation and its possible extension into commodities, with inevitable inflation" and against "the over extension of installment buying." He drew attention to and deplored "the fever of speculation" resting on "over optimism" that "can only land us on the shores of over depression."[125]

The stock market crash came on October 24, 1929, triggering the worst depression in history. Hoover's efforts to deal with the depression were ineffective due to his poor leadership.

The Smoot-Hawley Tariff Act was passed. It was counter-productive. Its high rates hurt the United States economy and foreign economies as well. Hoover wanted a strengthened tariff commission which, with executive approval, could raise or lower rates by up to 50 percent. He was unable to secure congressional approval for the commission. Although he signed the Smoot-Hawley Tariff in the spring of 1930, he was angered by the high rates.

Hoover retained only Andrew Mellon and James J. Davis from the Coolidge Cabinet. Three of his Cabinet appointments were excellent: Henry L. Stimson as Secretary of State, Charles Francis Adams as Secretary of the Navy and William D. Mitchell as Attorney General. The others were weak. All of his Cabinet members were white males. None were Catholics, Jews or Southerners. Most were millionaires. He put many postmasters under Civil Service. His appointees were not corrupt or involved in scandal.

Hoover signed the Norris-LaGuardia Act. He created the National Institutes of Health. The Reconstruction Finance Corporation (RFC) lent funds for the eradication of slums. The Agricultural Marketing Act of 1929 was passed. A conservationist, he supported the building of Boulder Dam and planned to build the Grand Coulee Dam. He vetoed a bill providing for government operation. He vetoed a bill for federally subsidized state employment. The RFC was ineffective as a relief agency. Hoover signed the Wagner-Graham Stabilization Act, but delayed months in appointing a director.

Two days after he took office, President Hoover conferred with Federal Reserve officials about restraining stock speculation. When the stock market crash came, Hoover responded quickly. He met with business leaders and asked for voluntary arrangements to keep workers employed at decent wages. He asked Congress to help workers keep their jobs and wages. He requested greater public works appropriations. The government focused on reviving finance rather than dealing directly with unemployment, unprofitably low prices, and agricultural unemployment. Hoover started a few new programs, but he relied mainly on publicity and voluntary response.

Hoover was not anti-labor. In 1928, as a presidential candidate, he called for a shorter workday accompanied by the laborer's purchasing power. He refused to exempt oil companies from compliance with antitrust laws. More indictments for violating anti-trust laws came under Hoover than any other president.

The army drove the veterans' Bonus Army from the Capitol lawn and evicted the veterans from the downtown area. Ignoring the president's orders, General Douglas McArthur burned the veterans' tents. Colonel Dwight Eisenhower was second in command.

Hoover signed the Revenue Act of 1932 and the Economy Act of 1932. Hoover treated African-Americans and Native Americans well.

Hoover favored an anti-lynching law. He appointed more African-Americans to middle-level government jobs than Harding and Coolidge combined. He proposed helping African-Americans secure ownership of land on which they worked as tenants and sharecroppers. His Indian policy was to help Native Americans become independent and to preserve Indian culture. He favored collective tribal ownership of Indian lands. He wanted integration, but not assimilation, of Indians into the nation. He thought the reservation system should be ended. He doubled appropriations for Native Americans. Hoover defended civil liberties.

Herbert Hoover was no politician. According to William Allen White, "The President has great capacity to convince intellectuals. He has small capacity to stir people emotionally and through the emotions one gets to the will, not through the intellect. He can plow ground, harrow it, plant the seed, cultivate it, but he seems to lack the power to harvest it and flail it into a political merchantable product."[126]

Hoover wrote, "I have never liked the clamor of crowds. I intensely dislike superficial social contacts. I make no pretensions to oratory and I was terrorized at the opening of every speech."[127]

Charles Michelson classified Hoover among "the amateurs in the art of politics" as one who "did not know how to chart the process of overcoming opposition."[128] He wrote, "The Old Guard of the Senate, most concerned as to who is going to win the next presidential nomination, don't like Hoover, don't understand him, and are doubtful of their ability to deal with him.... It is bad enough to have Coolidge in the White House with his reticence and the uncertainty where his favor lies but Coolidge at least is a politician, thinking their language, if he does not speak it much; while Hoover revolves in a different orbit."[129]

A friendlier reporter stated that Hoover "seems not to have the least appreciation of the poetry, the music and the drama of politics."[130]

The Secretary of Commerce had addressed a banquet of the National League of Women Voters in Baltimore. Afterward he was praised by Lady Astor. Fifteen hundred exploded in applause and Hoover blushed crimson. Lady Astor said, "Look at him. He is not an ideal politician. He lacks the glad hand and the perpetual smile, thank goodness."[131]

E. M. Sait wrote of Hoover, "Unfortunately, he had been trained as an engineer, not a politician; his contact with public life had been limited to his service as Secretary of Commerce under Harding and Coolidge; and his temperament, like his training, did not accommodate itself to the peculiar rules of the great game of politics."[132]

A *Christian Science Monitor* editorial many years later stated, "Mr.

Hoover was never in his proper place as a politician. His trouble in office was not merely that he lacked political dexterity; there is in him none of that glibness, none of the superficial good fellowship, especially none of those arts of accommodation which mark the political craftsman."[133]

No, Hoover was no politician. Arch Shaw said, "The process of politics in the sense that so many Americans envisage the word suggests opportunism, intrigue, insincerity and the use of patronage, which lead by devious paths into intellectual dishonesty. In that sense he was not a politician. In the sense of being alert to political currents and the needs and tendencies of his time, of steadfastness to principle and of inspirational leadership, he always has been."[134]

Hoover, who admitted that he was terrorized at the opening of every speech, had a great relish for private talk. Hinshaw found the explanation for this and most other Hoover traits in Quakerism: "Hoover the Quaker, given to reticence, distinctly modest, quick in sympathy for the oppressed, with great strength and instinctive generosity and with astounding audacity of the spirit, is full of the manners and methods of his peculiar people. He does not represent Quakerism in its rigid form, but the indelible impressions of his childhood have motored in a manhood concerned with things of the spirit, and the fiber of that spirit makes it pliable but unbreakable."[135]

Of the top one hundred men and women whom Hoover had appointed to office during his term in the White House, some died, a few retired for reasons of health, and many were promoted, but not one resigned, not one had to be dismissed.

The Chief's humor, Hinshaw wrote, was of the special Quaker brand: "It is unbarbed and usually comes from a turn of thought. It produces grins and smiles, almost never belly laughs. Since it has the qualities of the rippling clear brook rather than the rush of the cataract, it pleases rather than pains. It is never cynical and it never discomforts the other fellow."

John Spargo writes, "There is yet another Herbert Hoover ... the general companion and friend ... singularly modest without affectation or a trace of pomposity, he is a delightful conversationalist."[136]

In his post-presidency, Hoover served his government thirty-one years. In 1946 President Truman asked Hoover to find ways to avert global famine. Truman and Hoover became friends.

Six presidents, Hoover included, had tried and failed to persuade the legislation to reorganize the executive branch of government. Red tape and costly confusion were easily denounced on the campaign platform and all but impossible to eliminate in Washington, failed by special interest groups tainted with corruption. Hoover's entire career had revolved around organizing people to the public good.

In October 1945, Hoover expressed interest in another attempt at executive housecleaning. President Harry Truman responded with hearty approval. Congress created the Commission on Organization of the Executive Branch of Government, which became known as the Hoover Commission. The Hoover Commission was very successful.

Franklin D. Roosevelt

A former New York State senator, Assistant Secretary of Navy and governor of New York, Roosevelt was elected president in 1932. He had lost races for the U.S. Senate in 1914 and vice president in 1920. He was re-elected president in 1936, 1940 and 1944. Roosevelt was stricken with polio in 1921 and could never again walk unaided or without braces. He concealed the extent of this disability from the public.

Roosevelt, a liberal Democrat and reformer in the Progressive tradition, called his domestic program the New Deal. He was a pragmatist who was willing to experiment. The New Deal had three purposes: recovery, relief and reform.

Roosevelt's first inaugural address came in the midst of America's worst depression. "First of all," he began,

> Let me assert my firm belief that the only thing we have to fear is fear itself— nameless, unreasoning, unjustified horror.... Only a foolish optimism can deny the dark realities of the moment.... Values have shrunken to fantastic levels ... the means of exchange are frozen in the currents of trade; the withered leaves of individual enterprise lies on every side; farmers find no markets for their produce; the savings of many years in thousands of families are gone ... a host of unemployed ... face the grim problem of existence.... Rulers of the exchange of mankind's goods have failed through their own stubbornness and their own incompetence, have admitted their failure and have fled from their high seats in the temple of our civilization. We may now restore that temple to the ancient truths.... This Nation asks for action and action now. Our first task is to put people to work.... I shall ask Congress for the remaining instrument to meet the crisis-broad Executive power to wage a war against the emergency.[137]

Franklin Roosevelt was unafraid of power and responsibility, like Theodore Roosevelt and Woodrow Wilson. Franklin Roosevelt sometimes said Theodore Roosevelt was the greatest man he had ever known. He also admired Wilson.

Franklin Roosevelt refreshed the hopes of Americans, even those who had twisted the rule of exchange. Congress also stirred, granted him emergency powers and rushed through his first proposals.

Roosevelt was the first president to try to alleviate poverty on a large scale in the United States. He used the full powers of the federal government to combat the Great Depression. When he took office unemployed workers were standing in bread lines, many farmers and city workers had lost their homes and more were about to lose them because they could not make the mortgage payments. President Roosevelt declared a bank holiday. He called a special session of Congress and proposed legislation.

The Emergency Banking Act of 1933 passed on March 9. The measure permitted liquid banks within the Federal Reserve System to reopen under license from the Treasury Department, as most banks did. In order to make them liquid, the act enlarged the kinds of paper they could hold as reserves. It provided for the appointment of federal conservators or receivers to assist banks still closed to return to a healthy state.

Roosevelt saved the banks. In the blackest hour they had ever known, the legislation he sponsored saved them from permanent collapse and reduced the risks on which they made their profits. Roosevelt did not want to nationalize banking. He did not want to abolish capitalism, but to enact reforms.

The Emergency Banking Act of 1933 stopped the panic but did not solve the problems that had caused it. The Banking Act of June 1933 established the Federal Deposit Insurance Corporation (FDIC). Individual bank deposits were guaranteed up to $5000 and the figure has since continually increased. The guarantee eliminated fears about banks for most Americans and assured banks of their normal business activities. The act curtailed speculation on credit.

On the same day, Congress passed the Farm Credit Act, a bill that encouraged the refinancing of farm mortgages on long terms and at low interest rates. Important as it was to farmers, it also helped banks, which sold illiquid mortgages they held to the Farm Credit Administration. The Home Owners Loan Corporation (HOLC), created three days earlier, refinanced the illiquid mortgages, particularly of middle-class householders, and increased the liquid assets of the banks. The new laws saved millions of American farms and homes from foreclosure, eased monthly payments, and made the banks beneficiaries of these laws. However, as the program of the New Deal developed, bankers by and large accepted their salvation as their due and rewarded Roosevelt with a surly animosity.

The Agricultural Adjustment Act (AAA) was a comprehensive plan for the rehabilitation of agriculture. It was declared unconstitutional in 1936 and passed again with revisions in 1938 as a soil conservation measure with acreage allotments, benefit payments, storage loans for surpluses, and marketing quotas. Crop rotation was promoted, as was contour plowing on hills. The Frazier-Lemke Moratorium Act of 1935 prohibited creditors from holding foreclosure sales for a period of five years, providing that the farmers involved could make reasonable payments on their mortgaged property. The law was declared unconstitutional. It was passed again with minor changes and withstood court scrutiny.

The Farm Security Administration was established in 1937 to help impoverished tenants and migrants receive federal assistance. Roosevelt's Secretary of Agriculture Henry A. Wallace established the ever-normal granary, a system that kept supplies and prices at levels satisfactory to growers and consumers alike. Roosevelt and Wallace did not plan it this way, but their farm programs helped the big business of commercial farming more than small farmers.

The National Recovery Act (NRA) of 1933 was passed. It carried Roosevelt's enthusiastic hopes for recovery. It brought together several different expectations about national economic planning. Roosevelt depended less on his Cabinet than on his "brain trust," a group of devoted social reformers who believed that an orderly management under government direction could result both in greater production and more general and equitable distribution of the wealth produced. Organized labor would play a role in national industrial planning.

Roosevelt established the National Recovery Administration to implement the act. He appointed General Hugh S. Johnson to direct it. Johnson used propaganda and public relations to promote voluntary adherence. He set standards for minimum wages and maximum hours. Rallies and parades were organized and a blue eagle became the symbol. Two million employers signed the code. Roosevelt forced Johnson out in 1934. The Supreme Court declared the National Recovery Act unconstitutional in 1935, but the NRA had succeeded in furthering social reform. The Fair Labor Standards Act of 1938 preserved the principles of the NRA.

The Supreme Court invalidated legislation establishing a pension system for railroads and minimum wages and maximum hours in the coal industry. President Franklin D. Roosevelt described Supreme Court decisions as "horse and buggy" jurisprudence. According to critics, the court was saying in effect that the federal government could do nothing for industry, labor, or agriculture to lessen economic crises. Roosevelt decided to pack the Supreme Court. After consulting with the Attorney General, he sent a message to Congress when it convened in 1937. It called for the appointment of an extra justice for each sitting justice past the age of seventy. This plan angered everyone, all the justices including the chief justice, as Roosevelt could have appointed six new judges, bringing the total to fifteen. It offended the liberals as well as conservatives. The president's bill failed. It split the Democratic Party. This attempt to pack the Supreme Court hurt the President politically.

Most of the older justices retired anyway and Roosevelt appointed eventually nine Supreme Court justices, more than any other president. He appointed Hugo L. Black, Felix Frankfurter and William D. Douglas, who were outstanding jurists. Others, less distinguished, were all competent.

President Roosevelt took the country off the gold standard in 1933. He embarked on a spree of gold buying. It failed. The Gold Act of 1934 passed which created a stabilization fund within the Treasury. This fund could buy and sell gold and other currencies. With the Gold Act of 1934, the Treasury, Roosevelt's own arm, gained control over monetary policy for the duration of his administration. Political Washington eclipsed financial New York and cheap money prevailed. Wall Street was infuriated. J.P. Morgan so detested Roosevelt by 1934 that he forbade the mention of Roosevelt's name in his presence.

The Banking Act of 1935 increased the range of authority of the Federal Reserve Board and reduced the independence of the regional federal reserve banks. Conservatives of both parties resisted, but even in amended form it made fundamental revisions in the banking system. As long as Roosevelt remained in office, the Federal Reserve Board provided the quality of public service that the New Dealers expected from an expert federal agency.

The New Deal monetary policy and banking reform did not produce recovery. Roosevelt had to resort to deficit spending with two objectives: to provide funds to assist the indigent unemployed and to finance public work projects that would "prime the pump"—put enough charge into the economy to start it to function automatically. Recovery did not come but both had important social consequences.

President Franklin D. Roosevelt made relief a top priority of his administration. With the Emergency Relief Act of 1933, the federal government for the first time in history recognized and assumed responsibility to assist directly the victims of depression. The act appropriated funds for disbursement to the states, which then distributed the money to needy unemployed. The president appointed Harry Hopkins to take charge of the program. Hopkins, a former social worker whom Roosevelt had first recruited to public service in New York, acted fast. Hopkins had a practical zeal for experimentations and a personal style and charm that made him the most striking and useful of the New Dealers. An intimate of President Roosevelt, he became a favorite target of attack by Republicans.

Hopkins, dissatisfied with the dole, developed a system of work relief which Congress authorized in a number of acts, the most important in 1935. It set up the Works Progress Administration (WPA) and various subsidiary agencies. The WPA hired the unemployed to work directly on a variety of public projects including schools, parks, airports, post offices and roads. Other WPA projects provided federal jobs for unemployed authors, actors, painters, musicians, schoolteachers, lawyers and engineers. One WPA subsidiary made grants to colleges to finance part-time employment for needy students. Hopkins succeeded in using relief not only to feed the unemployed but to renew their sense of self-esteem and of the dignity of work, and to nourish and preserve professional skills essential for American society and culture.

The nation needed new highways, modern urban housing, and great dams to control flooding and generate hydroelectric power. These needs were beyond private enterprise. Congress established the Tennessee Valley Authority (TVA) in 1933.

Roosevelt requested and Congress granted three billion dollars for the NRA for public works. This program was Roosevelt's chosen means for "priming the pump." Harold Ickes was selected to oversee the program. Ickes and Roosevelt were committed to fiscal jurisprudence. Billions were spent on public works through the New Deal, all of them of national value.

The Revenue Act of 1935 tried to strike at corporate size by taxing intercorporate dividends. The New Deal turned toward anti-trust. Another attempt was made in the Revenue Act of 1936, intended to force the distribution of profits by family-held corporations like the Ford Motor Company; for as long as profits were retained, the members of the family received little taxable income but the value of the stock they owned rose.

The Revenue Act of 1936 raised tax rates on middle and high incomes and larger estates. With Roosevelt's approval, the Treasury proposed a graduated tax on undistributed earnings that exempted necessary reserves, gave special treatment to small corporations and replaced all other existing taxes on corporations.

The advocates of the new tax believed that many large corporations were retaining much of their profits and not investing them. A tax that forced them to distribute all but a safe margin of profits would either provoke them to investment or consumer spending, both of which the economy needed.

The investors reacted adversely to the administration's decision to "soak the rich." The rich could afford it. Roosevelt said, "They are unanimous in their hatred of me — and I welcome their hatred."[138]

The conservatives continued to lobby against the Revenue Act of 1936. It was repealed in 1938.

Congress passed the Social Security Act upon the president's urging in 1935. A long-deferred and vital reform, it had emerged from the deliberations of a special committee Roosevelt appointed in 1933 to consider federal unemployment and old age insurance. The financing of the program rested on contributions from both employers and employees. For seventy years Social Security has been a successful government program helping millions of people. Now, George W. Bush and others want to privatize Social Security.

The Wagner Act, passed in 1935, encouraged the organization of industrial unions and created the National Labor Relations Board to resolve disputes between management and labor. Big labor grew within the Democratic Party and by 1941 was a powerful force.

The Civilian Conservation Corps (CCC) was established to provide jobs for men between the ages of 18 and 25 in reforestation and other conservation projects. The National Industrial Recovery Act (NIRA) established the Public Works Administration (PWA). The Act created the NRA (discussed earlier in this chapter). The Securities and Exchange Commission (SEC) was created in 1934 and given broad authority over the activities of stock exchanges. The Rural Electrification Administration (REA) lent money at low interest rates to utility companies and to farmer cooperatives interested in bringing electricity to rural areas.

In the election of 1938, with Democratic losses due to the Great Depression, a coalition of Republicans and conservative Democrats ended Roosevelt's Domestic Reform Program in 1939. Also in 1939, war in Europe brought an end to the Depression.

Roosevelt, by executive order, banned discrimination in defense industries and in government because of race, creed, color or national origin. He created the Fair Employment Practices Commission and appointed qualified persons to office, regardless of gender or religion. FDR appointed Frances Perkins as Secretary of Labor, making her the first female Cabinet member in the history of the United States. His Four Freedoms speech

was   an
inspirational statement for civil liberties and human rights. He stated the goals of freedom of speech and worship and freedom from want and fear in the United States. He spoke on January 6, 1941.

During World War II, however, there were two blots on Roosevelt's human rights record. He interred Japanese Americans in concentration camps, and he did not admit Jewish refugees to the United States above their quota until 1944.

More than any previous president, Roosevelt used the power of the presidency to promote the general welfare of all people. He was truly a great president in the area of domestic programs.

Franklin D. Roosevelt won a record four presidential elections. He died in office in April 1945.

Harry S Truman

A former election clerk, road overseer and postmaster, Harry Truman joined the Missouri National Guard. He served in France in World War I as commander of a field artillery battery. He rose to the rank of major. In 1922 with support of the corrupt Prendergast machine, Truman won election as county judge, and he was re-elected until 1934 when he was elected to the U.S. Senate. He was re-elected to the Senate in 1940 and chaired the Truman Committee, which uncovered waste and inefficiency in the national defense program. The Truman Committee saved the government about one billion dollars and greatly speeded war production.

Harry Truman rose to national prominence. He was elected vice president in 1944. He became president in April 1945 when Franklin D. Roosevelt died in office.

After Roosevelt's death, Truman's popularity declined. A contemporary Gallup poll reported his approval rating at only 36 percent. "Must it be Truman?" asked *The Nation*. "Truman should quit," said *New Republic*. "Harry Truman has none of the qualities demanded by the presidency." He was "colorless," "a little man" with a known difficulty understanding the printed word. In the *New York Times*, Arthur Krock wrote, "When he [Truman] vetoed the 'rich man's' tax bill, which Congress had substituted for his own 'poor man's' bill, numerous Democrats voted to override the veto."

Truman's domestic program was called the "Fair Deal." As predicted, after the war, depression did not occur. Truman, a liberal Democrat, was able to maintain prosperity throughout his administration. He took strong action to keep the nation prosperous by intervening in labor-management disputes and using the powers of government to help in the transition from a war-time to a peacetime economy. When he left office, unemployment was low. Farm income, corporate income and dividends were all at an all-time high. Truman kept price controls and worked against wage raises and price increases. Although there were some price increases, there was no runaway inflation while Truman was president.

The Republican-controlled Congress passed by large majorities the Taft-Hartley Act, which outlawed the closed shop, made unions liable for breach of contract, prohibited political contributions from unions, required them to make financial reports, and required their leaders to take a non-communist oath. On June 20, 1947, Harry Truman vetoed the Taft-Hart-ley Act. Thousands of letters poured into the White House favoring the veto. Truman, who genuinely believed it was a bad bill, knew a veto would go far to bring labor back into Democratic politics. His daughter, remembering the Taft-Hartley veto, later wrote, "While he was responding to his presidential conscience, my father did not stop being a politician. The two are by no means incompatible."[139] Congress voted to override the veto. A majority of Democrats voted for the Taft-Hartley Act and then to override the veto.

In 1947 Truman proposed strengthening anti-trust laws, but Congress failed to act. He vigorously opposed strikes by coal miners, railroad workers, and steel workers when he regarded such strikes to be against the national interest. He proposed striking railroad workers be drafted into the army. He proposed increased support for farmers, including crop insurance. Truman favored hydroelectric projects, irrigation, and conservation of natural resources.

Truman reaffirmed the Fair Deal. He proposed increased unemployment insurance, federal aid to housing, slum clearance, veterans' housing loans, federal aid to education and medical insurance programs. Not all of his programs made it through Congress but his programs, such as the health plan, showed his concern for people.

Truman promised Alben Barkley, his vice-presidential running mate in the election of 1948, to "give 'em hell." Crowd's shouts of "Give 'em hell, Harry!" always brought whoops, laughter and yells of approval, especially when he attacked the Eightieth Congress.

Truman blamed Congress for the high cost of living, for failing to vote for grain storage bins, for the Taft-Hartley Act, for the "rich man's tax bill," for slashing federal support for irrigation and hydroelectric power projects in the West. It was the Republicans in Congress who were holding back progress in the central valley of California. Republicans at heart had no real interest in the West — not in water, not in public power. The Republicans who controlled the Appropriations Committee in the House and Senate were not Californians, they were not westerners. "They are eastern Republicans." ("I never gave anybody hell," he later said. "I just told the truth and they thought it was hell."[140])

Truman refused to invoke the Taft-Hartley Act on the steel workers because they had remained on the job 80 days without an increase in pay. It seemed unfair to Truman and he did not resort to a law he disliked and labor despised. He considered the industry's proposed price increase a little better than profiteering that would lead to inflation. He said, "The attitude of the companies seemed wrong to me, since under the accelerated defense program the government was by far the biggest customer for steel and steel products. To hike prices at this time meant charging the government more for the tools of defense."[141]

On April 8, 1952, Truman seized the steel mills by signing Executive Order No. 10340 just hours before the strike was scheduled. Truman went on the air to address the country at 10:30 that night.

He said, "The plain fact of the matter is that the steel companies are recklessly forcing a shutdown. They are trying to get special, preferred treatment.... And they are apparently willing to stop steel production to get it. As President of the United States it is my plain duty to keep this from happening.... At midnight the Government will take over the steel plants."[142]

President Truman established the Everglades National Park. He established the Atomic Energy Commission (AEC) under civilian, not military, control, saying, "The release of atomic energy constitutes a new force too revolutionary to consider in the frame work of old ideas."[143] He said that the way to get along in the world was to apply the Golden Rule: "We can't stand another global war. We can't ever have another war, unless it is total war, and that means the end of our civilization as we know it. We are not going to do that. We are going to accept that Golden Rule and we are going forward to meet our destiny which I think Almighty God intended us to have."[144] He appointed David Lilienthal to the Atomic Energy Commission.

When Russia started work on the hydrogen bomb, Truman issued a handout, a mimeographed sheet. "It is part of my responsibility as Commander in Chief of the Armed Forces to see to it that our country is able to defend itself against any possible aggressor. Accordingly, I have directed the Atomic Energy Commission to continue its work on all forms of atomic weapons, including the so called hydrogen or super bomb."[145]

On September 6, 1945, Truman presented a 21-point domestic program that included unemployment compensation, an immediate increase in the minimum wage, a permanent Fair Employment Practices Committee, tax reform, crop insurance for farmers, and a full year's extension of the War Powers and Stabilization Act, meaning the government would keep control over business and federal housing to make possible a million new homes a year. He wrote, "We must go on. We must widen our horizon further. We must consider the redevelopment of large areas of the blighted and slum sections of our cities so that in the truly American way be remade to accommodate families not only of low-income groups heretofore, but every income group."[146]

It was a comprehensive statement of progressive philosophy and a sweeping liberal program of action. For Republicans and conservative Democrats who thought the New Deal was over, it was a rude awakening.

Truman decided to run for president in 1948. On January 7, 1948, he delivered a message before Congress reaffirming his liberal program. Truman again called for a national health insurance program, a massive housing program, increased support for education, increased support for farmers, the conservation of natural resources and a raise in the minimum wage from 40 to 75 cents an hour. To compensate for rising prices he proposed a "poor man's" tax cut whereby each taxpayer would be allowed to deduct $40 for himself and each dependent from his final tax bill.

On February 2, 1948, he sent a civil rights message to Congress. It was a strong message based on the findings of his own Civil Rights Commission. Until this time there had never been a special message on civil rights. It began, "Not all Americans are free of violence. Not all groups are free to live and work where they please or to improve their conditions of life by their own efforts. Not all groups enjoy the full privileges of citizenship.... The Federal Government has a clear duty to see that the Constitutional guarantees of individual liberties and equal protection under the laws are not denied or abridged anywhere in the Union. That duty is shared by all three branches of the Government, but it can be filled only if the Congress enacts modern, comprehensive civil rights laws, adequate to the needs of the day, and demonstrating our continuing faith in the free way of life."[147]

Truman called for a federal law against the crime of lynching. He wanted more effective protection of the right to vote everywhere in the country. He wanted a law against poll taxes.

He had established the Civil Rights Commission and the Fair Employment Practices Commission with authority to stop discrimination by both employers and labor unions alike. He ended discrimination in interstate travel by rail, bus and airplane. He asked the Secretary of Defense to stop discrimination in the Armed Services. He asked that claims of Japanese Americans forced from their homes during the war solely because of their racial origin be acted upon. Asked at a press conference a few days later what he had drawn on for background, he replied, "The Constitution and the Bill of Rights." Harry Truman did more for civil rights in America than any president since Abraham Lincoln.

Stepping up the attack on Congress, he called for action on price controls, housing, farm supports, health insurance and a broader base for Social Security. He spoke on June 14, 1948. Only that morning he had vetoed a Republican bill that would have taken 750,000 people off Social Security.

Through government support (the GI Bill), 8 million veterans had been to college, Social Security benefits doubled, and minimum wages increased. Sixty-two million Americans had jobs, a gain of 11 million in seven years. New census reports indicated gains in income, standards of living, education and housing unparalleled in American history. Progress was made in slum clearance, with millions of homes built through government financing. Prices were higher but income outpaced them. Real living standards were considerably higher than seven years earlier. Truman issued executive orders ending segregation in the Armed Forces and in the federal civil service.

Truman established a Federal Loyalty and Security Program. This was the era of McCarthyism. By 1951 three million government employees were investigated and cleared by the Civil Service Commission and another 14,000 by the FBI. Several thousand resigned but only 212 were dismissed as being of questionable loyalty. None were indicted and no evidence of espionage was found.

Senator Joseph McCarthy of Wisconsin, a hopeless failure, seized on the issue of Communist infiltration in government to bring him fame. He falsely accused people in government of being Communists. He had no evidence but became the leader of the "Red Scare." By the end of six weeks, McCarthy had not named a single Communist.

McCarthy announced Owen Lattimore was a "top Russian espionage agent." Time would show that Lattimore was neither a Communist nor even influential at the State Department where he worked four months. The accusation was a fraud. McCarthy told the Senate Foreign Relations Committee, "If you crack this case it will be the biggest espionage case in this country."[148]

About this time Truman agreed to an exclusive interview. As the journalist reported, "In an age of atomic energy, transmuted into a weapon which can destroy great cities and the best works of civilization, and in the shadow of a hydrogen detonate which could multiply many times that agent of destruction, a serene President of the United States sits in the White House with undiminished confidence in the triumph of humanity's better nature and the progress of his own efforts to achieve an abiding peace.... His faith in the future has a 'luminous' quality. He sits in the center of a troubled and frightened world.... But the penumbra of doubt and fear in which the American nation pursues its great and most perilous adventure ... stops short of him. Visitors find him undaunted and sure that, whether in his time or thereafter, a way will be discovered to preserve the world from the destruction which to many seems unavoidable."[149]

"I think," Truman said with a hard look, "the greatest asset that the Kremlin has is Senator McCarthy."[150]

Truman was asked, "Was Owen Lattimore a Russian spy?" Truman in anger replied, "Why of course not. It's silly on the face of it."[151]

The president wrote to Owen Lattimore's sister, "I think our friend McCarthy will eventually get all that is coming to him. He has no sense of decency or honor. You can understand, I imagine, what the President has to stand — every day in the week he's under a constant barrage of people who have no respect for the truth and whose objective is to belittle and discredit him. While they are not successful in these attacks they are never pleasant. So I know how you feel about the attack on your brother. The best thing to do is to face it and the truth will come out."[152]

Republican Senator Henry Cabot Lodge, Jr., member of the Tydings Committee, announced that weeks of effort at the White House going over the eighty-one cases charged by Senator McCarthy had produced no evidence of consequence. The Korean death trap, charged Joe McCarthy, lay at the doors of the Kremlin and those who sabotaged rearming, including Acheson and the president. Senator McCarthy called on Acheson and Marshall to resign and talked of impeaching Truman.

On November 1, 1950, two Puerto Rican nationalists decided to assassinate President Truman. Shots were fired. Truman and his wife were unharmed. The assassins were shot. One was killed, the other was still alive. White House policeman Joseph Downs was shot three times. Secret servicemen Donald Birdsell and Floyd Boring were shot. Leslie Coffelt was shot and died later.

When MacArthur was fired, Joe McCarthy called President Truman a "son of a bitch." He charged the decision had been influenced by "bourbon and Benedictine." McCarthy continued to charge treason and espionage. He aimed his main attack at Marshall. On September 12, 1951, General George

C. Marshall resigned. McCarthy said the mysterious, powerful Marshall and Dean Acheson were part of a Communist conspiracy of infamy so immense that it surpassed any "such venture in history."[153]

Truman called a secret meeting at Blair House attended by Attorney General McGrath, four Democratic senators — Anderson, Monroney, Henning and Sparkman — a veteran Kentucky congressman named Brent Spence, Solicitor General Phillip B. Perlman, Democratic Party Chairman William Boyle, Clark Clifford and John Hersey. Truman wanted confidential advice. What could be done about McCarthy?

Truman gave a "pithy and bitter" summary of McCarthy's methods — "his hectoring and innuendo, his horrors and dirty tricks... his bully's delight in the ruin of innocents."[154] All this was tearing his country apart, Truman said. But what antidote could he as president use against such poison?

Senator Clinton Anderson mentioned a "devastating" dossier that had been assembled on McCarthy, complete with details on his bedmates over the years, enough to "blow Senator McCarthy's whole show sky high."[155] Suggestions were made that the material be leaked to the press. But Truman smacked the table with the palm of his hand. The president, outraged, wanted no more such talk.

Hersey wrote, "Three pungent comments of Harry Truman's on the proposal that had just been made have stuck in my mind ever since. This was their gist, you must not ask the President of the United States to get down in the gutter with a guttersnipe. Nobody, not even the President of the United States, can approach too close to a skunk in skunk territory, and expect to get anything out of it but a bad smell. If you think somebody is telling a big lie about you, the only way to answer is with the whole truth."[156] The president would answer, "No comment," on questions about McCarthyism. Marshall also refused to answer.

Truman unified the armed services under the Department of Defense. He appointed some very good Cabinet members in George Marshall, Dean Acheson, James Byrnes, James Forrestal, Averill Harriman and Robert Lovett.

Truman improved the organization of the executive branch through his own efforts and by the recommendations of a commission headed by former president Herbert Hoover, whom Truman brought back into public life.

Harry Truman won the 1948 presidential election even though the South formed an anti-civil rights party called the Dixiecrats, and those to the left of Truman nominated Henry A. Wallace as the Progressive Party candidate. Truman came out fighting, attacking the "Do-nothing Eight-ieth Congress." He defeated Thomas Dewey, the Republican candidate who had been favored to win.

Truman's immigration policy, his civil rights proposals, his actions to end discrimination, and his help to the economically needy demonstrated his commitment to human rights. Truman's domestic program advanced the cause of dignity for all.

Truman had a concept of what the nation should be like. He wanted a nation where all the people were free to live and work where they please, where individual liberties and equal protection of the laws were honored, and where the common man could get an education, a job at a fair wage, medical care and a decent standard of living. The achievements of the Truman Administration were great.

Eric Severeid said nearly forty years later of Truman, "I am not sure he was right about the atomic bomb, or even Korea. But remembering him reminds people what a man in that office ought to be like. It's character, just character. He stands like a rock in memory now."[157]

Dwight D. Eisenhower

War hero and five star General of the Army Dwight D. Eisenhower served as Supreme Commander of all the Allied forces in Europe during World War II. He accepted the position of Supreme Commander of North Atlantic Treaty Organization (NATO) on January 31, 1951. "Ike" was president of Columbia University from 1948 to 1953.

Eisenhower, a Republican, was elected president of the United States in 1952 and re-elected in 1956. Ike was very popular with the American people, but had mostly ineffective domestic programs. There were depressions in 1954 and in 1957–1958. Eisenhower was pro-business. He was anti-labor and anti-farmers. Most of his Cabinet was made up of millionaires. Secretary of Agriculture Ezra Taft Benson was hated by farmers. As president, Eisenhower believed that his primary responsibility was to promote and maintain American national security. He intended to be first and foremost a foreign policy president. In the 1952 presidential race, Ike sought the Republican nomination as an internationalist, while his Republican opponent, Robert A. Taft, favored isolationism.

Ike finally turned against Senator Joseph McCarthy when his own appointees were attacked in the winter of 1953-1954. On October 3, 1952, McCarthy was running for re-election and was campaigning on the same train as Eisenhower. Ike had already unmistakably made known his esteem for Marshall.

Eisenhower wanted to restore the United States to a society marked by enlightened corporate leadership. He opposed farm groups, labor unions, and minority advocates as interest groups. He did not consider businessmen as special interests. He counted among his best friends and most influential advisors the chief executive officers of some of the largest American corporations. He preferred their company to that of farm or labor unions. He appointed huge numbers of business leaders to government boards, commissions and advisory committees.

Among the domestic problems facing the president were inflation, unemployment, and budget deficits. He had some success. He believed that voluntary action was preferable to controls. He opposed governmental programs for poverty, health care, and regulation of business.

Ike was asked if he agreed with McCarthy that Marshall was a traitor. Would he back a senator who called Marshall a traitor? Eisenhower, face red, replied, "George Marshall is one of the patriots of this country.... Maybe he has made mistakes. I do not know about that, but from the time I met him on December 14, 1941, until the war was over, if he was not a perfect example of patriotism and a loyal servant of the United States, I never saw one. If I could say more, I would say it, but I have no patience with anyone who can find in his record of service for this country anything to criticize.... There was nothing to disloyalty in General Marshall's soul."[158]

Well, then, what about McCarthy? "I am not going to support anything that smacks of un–Americanism."[159]

On October 2 Eisenhower called for McCarthy to come to his hotel room at 5:30 alone. From the hallway outside a speechwriter couldn't help overhearing Eisenhower's "white-hot anger." It had been building up for days and now it exploded. "He just took McCarthy apart. I never heard the General so cold-bloodedly skin a man. The air turned blue.... McCarthy said damned little."[160]

The American people grew tired of McCarthy on TV. And the Senate voted to condemn McCarthy's conduct in December 1954. McCarthyism ended. McCarthy failed because he didn't act like a senator and Eisenhower won because he acted presidential. He created a new federal internal security review program.

Eisenhower, a conservative, turned away from the New Deal and the Fair Deal. On the recommendation of the Hoover Commission on the Reorganization of Government, Congress created the Department of Health, Education and Welfare in 1953. Ike appointed Oveta Culp Hobby as Secretary of the HEW. She became the second woman Cabinet member in United States history.

In 1953 Eisenhower appointed California's governor, Earl Warren, as Chief Justice of the Supreme Court. Warren was convinced that the Court must take the offensive in the cases of civil rights. Warren succeeded in welding his associates into a unit on the question.

In 1954 an NAACP-sponsored case, *Brown v. Board of Education of*

Topeka, came up for decision. Thurgood Marshall, the NAACP lawyer, challenged the "separate but equal" doctrine and submitted a mass of sociological evidence to show that the mere fact of segregation made equal education impossible and did serious psychological damage to both black children and white. Speaking for a unanimous Court, Warren reversed the *Plessy v. Ferguson* ruling of 1896. "In the field of public education, the doctrine of 'separate but equal' has no place," he declared. "Separate education facilities are inherently unequal."[161] The next year the Court ordered the states to proceed "with all deliberate speed" in integrating their schools.

Despite these decisions, few districts in the southern and border states seriously tried to integrate their schools. Riots broke out in Tennessee, Virginia and Alabama. Eisenhower, opposed to the Court decisions, failed to act. Finally, in 1957, events compelled him to act. When the school board of Little Rock, Arkansas, opened Central High School to a handful of African-American students, the governor of the state, Orval M. Faubus, called out the National Guard to prevent them from attending. Unruly crowds taunted the students and their parents.

Eisenhower could not ignore the direct flouting of federal authority. After the mayor of Little Rock sent him a telegram — "situation is out of control and police cannot disperse the mob"[162] — Ike dispatched 1000 paratroopers to Little Rock and summoned 10,000 National Guardsmen to federal duty. The African-American students then began to attend class. A token force of soldiers was stationed at Central High for the entire year to protect them.

Resistance strengthened the determination of African-Americans and many northern whites to make the South comply with the desegregation decision. Besides pressing cases in the federal courts, leaders of the movement organized a voter registration drive among African-Americans in the South. The result was the Civil Rights Act of 1957. It authorized the attorney general to obtain injunctions to stop election officials from interfering with African-Americans seeking to register and vote. The law also established a civil rights commission with broad investigative powers and a civil rights commission in the Department of Justice. Enforcing this Civil Rights Act, however, was difficult. Warren restored the "clear and present danger" principle to the Smith Act.

The Tax Code of 1954 was a major overhaul of the nation's tax system, which lowered taxes on industry and capital. The anti-union provisions of the Landrum-Griffin Act of 1957 pleased corporate lobbyists, while the administration's reluctance to invoke injunctions against strikes pacified labor.

Eisenhower endorsed the creation of the St. Lawrence Seaway Development Corporation in 1956 to build a deep-water navigation channel. He promoted the Interstate Highway Act. While this was a major improvement for automobile travel, it led to erosion of the urban tax base, and through suburban sprawl, disincentives to mass transit and energy conservation and increased air pollution.

Ike opposed governmental programs to alleviate poverty, provide healthcare or to regulate business in the interests of the public. Although he disapproved of Social Security, he knew it was too popular to be attacked; he broadened it. He removed price and wage controls and increased the minimum wage. The Housing Act of 1959 did very little for low-income people.

He signed the National Defense Education Act in 1958 reluctantly, as he opposed federal aid to education. Additional voting rights were approved in 1960.

Ike made some excellent appointments to the Supreme Court. The greatest of these was Chief Justice Earl Warren.

John F. Kennedy

In the summer of 1936 John F. Kennedy studied at the London School of Economics, where he contracted jaundice. That fall he entered Princeton University, but a recurrence forced his withdrawal. When he recovered, he entered Harvard University, from which he graduated cum laude in 1946. He attended the Stanford University Graduate School of Business briefly. He volunteered for the army but was rejected for health reasons. Soon after he joined the Navy and was stationed in Washington, D.C. Following the attack on Pearl Harbor, he applied for sea duty. On August 2, 1943, the PT boat he commanded was cut in half by a Japanese destroyer. For his heroism in rescuing members of his crew, he was awarded the Navy and Marine Corps Medal. He injured his back, for which he received the Purple Heart. His back gave him great pain the rest of his life.

Kennedy worked briefly as a newspaper reporter. He was elected to Congress in 1946 and re-elected twice. In 1952 he was elected to the U.S. Senate. At the Democratic convention in 1956 Kennedy made the nominating speech for Adlai Stevenson. When Stevenson opened the vice-presidential choice to the floor, Kennedy worked for that nomination but lost to Estes Kefauver. He immediately began working for the 1960 presidential nomination. In 1958 he was re-elected to the Senate but his goal was the presidency in 1960.

As no Catholic had ever been elected, Kennedy thought his only chance was by proving his vote-getting abilities in the primaries. He entered eight primaries; his chief rival, Hubert Humphrey, entered five. The other leading contenders — Stuart Symington and Lyndon Johnson — stayed out of the primaries, pinning their hopes on political maneuvering during the convention. The first primary was in Wisconsin. Kennedy won, carrying the Catholic districts but losing in the Protestant areas. The crucial test came in West Virginia, which was 95 percent Protestant. Kennedy swept the remaining primaries. Kennedy won the Democratic nomination and chose Johnson as a running mate. The Republicans nominated Richard Nixon for president and Henry Cabot Lodge, Jr., for vice president.

Kennedy charged in domestic programs; there was a stagnant economy and a failure to meet the needs of a growing population. He said the United States was failing to modernize itself. Needs in public services, health, transportation and urban renewal were not being met. The race appeared very close. Kennedy won the election by getting the best of Nixon in four televised debates. Kennedy looked better than Nixon. Kennedy outclassed Nixon in the style and substance of his arguments. Kennedy won a plurality of the popular vote. Kennedy received 303 electoral votes to 219 for Nixon.

In his inaugural address, Kennedy said, "Let the word go forth from this time and place, to friend and foe alike, that the torch has been passed to a new generation of Americans.... Let every nation know, whether it wishes us well or ill that we shall pay any price, bear any burden, meet any hardship, support any friend, oppose any foe to assure the survival and success of liberty.... Now the trumpet summons us again — not as a call to bear arms, though arms we need — not a call to battle, though embattled we are — but a call to bear the burden of a long twilight year in and year out.... And so, my fellow Americans: ask not what your country can do for you — ask what you can do for your country."[163]

President Kennedy had a strong Cabinet, which included Dean Rusk as Secretary of State, Douglas Dillon as Secretary of the Treasury, Robert McNamara as Secretary of Defense, his brother Robert Kennedy as Attorney General, Arthur Goldberg as Secretary of Labor and Robert C. Weaver, an African-American, as head of the Housing and Home Finance Agency, which Kennedy made a Cabinet post. He recruited distinguished scholars and appointed several Republicans to his team.

A liberal Democrat, Kennedy called his domestic program the New Frontier. He inherited a recession that soon ended. By Executive Order No. 1, on his first day in office, he doubled the food rations of four million needy Americans. His proposals to create the Department of Urban Affairs and medical care for the aged were both rejected by Congress. He proposed an increase in the minimum wage from $1.00 to $1.25. He increased aid to dependent children. He increased Social Security benefits. Congress passed his Aid to Depressed Areas bill. Kennedy promoted conservation and environmental protection. He introduced measures against air and water pollution. He proposed aid for mass transit.

Inflation was low and Kennedy was determined to keep it low by establishing voluntary wage-price guidelines. In 1962 the steelworkers agreed to a contract with no wage increase, but several companies raised prices anyway. Kennedy went on television and denounced the steel executives. Under administration pressure, companies rolled back the increases.

Kennedy was generally pro-labor. Attorney General Robert Kennedy vigorously prosecuted both labor racketeering and anti-trust violations. John Kennedy's farm bill was not passed by Congress. In 1963 he proposed a tax cut to stimulate the economy. The cut had not been acted upon at the time of his assassination.

Kennedy supported federal aid to public but not to parochial schools. He established the President's Advisory Council on the Arts. Artists, writers, musicians and Nobel Prize winners were invited to the White House. Kennedy proposed manpower development and training. He established the President's Committee on Equal Opportunity.

John F. Kennedy strongly supported separation of the church and state. He effectively opposed religious bigotry. He ended, by executive order, racial discrimination in housing owned, operated, or financed by the federal government. He appointed African-Americans to prominent government jobs. Kennedy was not the tool of any special interests. He always wanted to do what was best for the country. He used government power to back his efforts for social justice. Kennedy had a vision of the future. He was good at analyzing situations and conceiving progressive strategies for their solutions. He made tough decisions time after time. His domestic program brought hope and pride to the American people.

Because of the seriousness of foreign relations, domestic programs were given a low priority by the Kennedy Administration; however, Civil Rights became so important that Civil Rights itself became a priority. A 38-year-old African-American novelist named James Baldwin, the son of a Harlem minister, wrote:

> Try to imagine how you would feel if you woke up one morning to find the sun shining and all the stars aflame ... you would be frightened because it is out of the order of nature. Any upheaval in the universe is terrifying because it so profoundly attacks one's sense of reality. Well, the black man has functioned in the white man's world as a fixed star, as an immovable pillar and as he moves out of his place, heaven and earth are shaken to the foundations....
>
> The Negroes of this country may never be able to rise to power, but they are very well placed indeed to precipitate chaos and bring down the curtain on the American dream. There is a limit to the number of people

any government can put in prison, and a rigid limit indeed to the practicality of such a course.... A bill is coming in that I fear America is not prepared to pay.

If we — and now I mean the relatively conscious whites and the relatively conscious blacks, who must, like lovers, insist on or create the consciousness of the others — do not falter in our duty now, we may be able, handful we are, to end the racial nightmare, and achieve our country, and change the history of the world.

If we do not now dare everything, the fulfillment of that prophecy, recreated from the Bible in song by a slave, is upon us; God gave Noah the rainbow sign, no more water, the fire next time.[164]

John Kennedy did not disagree with Baldwin but he thought it was too soon to act. He thought America wasn't ready to accept African-Americans as part of American society.

The army was called out to integrate the University of Mississippi on October 1, 1962. An African American student, James Meredith, was enrolled.

Governor George Wallace vowed to stand in the doorway of the University of Alabama to prevent court-ordered integration. Kennedy said, "The courts have made a final judgment on this matter.... I am obligated to carry out the court order. That is part of our Constitutional system. There is no choice in the matter.... We are a people of laws and we have to obey them."[165] The African-American students were enrolled June 11, 1963.

President John F. Kennedy was assassinated on November 22, 1963. The White House transcripts said, "After the breakfast at the Texas Hotel in Fort Worth the President flew to Love Field in Dallas. There he acknowledged greeters for a brief period and then entered an open car. The motorcade traveled down a 10-mile route through downtown Dallas on its way to the Trade Mart, where the President planned to speak at a luncheon. At approximately 12:30 (CST) he was struck by two bullets fired by an assassin. The President was declared dead at 1:00 P.M. at the Parkland Hospital in Dallas."[166]

Following are some of the words of John F. Kennedy.

"There is no sense in trying to do anything unless you give it your maximum effort. You may not succeed, but at least the effort and dedication and interest should be there."[167]

"Those societies that have produced great creative and political achievements have almost always given a high place to the physical vigor of the individual citizen. For it is only upon a foundation of individual hardiness and vitality that we can build an 'exercise of vital powers along the lines of excellence.'"[168]

"Leadership and learning are indispensable to each other. The advancement of learning depends on community leadership for financial and political support — and the products of that learning, in turn, are essential to the leadership's hopes for continued progress and prosperity."[169]

"It is well to remember that this nation's first great leaders, our founders, Jefferson, Madison, Monroe ... Mason, Bryant and all the rest were not only the political leaders of this country, but they were also among the most educated citizens that this country had ever produced."[170]

"We are politicians in the sense that we believe political action through one of the political parties ... is the best means of achieving service for our country.... These matters do not end on Election Day. All this is a means to an end, not an end in itself, and the end is service to our country."[171]

"We shall be judged more by what we do at home than by what we preach abroad.... These domestic tasks do not divert our energy or our security — they provide the very foundation for freedom's survival and success."[172]

"I hope, in other words, that we will take this rich country of ours, given to us by God and by nature, and improve it through science and find new uses for our natural resources."[173]

"Our national conservation effort must include the complete spectrum of resources: air, water and land; fuels, energy and minerals; soils, forests and forage; fish and wildlife. Together they make up the world of nature which surrounds us — a vital part of the American heritage."[174]

"I think, of course, great times make great Presidents and great men.... A sense of the future and the past and a wide cultural experience which makes it possible for them to draw on the lines of other men and the experiences of other men and apply it to a particular situation, moral courage, a sense of the future, a sense of the past, a physical vitality, intellectual curiosity and purpose. I would say those are the qualities."[175]

"It is in times such as these that many men, weak in courage and frail in nerve, develop the tendency to turn suspiciously on their neighbors and leaders. Unable to face up to the dangers from without, they become convinced that the real danger is from within."[176]

"Members of the Congress, the Constitution makes us not rivals for power but partners for progress. We are all trustees for the American people, custodians of the American heritage. It is my task to *report* the State of the Union — to *improve* it is the task of us all."[177]

"The other point is something that President Eisenhower said to me on January 19th. He said 'There are no easy matters that will ever come to you as President. If they are easy, they will be settled at a lower level.'"[178]

"I know few significant questions of public policy which can be safely confided to computers. In the end, the hard decisions inescapably involve imponderables of intuition, prudence and judgment."[179]

"If a Negro baby is born — and this is true also of Puerto Ricans and Mexicans in some of our cities — he has about one-half as much chance to get through high school as a white baby. He has one-third as much chance to get through college as a white student. He has about a third as much chance to be a professional man, and about half as much chance to own a house. He has about four times as much chance that he'll be out of work in his life as the white baby. I think we can do better."[180]

"If a free society cannot help the many who are poor, it cannot save the few who are rich."[181]

"With a good conscience our only reward, with history the final judge of our deeds, led us go forth to lead the land we love, asking His blessing and His help, but knowing that here on earth God's work must truly be our own."[182]

"Though we like to think of ourselves as a young country — this is the oldest republic in the world."[183]

"Nor is it accidental that many of our outstanding Presidents, men such as Jefferson or Wilson or Truman, have had a deep sense of history. For all of the disciplines, the study of the folly and achievements of man is best calculated to help develop the critical sense of what is permanent and meaningful amid the mass of superficial and transient events and decisions which engulf the Presidency. And it is on this sense, more than any other, that great leadership depends."[184]

"Democracy is a difficult kind of government. It requires the highest qualities of self-discipline, restraint, a willingness to make commitments and sacrifices for the general interest, and also it requires knowledge."[185]

"Our greatness today rests in part of this gift of geography that is the United States."[186]

"We are reaching the limits of our fundamental needs — of water to drink, of fresh air to breathe, of open space to enjoy, of abundant sources of energy to make life easier."[187]

"The history of America is, more than that of most nations, the history of man confronted by nature."[188]

"From the beginning, Americans had a lively awareness of the land and the wilderness. The Jeffersonian faith in the independent farmer laid the foundation for American democracy; and the ever-beckoning, ever-receding frontier left an indelible imprint on American society and the American character."[189]

"It is not always the other person who pollutes our streams, or litters our highways, or throws away a match in a forest, or wipes out game, or wipes out our fishing reserves."[190]

"The great movements in this country's history, the great periods of intellectual and social activity, took place in those periods when we looked long range to the future.... It was in the days of Theodore Roosevelt, when the whole national conservation movement began, and all of the decisions [were made] in a much easier period, when we had far fewer people ... which makes it possible for us to travel throughout the United States and still see green grass and still have some hope for the future."[191]

"I want us in 1963 to make the same decisions here in the United States."[192]

"The overseas success of our Peace Corps volunteers, most of them young men and women carrying skills and ideals to needy people, suggests the merits of a similar corps serving our own community needs: in mental hospitals, on Indian reservations, in centers for the aged or for young delinquents, in schools for the illiterate or the handicapped. As the idealism of our youth has served world peace, so can it serve the domestic tranquility."[193]

"The Emancipation Proclamation was not an end. It was a beginning. The century since has seen the struggle to convert freedom from rhetoric to reality. It has been in many respects a somber story.... Despite humiliation and deprivation, the Negro retained his loyalty to the United States and to democratic institutions. He showed this loyalty by brave service in two world wars, by the rejection of extreme or violent policies, by a quiet and proud determination to work for long-denied rights within the framework of American Constitution."[194]

"Children are the world's most valuable resource and its best hope for the future. It is a real tragedy that in an area of vast technological progress and scientific achievement, millions of children should still suffer from lack of medical care, proper nutrition, adequate education, and be subjected to the handicaps and uncertainties of low-income, substandard environment."[195]

"I think politicians and poets share at least one thing, and that is that their greatness depends upon the courage with which they face the challenges of life. There are many kinds of courage — bravery under fire, courage to risk reputation and friendship and career for convictions which are deeply held. Perhaps the rarest courage of all — for the skill to pursue it is given to very few men — is the courage to wage a silent battle to illuminate the nature of man and the world in which he lives."[196]

"A man may die, nations may rise and fall, but an idea lives on. Ideas have endurance without death."[197]

Lyndon B. Johnson

A graduate of Southwest Texas State Teachers College, Lyndon Johnson taught high school only briefly before leaving for Washington, D.C., as the secretary of a Texas Democratic Congressman. Captured by the excitement of the New Deal, Johnson returned to Texas to manage the state's branch of the National Youth Administration, a responsibility he discharged with both psychological and political reward. Johnson was elected to the House of Representatives in 1937. He attached himself to Sam Rayburn, the shrewd Texan who served many years as Speaker, and to Franklin Roosevelt, whom Johnson viewed as a patron rather than the president.

In 1948 Lyndon Johnson won election to the Senate after a close victory in the primary. In the Senate he took a position just enough to the left of his conservative southern colleagues to permit him to keep their trust while he cultivated liberals. In 1953 Johnson became minority leader and, in 1955, after the Democrats regained control of the Senate, he became majority leader, a position he enjoyed and mastered.

By 1960 Johnson had more influence in Washington than any other Democrat, a national reputation, a demonstrated capacity for leadership, and a hunger for the presidency. The preferred candidate of the South and of many conservative Democrats elsewhere in 1960, he lost the nomination to John F. Kennedy who picked Johnson as his running mate partly because of Johnson's obvious abilities, partly because of his strength in southern states Kennedy needed to carry.

As Kennedy also realized, Johnson had a genuine concern for the poor. His memories of his own youth, his sensitivity to the needs of his rural neighbors, his continuing affection for the New Deal, and his vaulting view of American possibilities built his commitment to social reform beyond the limits of the prudential politics he had practiced during the preceding decade. Though he had absorbed much of the culture and manner of the "good ol' boys," Johnson was authentically democratic in his distaste for racial prejudice. He had managed the civil rights bills of the 1950s with a compelling sense of urgency and a precise calculation of possibility.

Kennedy's New Frontier operated with just that balance, but Johnson was not comfortable with his office or his environment. He was never content as a subordinate to anyone. He also resented what he took to be a disdain for the South and for himself among Kennedy's circle of friends. He had reservations about the Ivy League background of Kennedy's intimates. Insecure in their company, Johnson bolstered his courage by recourse to the macho vocabulary of the ranch, a language Kennedy also knew but used only in private. Johnson's more public vulgarity tended to confirm the suspicions of those who considered him gauche and also vain, devious, emotional and egocentric. That assessment, partially valid, underestimated the political intelligence, social consciousness, and personal command of Lyndon Johnson.

His critics also underrated his understanding of the past and his anxiety about his place in history. Johnson knew what the pattern of American reform had been, how much remained to be done, and how large was the role of the president was in furthering change. Johnson had served in Congress during the long dry season that began in 1939 and had not ended in 1963. In that time reform legislation was blocked by Republicans and conservative Democrats, mostly southern.

When Kennedy was assassinated in November 1963, Johnson immediately espoused Kennedy's program, in which he also believed. He responded to his new office as Theodore Roosevelt had, with a spontaneous sense of its possibilities. He had had twenty-three years in Congress, where his prestige remained high. He had an excellent knowledge of the federal government. He had an excellent personal staff and persuaded most of Kennedy's senior associates also to remain. He had no doubts about the significance of his objectives.

Johnson focused first on two measures, revenue and a civil rights bill. The revenue bill proposed a tax reduction in order to encourage investment and spur economic growth. A resulting increase in national income would lift federal revenues to support poverty-related programs. Kennedy's advisors, adherents of the new economics derived from J. M. Keynes, even gave up the possibility of tax reform for the sake of their stimulation. But business and conservatives in Congress did not trust the new frontiersmen, who they considered latter-day New Deal spenders. Johnson spoke the language of prudence. He spread the word that he would pare the budget so as to reduce the projected deficit from $9 billion to $5 billion. By appearing the champion of fiscal conservative, he won Congress over and the tax bill passed. It produced the anticipated economic effects. It also eased the taxes of both the wealthy and the middle class, of both big business and smaller enterprises with the result of enhancing Johnson's standing with those groups. Johnson had made prudence and prosperity his issues for 1964 and built an enlarged constituency for the rest of his program.

The civil rights bill, central to that program, had emerged from Kennedy's increasing responsiveness to the momentum of the civil rights movement. By 1963 the leadership of the movement ushered in Dr. Martin Luther King, Jr. Confrontations between King's followers, black and white devotees of civil disobedience, and the segregationists gave urgency to King's cause. As chairman of Kennedy's committee on equal employment opportunity, Johnson said he had again come "face to face with the deep-seated discrimination"[198] that obstructed the employment and the education of blacks. "In the spring of 1963," he later wrote, "events in Birmingham, Alabama, showed the world the glaring contrast between the restraint of the black demonstrators and the brutality of the white policemen."[199] King's march on Washington that summer further moved the nation. For Johnson, nothing made "a man come to grips more directly with his conscience than the Presidency ... the burden of his responsibility literally opens up his soul ... so it was with me.... I would use every ounce of strength I possessed to gain justice for the black Americans."[200]

Johnson put his prestige as president on Kennedy's civil rights bill, which was designed to end segregation in public restaurants and hotels. If southern Democratic senators, assisted as they had been so often by Republicans, could prevent cloture, they could threaten a filibuster in order to force a weakening of the measure. Johnson cut off that possibility. He had an easy familiarity with senators that Kennedy had lacked. Using that advantage, he made it clear that he would accept no compromise. He also used his power on the minority leader, Republican Senator Everett Dirkson. He appealed to Dirkson's vanity. Dirkson enjoyed his unusual role as a champion of democracy. Senator Hubert H. Humphrey established a bipartisanship among liberals. The attempt to cloture failed and the Civil Rights Act of 1964 passed. It ended legal discrimination in public places, in employment, and in voter registration. It authorized the attorney general to institute suits on behalf of injured individuals. It was a major triumph for Johnson.

In January 1964, President Johnson called for an unconditional war on poverty in America. His program had been due to the planning of the Kennedy Administration, which had addressed the special problems of the aged and the ill and of the untrained and unemployed in Appalachia and in urban slums. Johnson sponsored versions of those plans in a personal style which he associated with the late-nineteenth-century populism of his native Southwest. With skill he shepherded through Congress the Economic Opportunity Act of 1964, which authorized $750 million for jobs and training, for the support of community efforts to attack poverty, and for creating a domestic social service corps modeled upon Kennedy's overseas Peace Corps and called VISTA, "Volunteers in Service to America." The act also enabled the establishment of the Head Start program for disadvantaged preschool children and the Upward Bound program for poor but aspirant college students. Republicans forced Congress to table Johnson's proposal for national medical insurance, but this important reform awaited only the president's re-election.

During the Johnson Administration, profits soared and poverty declined. Unemployment was reduced to four percent. The minimum wage was increased to $1.60 per hour and coverage was expanded. Prices started increasing in 1965 and LBJ urged suspension of the business tax credit to combat inflation. He did not raise taxes or impose mandatory wage-price controls. He preferred voluntary guidelines. He asked for cutbacks in spending. He pressured the aluminum, copper, and steel industries to rescind or modify price increases. However, his anti-inflation actions were not entirely successful. In 1968 a surcharge on income taxes to support the war and his domestic programs was passed by Congress.

Johnson promoted religious freedom. He proposed improved schooling for Native Americans, vocational training for the unskilled, and federal participation in the JFK Center for the Performing Arts. He signed a bill eliminating immigration quotas based on national origin. President Lyndon B. Johnson believed all persons were deserving of respect, regardless of status. He tried to improve the lot of the homeless, to alleviate poverty, and to insure justice for any unfavored group.

Lyndon Johnson yearned for election in his own right. He later recalled hesitations born of his self-consciousness as a Southerner, his fear that the country would not accept his leadership, and his worry about his health. Nine years earlier he had a serious heart attack, but his health had been excellent since then. In fact he had no real doubt. He believed he would become the greatest of presidents and he wanted the job desperately. He rejoiced in his strategy and his achievements. He had obtained civil rights legislation without alienating the South or its representatives. His poverty program succeeded with the eastern liberals whose regard he privately valued. The coalitions he had put together in Congress foreshadowed the construction he had begun of a consensus so broad that he won election by an overwhelming majority. In addition to blacks and white liberals, usually conservative Democrats liked the tax reduction, as did business, which was prospering as the economy boomed and reconciled to a poverty program in which corporations were to play an altruistic but potentially profitable part. Unlike Franklin Roosevelt in 1936, Lyndon Johnson in 1964 cultivated the managers of American industry, a departure from previous liberal practice. Outside of the president's fold were some Republicans, some southern segregationists and a few blue-collar whites disgruntled by the gains of the black and the poor.

Johnson and Attorney General Robert F. Kennedy did not get along. Johnson believed Robert Kennedy opposed Johnson's selection as vice president. Robert Kennedy felt Johnson had given John Kennedy small credit for the achievements of 1964.

The clash came over Johnson's choice of a vice president. Robert Kennedy thought about that office, but he never declared his candidacy. He knew Johnson did not want him, but he refused to drop out of the race and he wished to remain in public life. The president, in July 1964, announced it inadvisable to recommend for vice president any member of the Cabinet. This eliminated Kennedy and several others unacceptable to the president. As it worked out, Kennedy ran successfully for United States senator from New York, a position from which he enhanced his stature. Johnson chose Hubert Humphrey as his running mate. Humphrey was a liberal whose promises of personal loyalty made him a satisfactory vice president.

The Republicans guaranteed Johnson's victory by nominating Senator Barry Goldwater of Arizona. Goldwater, a conservative, believed that active government endangered freedom, called for the abolition of the income tax, the sale of the Tennessee Valley Authority, and the reduction or elimination of Social Security. It was Goldwater who seemed radical, threatening to rip apart the social fabric, which decades of reform had knit. Johnson carried forty-four states with over 60 percent of the popular vote. The Democrats won big majorities the House and Senate.

Johnson called his domestic program the Great Society. It included the war against poverty and the struggle for racial equality and, as he said in his inaugural address in 1965, it also asked "not only how much, but how good; not only how to create wealth, but how to use it; not only how fast we are going, but where are we headed. It proposes as the first test of a nation: the quality of its people."[201] In order to fulfill the needs of the spirit, he said the nation had first to establish freedom from the wants of the body. He urged Congress to do both, to beautify the country, eliminate water and air pollution, clean up the cities, provide medical care for the aged and education for the young, and guarantee voting rights to blacks still ordinarily barred from the polls in the South. Those objectives grew out of Franklin Roosevelt's Economic Bill of Rights of 1944, now expanded, and they projected forward the agenda of gradual reform, the American dream at a time propitious for its achievement.

Johnson had the votes in Congress, the skill to muster them and the weight of public opinion on his side. He served in a time of prosperity. In March 1965 an Appalachian aid bill was passed. Twenty-three billion dollars went for economic development of the Appalachian region and for slum clearance and the creation of model urban communities. The Elementary and Secondary Education Act of 1965 was passed in April. It provided federal aid for elementary and secondary schools not on a general basis but according to a selective formula which took into account both the poverty of the school district and the amount of the state's average educational expenses per child. Johnson's bill also required each school district to make available resources such as textbooks and television to children in private and parochial as well as public schools.

At the president's urging, Congress passed the Medical Act in July. It provided $6.5 billion for Medicare under Social Security for all Americans 65 or older. Medicaid, supported by federal grants to the states, furnished special help to the poor.

In August 1965 a housing bill passed. Also in August, a voting rights bill was introduced. Johnson addressed Congress, supporting the voter rights bill: "I speak tonight ... for the dignity of man and the destiny of democracy.... There is no issue of state's rights.... There is only the struggle for human rights.... Even if we pass this bill the battle will not be over.... The effort of American Negroes to secure for themselves the full blessings of American life ... must be our cause, too. Because ... it is all of us who must overcome the crippling legacy of bigotry and injustice. And we shall overcome."[202]

Those last three words, the refrain of the hymn Martin Luther King made his anthem, reflected Johnson's commitment to the issue. Congress passed the Voting Rights Act of 1965. It eliminated discriminatory literacy tests, provided federal officers to assist black voter registration, and established severe penalties for interference with individual's rights to the ballot. It set in motion, for the first time in a century, the rapid inclusion of blacks in the southern electorate. Yet Johnson said it was not enough:

"We seek not just freedom but opportunity. We seek not just ... equality as a right and a theory but equality as a fact and a result."[203]

In 1965, Martin Luther King, Jr., led a civil rights march from Selma, Alabama, to Montgomery. Violence broke out when state troopers at Selma battered the marchers who had refused to turn back. Fifty or so demonstrators were injured. Several days later, a group of white vigilantes murdered a white Boston clergyman, a "nigger lover," they explained. The brutalities of the episodes, caught in part by television cameras, reached millions of homes in America and provoked a national demand for the use of federal troops to protect King and his company. With that sentiment behind him, President Johnson maneuvered the governor of Alabama into admitting he could not afford to mobilize the National Guard, a confession that permitted the president to federalize the Alabama guard under his command and order it to defend the rights of the marchers to proceed peacefully to their destination.

Between 1963 and 1969 blacks made substantial gains in employment, income, education and health, as well as in access to public facilities and to the vote. In the same period the poor in general benefited from federal support for child care, medical care, low income housing, job training, and community action organized for widespread participation. A bill to combat heart disease, cancer and strokes was passed in October 1965. In November, the Higher Education Act was passed, including federal aid to colleges and the creation of a National Teacher Corps. Johnson signed legislation establishing automobile safety standards. A law against age discrimination in employment was passed in 1967. Johnson had cause to boast about his record.

He accepted able blacks for major offices. For example, Robert E. Weaver served as secretary of the new Department of Housing and Urban Affairs and Thurgood Marshall as associate justice of the Supreme Court. Johnson expected his reforms soon to swell the number of qualified blacks and other minorities.

Johnson held a White House conference on civil rights in 1966. The Civil Rights Act of 1968 was passed. Opposition to the Vietnam War and the loss of the House of Representatives in the 1966 election slowed the Great Society reforms. Lyndon Johnson decided not to run for re-election in 1968. Johnson's enormous energy produced impressive results. His record in 1965–1966 rivaled those of Woodrow Wilson in 1913–1914 and Franklin Roosevelt in 1935.

Johnson had been a man of towering intensity and anguished insecurity, of grandiose ambition and grave self-doubt, a man who was brilliant, crude, intimidating, compassionate, overbearing, and driven.[204]

Richard M. Nixon

A Republican, Nixon was elected to Congress where he gained fame by attacking Alger Hiss. After a second term in the House, he was elected to the Senate in 1950. In both the congressional and senatorial races, he accused his opponents with being soft on communism. In 1952 and 1956 he was elected vice president. In 1960 he ran for president and lost. He ran for governor of California in 1962 and lost. Nixon was elected president in 1968 and re-elected in 1972.

Nixon was devious, manipulative, driven by unseen and unknowable forces, quick to blame, slow to forgive, passionate in his hatreds, self-centered, untruthful, untrusting, and at times so despicable that one wants to avert one's eyes in shame and embarrassment. Nixon was a strange man, a weird politician. He was always a man alone. He had uncomfortable shyness. He did not like groups. He trusted no one. He was an introvert when the presidency needed an extrovert. He was like Prince Niccolo Machiavelli who, in 1513, wrote:

> A prudent ruler, therefore, cannot, and should not, keep his word when keeping it is to his disadvantage, and when the reasons that made him promise no longer exist. For if all men were good, this precept would not hold, but since they are bad and would not keep their word to you, you do not have to keep yours to them. Nor is there ever a shortage of legitimate reasons to disguise your disregard.... Everyone understands how laudable it is for a prince to keep his word and live integrity and not cunning. Nonetheless, experience shows that nowadays those princes who have accomplished great things have had little respect for keeping their word and have known how to confuse men's minds with cunning. In the end they have overcome those who have preferred honesty.

Nixon was a modern counterpart of Machiavelli. It was no accident that Nixon preferred a White House of lies, organized for deception. Eventually

161

it was deceived and confused egos that undermined Nixon. There were so many lies even the president himself and his insiders did not know the truth.

Nixon demeaned the office of president by petty, small-minded, mean-spirited and crude conduct. Nixon was not trustworthy. His public life lacked morality.

Nixon had successes in foreign relations, which are not covered in this book. Nixon's domestic program was ineffective. He was the ultimate cynic, a president without principle in domestic politics. By executive order, Nixon created the office of Minority Business Enterprise within the Commerce Department, but he opposed school desegregation, affirmative action, anti-discrimination programs, and extending the Voting Rights Act of 1965.

He supported wiretapping and no-knock entry by police. He opposed the Miranda ruling. He secretly taped visitors to the White House. Nixon was accused of anti–Semitism. The Equal Employment Opportunity Act of 1972 was passed, but Nixon's entire Cabinet, White House staff and all his Supreme Court appointees were white males with the exception of his personal secretary.

Inflation increased, unemployment increased and the gross national product declined the first two years of the Nixon Administration. Then the president instituted wage-price controls and urged the Federal Reserve to expand monetary policy. These steps helped the economy temporarily, but when the controls were removed after the 1972 election, inflation soared. Nixon indexed Social Security payments to keep up with inflation. Because he lacked a coherent agenda, Nixon was unable to get support for his domestic program.

Nixon did not propose pro-labor legislation, but he courted labor leaders, especially George Meany, and received support from much of the rank and file. Nixon fought hard to abolish the Office of Economic Opportunity. Congress refused to eliminate legal services, economic development, and community action programs. Nixon impounded the funds that Congress had appropriated for these programs. Nixon opposed mandatory national health insurance. Nixon had no consistent fiscal policy. He supported the Philadelphia plan to integrate construction trades.

Nixon used his staff more than his Cabinet. His most dominant Cabinet member was Henry Kissinger. His vice president, Spiro Agnew, and his Attorney General, John Mitchell, were very corrupt and tarnished the Nixon Administration.

Nixon's first staff appointment was Rose Mary Woods as his personal secretary. It was a good choice.

His second appointment was Bob Halderman: his job Nixon described as "administrative rather than substantive.... He would be a funnel rather than a filter.... The gate keeper of the Oval Office."[205]

Halderman and Woods didn't get along. Nixon wanted it that way.

Nixon appointed Ron Ziegler as his press secretary. In practice Nixon would be his own press secretary. Herb Klein was named director of communications.[206] Henry Kissinger became National Security Advisor.[207]

William Rogers was appointed Secretary of State. Nixon appointed a Democrat, Daniel Patrick Moynihan, as director of the Urban Affairs Council which he described as the domestic-policy equivalent of the NSC.[208]

Nixon did not intend to make Moynihan his domestic-policy czar. Instead he created conflicting centers of power. On one side of Moynihan, he made John Ehrlichman the White House council, with primarily domestic responsibilities. On the other side, he created a new Cabinet-level position of Counselor to the President and named economist Arthur Burns to fill it. Nixon reasoned that Burns' conservatism would be a useful and creative counterweight to Moynihan's liberalism.[209] Steve Hess, who went to work for Moynihan, thought Nixon had done well, creating an atmosphere for an honest conflict of ideas for domestic affairs.[210]

A fourth man who would be intimately involved in domestic policy was Bob Finch, who accepted the post of Secretary of Health, Education and Welfare. George Schultz became Secretary of Labor. Nixon wrote, "Dr. Schultz has earned the respect of management and labor as one of the nation's outstanding mediators."[211]

Maurice Stans became Secretary of Commerce; David Kennedy of the Chicago banking community became Secretary of the Treasury; George Romney was named Secretary of HUD. Other appointments included Winton Blount as Postmaster General, Walter Hickel as Secretary of Interior, John Volpe as Secretary of Transportation and Clifford Hardin as Secretary of Agriculture.

Nixon selected Melvin Laird — in Nixon's view "a strong man and a shrewd politician" — as Secretary of Defense.[212] Nixon initially offered the post of Attorney General to John Mitchell who said no because of problems with his wife's health. Nixon then asked Ehrlichman, who declined because he wasn't qualified. Nixon then returned to Mitchell and persuaded him to accept. Nixon described Mitchell as "the strong man in the campaign team and its leader, not because he was named such but because he earned that place due to his immense competence ... he will provide leadership far beyond the technical problems of his department."[213] Nixon wrote that Mitchell was "tough, intelligent, and fair. Moreover, I counted him my most trusted friend and advisor, and I wanted to have his advice available, not just on legal matters but on the whole range of presidential decision-making."[214] Paul McCracken was named chairman of the Council of Economics adviser.

Nixon did little to try to improve the lot of the homeless, to alleviate poverty or to insure justice for unfavored groups. The White House tapes reveal a man who had little respect for human dignity.

Although he was the overwhelming favorite to win the election of 1972, Nixon set up the Committee to Re-elect the President (CREEP), which collected a record-breaking $60 million campaign fund. Much of this money was collected illegally and used for illegal purposes. The Committee was responsible for the break-in and illegal wiretapping of Democratic headquarters in the Watergate building.

Nixon was not effective utilizing two-way communication. One of the causes of the Watergate scandal was the failure to assign subordinates to appropriate roles and to hold them responsible for results. The Watergate cover-up was one example of withholding information, not only from the public, but from Congress and investigating committees. Nixon had long maintained an antagonistic relationship with the press. It reached a low point after his 1962 defeat for the California governorship. Even before Watergate Nixon was not very successful working with Congress. He had to compromise on budgets.

Two Supreme Court nominations — Clement Haynesworth, Jr., and George Carswell — were turned down by the Senate. Other acceptable appointees were Harry Blackmon, Lewis Powell, William Rehnquist, and Chief Justice Warren E. Burger. His appointments to lower courts were decried by many liberals and advocates of civil rights.

On June 6, 1974, the Watergate grand jury revealed that Nixon had been named an unindicted co-conspirator in the Watergate cover-up. The House Judiciary began public debate on articles on impeachment on July 24, 1974. The committee voted in favor of impeachment. Before the full house voted, the president resigned on August 9, 1974. Ex–Attorney General Mitchell and several others were sent to prison. President Ford granted Nixon a full pardon on September 8, 1974.

Gerald R. Ford

A football hero at the University of Michigan, Ford, after graduation from Michigan, obtained a law degree at Yale. He served in the navy in World War II, earning ten battle stars.

In 1948 he was elected to Congress. He was re-elected 12 times. In 1951 he was appointed to the Appropriations Committee. In 1963 Ford become chairman of the House Republican Conference. After the Kennedy assassination, President Johnson appointed Ford to the Warren Commission. In 1964 he became minority leader in the House.

When Vice President Spiro Agnew resigned in disgrace, President Nixon chose Ford to succeed him. When Nixon resigned to avoid impeachment, Ford became president. Ford is the only president in history of the United States to reach the presidency without having been elected either vice president or president. Ford's popularity dropped when he pardoned Nixon.

"I am a Ford, and not a Lincoln," he told America. "Our long national nightmare is over. The Constitution works." Ford viewed himself as "a moderate in domestic affairs, conservative in fiscal affairs, and a dyed-in-the-wool internationalist in foreign affairs."[215]

Ford inherited a bad economy and it got worse. Inflation was high. Unemployment was high. Ford announced the Whip Inflation Now (WIN) program and called on industry to exercise restraint. Ford vetoed environmental controls on strip mining, recommended that Congress repeal the requirements that the auto industry strengthen emission standards and vetoed a bill that would have required the transport of twenty percent of imported oil in high-cost U.S. tankers, employing union labor. In his first 14 months, Ford vetoed 39 measures. Although Ford's WIN buttons were much ridiculed, he was successful in reducing the rate of inflation by 1976 to one-half the 1974 rate.

Ford's main anti-recession proposal was a combination of tax rebates and investment tax credit. Congress passed a tax reduction bill greater than the president had requested, resulting in the highest deficits in U.S. history up to that time. Increases in oil prices kept the economy stalled. To combat inflation caused by price increases, Ford proposed to return billions of dollars to the public and to industry in tax rebates, tax reductions, and direct grants.

Ford favored capital over labor and industry over agriculture. He vetoed a bill that would have increased the power of construction unions, breaking his promise to sign it. His Secretary of Labor resigned in protest. Ford's tax reductions applied both to individuals and to corporations, but industry was the main beneficiary.

He did little to alleviate poverty. He did not favor using the power of the presidency to promote the welfare of the people. He did not act to support education, culture, national parks and recreation areas. He did not promote conservation and he vetoed environmental legislation.

Ford described himself as a moderate Republican when he ran for Congress. However, as president, Ford was conservative. His whole presidency was severely damaged by the unpopular Nixon pardon one month into his presidency before any criminal charges had been filed.

The president said, "Ladies and gentlemen, I have come to a decision which I felt I should tell you and all my fellow American citizens as soon as I was certain in my own mind and in my own conscience that it is the right thing to do.... Now therefore, I, Gerald R. Ford, President of the United States, pursuant to the pardon power conferred upon me by Article 11, Section 2, of the Constitution, have granted and by these presents do grant a full, free and absolute pardon unto Richard Nixon for all offenses against the United States which he, Richard Nixon, has committed or may have committed or taken part in during the period from July 26, 1969, through August 9, 1974."[216]

A national storm over the Nixon pardon struck the new president almost immediately. Neither Ford nor his advisers were prepared for its fury. What he had portrayed as an act of mercy for a broken man was bitterly attacked as a betrayal of justice, even as a deal secretly arranged in advance with Nixon. Newspapers, network commentators, and private citizens from coast to coast expressed their outrage and dismay. Instead of encouraging the healing process as he had hoped, Ford had reopened the Watergate wound and rubbed salt into the wound thus exposed.[217]

In 1975 President Ford signed Public Law 94-106, authorizing the admission of women into the service academies. In the fall of 1976, 119 women entered West Point, 81 entered the Naval Academy, and 147 enrolled in the Air Force Academy. Women also enrolled in the Coast Guard Academy and the Merchant Marine Academy.

Journalist Kenneth Quinn extolled Ford's policies:

> I would suggest that President Ford's most enduring legacy can be found in almost every city and town in America in the person of the more than 130,000 refugees he brought to this country immediately after the fall of Saigon, as well as the million other Indochinese refugees who followed in the next decade.
>
> These refugees from Vietnam, Laos and Cambodia have enriched the United States in an array of areas, achieving high standards in education and demonstrating a committed work ethic. Almost none of them would have gotten here except for the good-hearted and caring Gerald Ford.
>
> There was considerable opposition, even among the president's senior advisers, to bringing large numbers of Asian refugees to America. It would be enough, the argument went, to just take care of the top generals and South Vietnamese leaders. Ford disagreed. He lashed out at such attitudes, saying: "It just burns me up. We didn't do that to the Hungarians. We didn't do it to the Cubans. Damn it, we are not going to do it now."
>
> Jerry Ford had an instinctive trust that thousands and thousands of average Americans would open their homes and hearts to receive these unfortunate people who were at such risk. And his faith was rewarded across the country.
>
> Gerald Ford redefined the American attitude toward racially diverse refugees and launched what arguably became the single greatest international humanitarian endeavor since the Marshall Plan — an effort that resulted in more than 1.5 million refugees finding new homes in the United States, Canada, France and Australia.
>
> These refugees from Indochina, their children and grandchildren live in freedom today, thanks to Gerald Ford's concern for the suffering of "little people" with no one else to help them.[218]

Ford did poorly in his 1976 presidential debates with Jimmy Carter. Ford lost the presidential election of 1976.

On September 5, 1975, Ford survived an assassination attempt in Sacramento, California, by Lynette S. Fromme, a member of a cult once led by convicted mass murderer Charles Manson. Fromme was stopped by Secret Service agents before she could fire her handgun. On September 22, 1975, Ford survived another assassination, this time in San Francisco, by another female assailant. Sara Jane Moore fired a shot at the president, but a bystander diverted her aim.

On May 21, 2001, Ford received a Profile in Courage Award and in

1999 he was presented the Presidential Medal of Freedom. Gerald R. Ford died on December 26, 2006. He was 93 years old. Ford was the fourth former president to live to age 90. He will be remembered for his pardon of Richard Nixon. He told CBS that he had to pardon Nixon. He had no choice because it was necessary to heal the country by binding wounds, making progress possible. Ford said Nixon never said thank you.

At his funeral in the Capital Rotunda on December 30, 2006, the nation honored Gerald R. Ford. Ford's decision to pardon Richard Nixon, so divisive at the time, was hailed in his funeral services by his old Chief of Staff, Vice President Dick Cheney. "It was this man, Gerald R. Ford, who led our republic safely through a crisis that could have turned to catastrophe," said Dick Cheney. "Gerald Ford was almost alone in understanding that there could be no healing without pardon."[219]

"In our nation's darkest hour, Gerald Ford lived his finest moment," said Republican Senator Ted Stevens of Alaska. "He was the man the hour required."[220]

House Speaker Dennis Hastert said, "In 1974 America didn't need a philosopher king or a warrior prince. We needed a rock, we needed honesty and candor and coverage. We needed Gerald Ford."[221]

According to some historians, the strengthening of presidential power in the George W. Bush Administration and the weakening of congressional power had its roots in the Ford White House, where Cheney and Donald Rumsfeld also served. John Robert Greene, a Ford biographer and historian at Cazenovia College, said, "Ford dug in his heels as best he could to stop the erosion of presidential power." Cheney has explicitly linked actions of Ford and George W. Bush to a historic reassertion of power. Cheney said in an interview on ABC's *This Week* in 2002, "In 34 years, I have repeatedly seen an erosion of powers and the ability of the President of the United States to do his job." In December 2005, after the disclosure of the National Security Agency's eavesdropping without warrants, Cheney told reporters that the program was a proper assertion of the presidency. While the "nadir of the modern presidency had come in the 1970s," Cheney said, "I do think that to some extent now, we've been able to restore the legitimate authority of the presidency." Others disagree about Ford's and George W. Bush's strengthening the presidency.

At the funeral service at the Washington National Cathedral on January 2, 2007, the nation remembered Gerald R. Ford for what he didn't have — pretensions, a scheming agenda, a great golf game — as much as for the small-town authenticity he brought to the presidency.[222] Ford is remembered as a rock of stability.

President George W. Bush said, "In President Ford, the world saw the best of America and America found a man whose character and leadership would bring calm and healing to one of the most divisive moments in our nation's history. When President Nixon needed to replace a vice president who had resigned in scandal, he naturally turned to a man whose name was a synonym for integrity and eight months later, when he was elevated to the presidency, it was because America needed him not because he needed the office."[223]

Former president George Herbert Walker Bush called Ford a "Norman Rockwell painting come to life." He told gentle jokes about Ford's golf game. Tom Brokaw said Ford brought to office "no demons, no hidden agenda, no hit list or acts of vengeance." Henry Kissinger said, "In his understated way he did his duty as a leader, not as a performer playing to the gallery. Gerald Ford had the virtues of small town America."[224]

Jimmy Carter

A southern Democrat, Jimmy Carter defeated Gerald Ford in the presidential election of 1976. A populist, Carter was supported by liberal, moderate and conservative Democrats. Carter was a moral leader as well as a political leader. He promoted human rights in the United States and in the world. He was a Southern Baptist: a deacon and Sunday school teacher. He was evangelical but not fundamentalist. In his public life and in his private life he believed in doing what was right. He was strongly influenced by Reinhold Niebuhr. Throughout his career Carter had a consistent set of values and beliefs. Nothing sums up the philosophy of his public life better than his oft-repeated quote from Niebuhr that "the sad job of politics is to bring justice to a sinful world."

Carter, a graduate of the United States Naval Academy, served on battleships and submarines for seven years. In Plains, Georgia, he served as an officer in the Plains Baptist Church, state-certified Seed Organization, Lions Club, local planning commission, local library board, hospital authority and county school board. In 1962 he was elected to the state senate. He was re-elected in 1964. In 1966 he ran for governor but lost. In 1970 Jimmy Carter was elected governor of Georgia. In his inaugural speech the governor declared that the time for racial discrimination was over. The speech gave him national attention as a voice of the "New South." In 1974 Carter became chairman of the Democratic National Committee.

President Carter in 1977 inherited a bad economy with inflation, unemployment and deficits. Conditions had started to improve in 1976, but deteriorated again due to rising oil prices. The trade deficit for 1977 was the greatest it had ever been. Under Carter the budget deficit stayed under its 1976 peak, and unemployment was lower each year than it had been in the previous administration, but inflation increased each year of

Carter's administration. Carter proposed an energy program intended to check inflation. He wanted to improve conditions for the poor and the deprived and to reduce unemployment. He planned to reduce government spending, but also redirect it by targeting scarce resources toward the most needy. He wanted to reform the income tax and the welfare system to benefit lower income groups. He proposed a national health program. He had trouble getting his domestic program through Congress. A bill was passed taxing windfall profits in the oil industry.

Carter created the Department of Energy and the Department of Education. Five energy bills were passed by Congress in 1978. Carter signed a bill banning dumping raw sewage in the ocean. New laws were passed in 1977 regulating strip mining and in 1978 controlling the leasing of off-shore drilling areas. In 1980 bills were passed to clean up toxic waste and protect Alaskan wilderness. Carter strengthened education. He improved the Elementary and Secondary Education Act in 1977 and 1978. He doubled the portion of the budget going to education. President Carter supported civil liberties and human rights.

Congress granted $1.5 billion in aid to the financially endangered Chrysler Corporation. In 1980 Carter announced a recession had begun. President Carter resisted congressional pressure to enact a massive tax cut.

Jimmy Carter was at the helm of a vast array of humanitarian efforts. He embodied the qualities that the American public mourns having lost in its politicians: integrity, honesty, ethics and dedication. His was always less a political agenda than a moral one. He saw the office as a vehicle for constructive change, propelled by firm and very Christian convictions about right and wrong. Critics railed against his lack of political ideology. What made Jimmy Carter a unique and honorable man made his presidency an uphill battle.

Carter's roots were in Plains, Georgia, where the imbalanced society created by inherited wealth and segregation could not suppress the farm worker who held dear the tenets of social justice and strove toward the highest goals. Tenacity and self-confidence propelled Carter from the Naval Academy to the governorship to the presidency. Along the way, he remained devoted to his wife Rosalyn and his family, to his religion and to the idealogy that the state and government have a responsibility to create a better society.

In his post-presidency, Carter was active in the Habitat for Humanity program, in which houses for the poor are built in the United States and abroad. By the end of 1986, thousands of Habitat volunteers were in 171 U.S. communities and 17 foreign nations. The Habitat was committed to build at least one house overseas for each one constructed in the United States. This program had a special appeal to Jimmy and Rosalyn Carter.

Carter's administration was dominated by foreign relations, including the hostage crisis in Iran. While foreign relations are not considered a part of this book, something needs to be said here about Carter's efforts both when he was president and in his post-presidency concerning world affairs.

Jimmy Carter won the Nobel Peace Prize October 10, 2002, for his efforts to bring peace to the Middle East and his commitment to human rights and the promotion of democratic values around the world. He was honored for "his decades of untiring effort to find peaceful solutions to international conflicts, to advance democracy and human rights, and to promote economic and social development."[225]

Ronald Reagan

A former radio sports announcer and movie and TV actor, Reagan, a right-wing Republican, was elected governor of California in 1966. He was re-elected in 1970. Reagan narrowly lost the Republican nomination for president in 1976. In 1980 Reagan was elected president of the United States. He was re-elected in 1984.

Reagan's domestic program was supply-side economics known as "Reaganomics." His theory was that cutting taxes on corporations and high income individuals would lead to greater investment and enable businesses to expand and to modernize equipment, increasing production, strengthening the economy, generating more jobs, and creating more revenue, which, combined with spending cuts, would balance the budget and curb inflation. He stopped the war on poverty because he believed the poor would be helped more by trickle-down economics than by government programs. Reagan favored the interests of capital over labor and agriculture. He ordered the firing of 13,000 striking aircraft controllers, replacing them with less qualified personnel.

Reagan prohibited federally funded family centers. He cut food for the poor and federal health care and opposed environmental standards. He failed to balance the budget.

Reagan's 1981 tax cut was the largest in American history. In 1986 the most thorough revision in forty years was passed. The regressive income tax reductions in the higher brackets made a big windfall for the wealthiest Americans. The total taxes on the average citizen remained about the same or maybe a little worse. Reagan's refusal to raise taxes in his second term led to an exploding deficit, which he blamed not on his administration, but on Congress, special interests, and the media.

Secretary of Interior James Watt wanted to open wilderness to oil exploitation, to expand off-shore leasing, to dismantle the Office of

Surface Mining, and to declare a moratorium of national park legislation.

Areas of domestic policy included welfare reform, health care, Social Security, education, and domestic law enforcement. The issues were contentious and the participant departments were many. The domestic assignment was about the broadest in the White House, requiring the domestic head to reach out across thirteen of the fifteen Cabinet departments plus the Environmental Protection Agency (EPA).

The recession of 1981-1982 resulted in record unemployment, bank failures and farm foreclosures. Critics charged that such dire circumstances were the results of "Reaganomics"—substantial reductions in government assistance and services, coupled with tax cuts. For his part, Reagan maintained that the faltering economy was the legacy of his predecessors. He urged the nation to "stay the course," and promised better days were just around the corner.

Reagan lobbied Congress to enact significant tax cuts while he drastically scaled back government spending. As federal funding for many social services were cut, responsibility for efforts such as Aid to Families with Dependent Children and school lunches was shifted to individual states. Reagan called this "new federalism."

Midway through his first term, economic conditions did improve. Reagan's stimulus package resulted in decreased inflation and increased employment. An exploding federal deficit and increasing disparity between the rich and poor resulted. By 1984, thirteen million children lived below the poverty line. Conditions in the inner cities grew more desperate as relief services were cut off. While corporate executives enjoyed record profits, legions of blue-collar workers saw their jobs shipped to other countries where wages were lower. Observers used the term "social Darwinism" to describe an economy where only the strong survive. But Reagan believed that the poor would benefit from a trickle-down economy where increased wealth would find its way to every facet of society.

The stock market crashed in October 1987 due to recklessness encouraged by Reagan. The wisdom of Reaganomics was very much put into question.

Reagan had a lax management style and failed to control his executives. Attorney General Edwin Meese resigned under pressure for influence-peddling and bribery. Oliver North and John Poindexter were indicted for conspiracy, fraud and theft of government funds. Robert McFarlane pleaded guilty to misleading Congress. President Reagan was criticized by the Tower Commission for failing to oversee the implementation and consequences of his own policies.

Reagan said, in his autobiography, "I'd come to Washington to put into practice ideas I'd believed in for decades."[226] This attachment to ideas is unusual among presidents. He said, in his farewell address on January 11, 1989, "I won a nickname, 'The Great Communicator.' But I never thought it was my style or the words I used that made a difference: It was content. I wasn't a great communicator, but I communicated great things."[227] On November 25, 1986, Reagan had met with the leaders of Congress and told them that there had been a plan to use the proceeds from the sale of arms to Iran for support of the anti-government rebels in Nicaragua — known as the Contras. As a result of this discovery, the president's national security adviser, Vice Admiral John Poindexter, resigned and Lt. Col. Oliver North, a National Security Council staffer responsible for the Iran arms-sales project and the plan to divert funds to the Contras, was dismissed. The Iran-Contra affair became a full-scale scandal, the largest and most consequential of the Reagan presidency.

For the four months that the scandal continued, the administration was brought to a standstill. The Iran-Contra affair had a major impact on Reagan's effectiveness as president. The American people refused to believe his explanations. He was never again able to attain the creditability of his first six years. Reagan later wrote, "Those first few months after the Iran-Contra affair hit the front pages were frustrating for me. For the first time in my life, people didn't believe me. While I was unhappy, I never felt depressed about the situation.... I just went on with my job."[228]

By Iran-Contra, in the sixth year of his presidency, Ronald Reagan had achieved much of what he had set out for himself and his administration in domestic matters. Political embarrassment was not a great concern. If he worried about his place in history it was not apparent.

Ronald Reagan was not pragmatic. He was a conviction politician. An idealist, ideas and principles meant more than personal power or aggrandizement. President Reagan's definition of success was the adoption and success of his ideas. He had no desire for power alone, merely what he could do with it to achieve his purposes. The holding of power was not the point. Power needed to be used for a purpose.

Reagan refused to become involved in the details of his administration. His presidency was successful. The United States shook off economic stagnation and became highly efficient and competitive globally, leaving other nations far behind; the free market system President Reagan championed became the model for economic reform around the world. The

American people returned from a period of self-doubt and timidity to their accustomed self-confidence and sense of optimism.[229] According to Wallison, "The huge government deficits left no discernable scar on the American economy.... Reagan achieved all his major and ambitious goals and he made it look easy."[230]

According to Neustadt, Reagan lacked many of the skills and capacities that a successful president needs; "He seems to have combined less intellectual curiosity, less interest in detail, than any President at least since Calvin Coolidge.... Yet Reagan had to be accounted successful: His presidency restored the public image of the office to a fair approximation of its Rooseveltian mold: a place of programmic and symbolic leadership, both pacesetter and tone setter to both the world and America."[231]

Reagan made enormous changes in the nation's fiscal structure, changing the U.S. tax structure twice. Following a recession shortly after he took office, the U.S. economy roared back, economic growth continued into the next decade, and stock markets reached unprecedented levels. He changed the tax system in revolutionary ways.

Reagan was successful because, unlike any modern president, he led with ideas with a consistent philosophy expressed through his speeches and despite pressure he refused to be shaken from the core concepts with which he had sought election. The convictions and commitments, the apparent disinterest in detail, and the delegation of authority were ultimately the keys of Reagan's success. His dominant mode was delegation to his staff and to outsiders he was passive. He was polite, cordial and unassuming to everyone. He had a benevolent view of human nature and motivation.

As president, Reagan consciously decided to limit his intervention in the decisions of his administration in order to achieve some other objectives. This was another of the keys to his success as well as the appearance that he was "disengaged." Reagan represented a set of ideas and values that reoriented and reinvigorated the Republican Party as a party of change. How Ronald Reagan chose to implement his ideas and how he conducted his ideas and his presidency accounted for his popularity and success. He persuaded Americans that there was another way to think about government and created a historic turning point in the direction of the United States. The last quarter of the twentieth century in American history may be called the Reagan Era.

Ronald Reagan believed in limited government. He opposed big government because he thought its bureaucracy, its paternalism, and its taxation would reduce the ability and incentives of the American people to innovate, complete, and produce better lives for themselves. In his 1981 inaugural address, Reagan said, "In this present crisis, government is not the solution to our problem. Government is the problem." He was committed to reducing the role of government in the nation's life. Once he had removed what he regarded as obstacles to the American people's productivity — punitive tax rates, excessive regulation, trade restrictions — and raised national morale through his unique blend of faith, optimism, and stubborn insistence on distinguishing between right and wrong, Ronald Reagan could reasonably believe that he had done on the domestic front all that his presidency required. The efforts of the American people — whose potential, to him, was limitless — would take care of the rest.

Lou Cannon wrote, "Reagan's range was narrow, but his agenda is compelling. He wanted to get on with the business of cutting government spending, reducing income taxes, and building up the military. All other policies seemed to him beside the point."[232]

"Because he thought he had achieved most of what he set out to do, he was relatively unruffled by setbacks that did not undo his accomplishments — even including the Iran-Contra affair; because he was more concerned about establishing his core ideas than in maintaining decision-making control over his administration — and believed strongly in the value of delegation — he gladly delegated authority to those he trusted to follow his principles while he focused relentlessly on a few objectives — such as reducing the role of government in the economy — as foundational, and thus vastly more important than others; he could relegate to low priority many of the policies and programs that routinely come to the president's desk thus accounting for the appearance of disengagement."[233]

Reagan's administration was guided and given purpose by the president's philosophy and ideas. His major ideas and principles rose to the level of convictions.

Reagan wrote to Peggy Noonan in reply to her question, "I never thought of myself as a great man, just a man committed to great ideas. I've always believed that individuals should take priority over the state. History has taught me that this is what sets America apart — not to remake the world in our image, but to inspire people everywhere with a sense of their own boundless possibilities. There's no question I am an idealist, which is another way of saying I am American."[234]

At the end of his two terms in office, Ronald Reagan viewed with satisfaction the achievements of the innovative program known as the Reagan Revolution, which aimed to reinvigorate the American people and reduce their reliance upon the government. He felt he had fulfilled his campaign pledge of 1980 to restore "the great confident roar of American progress and optimism."

Dealing skillfully with Congress, Ronald Reagan obtained legislation to stimulate economic growth, curb inflation, increase employment, and strengthen national defense. He embarked on a course of cutting taxes and government expenditures, refusing to deviate from it when the strengthening of defense led to a large deficit.

George Herbert Walker Bush

A former congressman, ambassador to China, Republican national chairman, director of the Central Intelligence Agency (CIA) and vice president, Bush was elected president in 1988 as a Republican. In his acceptance speech at the New Orleans National Convention, Bush said, "My opponent won't rule out raising taxes. But I will. And the Congress will push me and I'll say no. And they'll push again and I'll say to them: Read my lips: no new taxes."[235] In the same campaign, a racist Willie Horton ad appeared on television.

In Bush's inaugural address, he said, "America is never wholly herself unless she is engaged in high moral principle. We as a people have such a purpose today. It is to make kinder the face of the Nation and gentler the face of the world. My friends, we have work to do."[236]

The Bush Administration was mainly involved with foreign relations — "Desert Shield" and the end of the Cold War. Despite unprecedented popularity from military triumph, Bush was unable to withstand discontent at home from a faltering economy, rising violence in inner cities, and continued high deficit spending.

The budget climbed to the highest it had ever been. Federal spending under Bush increased to 25 percent of the GNP (Gross National Product) in 1992, the highest since World War II. During the Bush administration, inflation fell, reaching a low of three percent annually. Other economic indicators worsened. Unemployment increased. Fewer jobs were created and more businesses failed than during any other administration since the Great Depression. The number of Americans qualified for food stamps jumped to a record ten percent of the population. The gap between rich and poor widened and continued widening. The annual budget deficit in 1992 doubled to $350 billion.

The Bush domestic program was troubled. He inherited deteriorating productivity, growing deficits, growing national debt and declining living standards for the poor and middle class. Although Reagan was to blame, Bush took no action to solve these problems.

Bush and Congress settled on a $157 billion bailout plan for the savings and loan industry. In August 1989, Congress approved the Financial Institution Recovery and Enforcement Act (FIRAEA). The Resolution Trust Corporation was formed to dispose of failed savings and loan companies at "fire sale" prices.

Bush's plan to stimulate the economy by encouraging growth in the private sector included cutting expenditures on taxes, especially on capital gains. After a prolonged battle with Congress, he agreed in October 1990 to a deficit reduction bill breaking his 1988 campaign pledge not to raise taxes. It was the right thing to do, but it angered Republican conservatives. Even more damaging was a prolonged international recession that resulted in stagnant growth at home, high levels of unemployment and increased concern about the ability of the United States to compete with Japan and other nations.

Bush supported NAFTA and GATT. These were helpful to business and agriculture, but were opposed by labor and small farmers. Bush favored capital over labor and farmers.

Bush failed to respond adequately to help veterans suffering from the Gulf War syndrome. He failed to support his own Secretary of Housing and Urban Development, who called for a renewal of the war on poverty, a national housing policy, and enterprise zones. Bush even vetoed a $27 billion tax bill to create enterprise zones designed to help residents of inner cities. He favored tax credits to help lower-income people buy insurance, the pooling of smaller business in larger insurance groups, reform of medical malpractice laws, and the encouragement of managed care programs to keep costs down. But he failed to send a detailed bill to Congress.

Bush's most important domestic achievement by the time the 101st Congress concluded was the passage of the Americans with Disabilities Act, which prohibited discrimination in jobs and in areas of public accommodations (patterned after the 1964 act). It was "a really forward looking piece of civil rights legislation affecting the disabled."[237] Bush's own enthusiasm reflected the public sympathy for such goals. Backed by a coalition of AIDS and civil rights activists, as well as public health groups, it went through Congress with largely bipartisan support. Senator Tom Harkin, an Iowa Democrat, was a major supporter. President Bush signed it into law on July 26, 1990. Critics nevertheless faulted it as too conducive to frivolous law suits and bureau rate-building and filled with mandates requiring costly structural changes to achieve such assistance. However, it remained not only the major accomplishment of the 101st Congress but his clearest push toward a "kinder and gentler society."[238]

He signed a Child Care Bill in 1990 after he persuaded Congress to include parental choice and federal aid for church-related child care. In 1990 Bush vetoed a Civil Rights Bill, falsely calling it a "quota bill." One year later he signed the Civil Rights Act of 1991, which was similar to the 1990 bill he had vetoed. Bush opposed affirmative action but in a primary election in Louisiana, an ex–Klansman, David Duke, ran a strong race after declaring himself a Republican, gave the president little choice but to go along with a compromise civil rights bill. This time, Bush did most of the compromising. "Where did the quotas go?" one Democrat scoffed during the House debate. "They swam upstream, as red herrings often do."[239]

A few months later Bush was embarrassed on civil rights over the acquittal of the police officers who were tried for the beating of Rodney King and the rioting that followed in Los Angeles. The King situation was the problem of local government. Yet it was an outrage. Bush, revolted by the original beatings, deplored the Los Angeles riots.

Bush's greatest administrative accomplishment of the summer of 1990 was getting David Souter onto the Supreme Court. John Sununu agreed; as New Hampshire governor he had appointed Souter to the state's Supreme Court. A Harvard Law School graduate and Rhodes Scholar recently named to the U.S. Court of Appeals for the first Circuit in Boston, he was neither a William Brennan nor a Robert Burk. Souter had left no paper trail.

President Bush made a bad choice when he appointed Clarence Thomas to the Supreme Court in the summer of 1991. Thomas does not consider *stare decisis* when he votes. He is an originalist. Although he benefited from affirmative action, he used his position in the Reagan Administration to restrict affirmative action and other civil rights. He did the same as a justice.

Bush appointed the first Secretary of Veterans Affairs. His chief advisor, John Sununu, after excessive use of government perks and abuse of travel expenses, was replaced by Samuel Skinner.

William Jefferson Clinton

An Arkansas Democrat, Clinton was elected president in 1992 and re-elected in 1996. In the campaign of 1992, Bill Clinton promised to "focus like a laser" on the failing economy. When Clinton took over, there was a high unemployment rate and a big deficit, but inflation was low.

One of Clinton's chief accomplishments was deficit reduction. When Clinton took office, the budget deficit was $290 billion. His program paid off rapidly. Annual growth in 1997 was 8.2 percent. The tax revenue this growth produced erased the deficit. It was $22 billion in 1997 and by the first week of 1998 was gone entirely.[240]

On September 30, 1998, Clinton announced a budget surplus of about $70 billion, the first one in twenty-one years. Clinton announced the budget's surplus would exceed $200 billion with a ten-year projected surplus of over $4 trillion. At Christmas 2000, Clinton announced there would be enough money from the budget to pay $600 million of national debt over four years. This did not happen because George W. Bush became president of the United States in 2001 and fiscal policy was changed.

Deficit reduction was not an end in itself but means to achieve economic growth, more jobs and higher incomes. Clinton's plan represented a fundamental change in the way government had been working, ending the irresponsibility and unfairness of the past by asking the wealthy big corporations and other special interests that had benefited disproportionately from the tax cuts and deficits of the Reagan-Bush era to pay their fair share.

Clinton appointed Janet Reno Attorney General. She had operated highly successful "drug courts" as prosecuting attorney of Dade County, Florida. In the campaign Clinton pledged to support federal funding to establish drug courts all across the country.

At the end of the first one hundred days of a new presidency, the press always does an assessment. On the positive side, Clinton had created a National Economic Council in the White House and put together an ambitious economic program to reverse twelve years of trickle-down economics and it was making progress in Congress. Clinton had signed the family leave law and the motor voter law to make voter registration easier. He had reversed the Reagan-Bush abortion policies, including the ban on fetal-tissue research and the gag rule. President Clinton put Vice President Gore in charge of "reinventing government." Clinton had reduced the size of the White House staff, despite its increasing workload. Clinton had sent legislation to Congress to create the national service program, to double the EITC and create empowerment zones in poor communities and to dramatically cut the cost of college loans.

On the negative side, he had temporarily dropped the middle-class tax cut in the face of growing deficit. He had lost the stimulus program to a Republican filibuster. He had delayed presenting the health care program and mishandled part of the Waco raid. President Clinton overestimated how much change he could quickly achieve. The country had been going the other direction for twelve years and it would take more than one hundred days to turn things around. But Clinton kept trying to do it all at once until Democrats lost the 1994 midterm elections.

Deficit reduction was essential to economic recovery but not enough to build a sustained, widely shared recovery. In the early months the administration filled out the agenda with initiatives to expand trade, increase investments in educational training, and promote issues aimed at trouble spots or targets of opportunity. Between 1993 and 2000, after changes were made in the 1977 Community Reinvestment Act, banks offered more than $800 billion in home mortgages and small business and community loans.

In late June 1993, the Senate passed the budget 50 to 49, with Gore breaking the tie. Then the House, which had already approved a budget plan, and the Senate had to reconcile their differences. There were $255 billion in budget cuts and $241 billion in tax increases. The budget passed the House, then the Senate, and Clinton signed it on August 20.

The president wanted Congress to approve a school-to-work program, to provide one or two years of high-quality training for young people who didn't want to get a four-year college degree. In late March, Clinton signed the Goals 2000 bill. Finally he had a congressional commitment to meet the national education goals he had worked on in 1989, to measure students' progress toward them and to encourage local school districts to adopt the most promising reforms.

In 1994, Jonathan Alter wrote in *Newsweek*, "In less than two years, Bill Clinton had already achieved more domestically than John F. Kennedy, Gerald Ford, Jimmy Carter and George Bush combined. Although Richard Nixon and Ronald Reagan often had their way with Congress, *Congressional Quarterly* says it's Clinton who has the most legislative success of any president since Lyndon Johnson. The standard for measuring results domestically should not be the coherence of the process but how actual lives are touched and changed. By that standard, he's doing well." All thirteen appropriation bills were passed by September 30, the last day of the fiscal year.

Newt Gingrich suggested words for labeling Democrats in a 1994 pamphlet entitled "Language: A Key Mechanism of Control": betray, cheat, collapse, corruption, crisis, decay, destruction, failure, hypocrisy, incompetent, insecure, liberal, lie, pathetic, permissive, shallow, sick and traitors.[241]

Clinton signed a welfare reform bill in 1995. It did too little to move people from welfare to work and too much to hurt poor people and their children. Progress was made by Clinton and Shalala on their own in reforming the welfare system; seventy-three percent of America's welfare recipients were covered by these reforms and welfare rolls were dropping.

On July 27, 1996, an act of terrorism occurred at the Olympics in Atlanta. A pipe bomb killed two people. In August Clinton signed the food Quality Protection Act, the Safe Drinking Act and the Kennedy-Kassenbaum Bill, which helped millions of people by allowing them to take their health insurance from job to job while prohibiting insurance companies from denying coverage because of a pre-existing health problem. Clinton announced the Food and Drug Administration's final rule to protect young people from the dangers of tobacco. On August 22, President Clinton signed a landmark welfare reform bill. A Welfare to Work Partnership was organized. Eventually 20,000 companies hired more than one million off welfare.

In his State of the Union Address on January 27, 1997, Clinton declared the country was in good shape, with 14 million new jobs, rising incomes, the highest rate of home ownership ever, the fewest people on the welfare rolls in twenty-seven years, and the smallest federal government in thirty-five years.

In his 1999 State of the Union speech, Clinton said that by 1999, the economic expansion was the longest in history, with eighteen million new jobs since he took office. Real wages were going up, income inequality was going down a little, and unemployment was at its lowest peacetime rate since 1957.

Hillary and Bill Clinton joined with Al and Tipper Gore at a White House Conference on Mental Health. The president announced the bald eagle was off the endangered species list and Gore would outline a plan for the restoration of the Florida Everglades. President Clinton reached an agreement with the Republican leadership on funding 100,000 new teachers and doubling the number of children in after-school programs. Clinton awarded the Congressional Medal of Honor to twenty-two Japanese-Americans who had volunteered to serve in Europe during World War II after their families were interned in camps.

By administrative regulations, Clinton doubled grazing fees and made a commitment to no net loss of wetlands. Some 6.6 million acres of California desert were set aside. Clinton obtained funds for the Environmental Protection Agency to move against pesticides. The North American Free Trade Agreement (NAFTA) passed. By executive order, Clinton created the Grand Staircase–Escalante.

George W. Bush

George W. Bush, a Republican, former governor of Texas and son of former president George Herbert Walker Bush, won the disputed presidential election of 2000. His opponent, Al Gore, received the most popular votes, but the electoral votes in Florida were disputed. The United States Supreme Court on December 12, 2000, awarded the presidency to Bush. He won a second term in the election of 2004.

The younger Bush scraped through Andover and Yale academically, never made a varsity team, earned no distinction in the Air National Guard, and was defeated in a run for Congress in 1978. He lost millions in the oil business and had to be rescued by his father's friends in 1983. It was after that last humiliation that he began drinking hard.[242]

In September 2002, Bush invited five religious leaders — three Christian, one Jewish and one Muslim — to meet with him in the Oval Office. He wanted them to know that the War on Terror had not ended and that some of its hardest battles still lay ahead. Then he asked them to pray for him. "You know, I had a drinking problem. Right now I should be in a bar in Texas, not the Oval Office. There is only one reason I am in the Oval Office and not in a bar. I found faith. I found God. I am here because of the power of prayer."[243]

"Leadership remains the greatest mystery in politics. George W. Bush was hardly the obvious man for the job. But by a very strange fate, he turned out to be, of all unlikely things, the right man."[244]

The Bush Administration has been dominated by foreign affairs, including wars with Afghanistan and Iraq. These wars will not be discussed here except in their detrimental effects on domestic programs.

The previous administration left a balanced budget and a budget surplus. Clinton had been paying the national debt. Instead of enacting badly needed domestic reform such as health care, the Bush Administration passed on June 7, 2001, a tax cut for the wealthiest Americans. This tax cut and the War on Terror led to large deficit spending and greatly increased the national debt.

The $128 billion budget surplus that Bush inherited in 2001 has turned into a deficit of at least $337 billion this year.[245] The Republican Senate voted to raise the debt ceiling to nearly $9 trillion. Senators passed a record $2.8 trillion budget.[246]

On September 11, 2001, the United States was attacked by four hijacked airplanes, two of which flew into the World Trade Center causing much loss of life, a third which crashed at the Pentagon and the fourth which crashed in rural Pennsylvania. This attack showed weakness in the U.S. intelligence community.

Bush combined Defense and Intelligence agencies under the Department of Homeland Security. Aliens, foreigners, and even American citizens were detained by the U.S. government in violation of the United Nations Charter and the Geneva Convention, as no charges were filed against those people who were detained. Many were victims of racial profiling.

The Iraq war has had a devastating effect on the Bush domestic program. One can't put a price tag on the national security. When America's survival is at stake, one spends whatever it takes. But the invasion of Iraq was a war of choice, not of survival. Americans should not only be aware of the costs of war, but also consider whether the money might have been spent better in the United States.

About $250 billion has been appropriated for the war so far, and roughly the same amount is projected yet to be spent. Those direct appropriations don't tell the whole story. Since the entire cost of the war is being borrowed, the interest expenses on the debt must be factored in. There is the cost of American deaths and care for the wounded. There is the cost of replacing all the ammunition and equipment expended in Iraq and the lost productivity to communities and employers in the United States when reservists and National Guard are called to active duty.[247]

Hurricane Katrina struck New Orleans, Mississippi and Alabama on August 29, 2005. The response by the federal government was much too slow and people died needlessly. The Federal Emergency Management Agency (FEMA) Director Michael Brown, who was criticized for his handling of Katrina, said he felt like a scapegoat for a government-wide failure and blamed his boss, Homeland Security Secretary Michael Chertoff.

"I was literally constrained by Secretary Chertoff," Brown said. "My hands were tied." Chertoff replaced Brown on September 9, 2005.[248] In

October 2005, Hurricane Wilma struck Florida; once again FEMA and state and local officials failed in their responsibility.

The United States should close the prison at Guantanamo Bay, Cuba, immediately and end violent treatment that amounts to torture, United Nations human rights investigators reported. The White House rejected the report. White House spokesman Scott McClellan said, "We know that these are dangerous terrorists that are being kept at Guantanamo Bay. They are people that are determined to harm innocent civilians or harm innocent Americans." He added, "U.S. service personnel must deal with prisoners who are trained to provide false information."[249]

Columnist David Broder maintains Bush must consult Congress prior to the use of secret wiretaps. As for the administration contention that Bush has "inherent power" as chief executive to order warrantless wiretaps, Senator Lindsay Graham said, "Its application, to me, seems to have no boundaries when it comes to executive decisions in a time of war. It deals the Congress out. It deals the courts out."

Broder says the president needs to come to Congress for statutory authority and court supervision of the program. If he won't, Congress needs to assert its responsibility by moving that legislation on its own.[250]

Lewis "Scooter" Libby, Vice President Dick Cheney's Chief of Staff, leaked classified information at the direction of President Bush. Ten days later, July 18, 2003, the information was declassified. Libby faces charges of perjury, obstruction and lying to the FBI. Bush's "selective declassification of highly sensitive intelligence is wrong," said House Minority Leader Nancy Pelosi.[251]

On May 10, 2006, George W. Bush reached his all-time low in popularity polls. His approval rating dropped to 31 percent according to the CBS at Times Poll. George W. Bush is still in office at the time of writing this book.

The low approval ratings led to a White House shake-up. Andrew Card was replaced as Bush's chief aide. Karl Rove, Deputy Chief of Staff, was demoted. Scott McClellan, press secretary, resigned. Porter Goss, CIA director, resigned. The American people are upset about the budget deficit, the national debt, mismanagement of hurricane relief, gasoline prices and domestic scandals.

Notes

1. George W. Nordham, *The Age of Washington, George Washington's Presidency 1789–1797* (Chicago: Adama Press, 1989), 221.

2. Nordham, *The Age of Washington*, 234.

3. James MacGregor Burns and Susan Dunn, *George Washington* (New York: Henry Holt, 2004), 156.

4. http://qwpapers.virginia.edu.

5. Nordham, *The Age of Washington*, 243.

6. Forrest McDonald, *The American Presidency, An Intellectual History* (Lawrence: University Press of Kansas, 1994), 229–230.

7. Ibid., 216.

8. Page Smith, *John Adams, volume II 1784–1826* (Garden City, NY: Doubleday, 1962), 975–978.

9. Paul Leicester Ford, "To Dr. Joseph Priestly," in *The Writings of Thomas Jefferson, Vol. 8*, ed. Paul Leicester Ford (New York: G. P. Putnam's, 1892).

10. Dumas Malone, *Jefferson and His Time, Jefferson the President: First Term 1801–1805* (Boston: Little, Brown, 1970), 302.

11. Daniel J. Boorstin, *The Landmark History of the American People: Volume 1: From Plymouth to Appomattox* (New York: Random House, 1987), 95.

12. Mary Kay Phelan, *The Story of the Louisiana Purchase* (New York: Thomas Y. Crowell, 1979), 136.

13. William P. Sherman Library and Archives, Great Falls, Montana.

14. Henry Adams, *History of the United States of America during the Administration of Thomas Jefferson* (New York: McGraw-Hill, 1971).

15. Peter S. Onuf, *Jefferson's Empire: The Language of American Nationhood* (Charlottesville: University Press of Virginia, 2000).

16. Woodrow Wilson, "What Jefferson Would Do," in *Jefferson Reader: A Treasury of Writings about Thomas Jefferson*, ed. Francis Coleman Rosenberger (New York: Dutton, 1953), 239.

17. Robert Allen Rutland, *James Madison, The Founding Father* (New York and London: Collier Macmillan, 1987), 226.

18. Robert Frost, *A Talk for Students* (New York: Fund for the Republic Publications, 1956).

19. Nordham, *The Age of Washington*.

20. John Quincy Adams, *Memoirs of John Quincy Adams, Vol. IV* (New York: Praeger, 1970), 375.

21. Ibid., 468.

22. W. P. Cresson, *James Monroe* (Chapel Hill: University of North Carolina Press, 1946).

23. *Annals of Congress* 15th Congress 2nd Session, I. 1204. *A Century of Lawmaking for a New Nation: U.S. Congressional Documents and Debates 1774–1875 Comprising the Period from November 16, 1818 to March 3, 1819* (Washington: Gales and Seaton 1855).

24. John Quincy Adams, *The Lives of James Madison and James Monroe* (Boston: Phillips, Sampson, 1850), 293.

25. Cresson, *James Monroe*, 468.

26. J. Q. Adams, "To Abigail and John

189

Adams," St. Petersburg, June 30, 1811, Adams Papers, private collection.

27. Adams, *Memoirs IV*, 531; Adams, *Memoirs V*, 4, 12, 21.

28. Adams, *Memoirs V*, 210.

29. Adams Papers, private collection.

30. Marquis James, *Andrew Jackson, Portrait of a President* (Indianapolis and New York: Bobbs-Merrill, 1937) 443; *Nashville Republican*, July 20, 1838; "Jackson to W. B. Lawrence, Aug. 24," in *Correspondence of Andrew Jackson, Vol. V*, ed. John Spencer Bassett and David Maydole Matteson (Washington, D.C.: Carnegie Institution of Washington, 1935), 565; John Parton, *Life of Andrew Jackson III* (New York; Mason Brothers, 1859–1860), 644–649.

31. Eric M. Eriksson, "The Federal Civil Service under President Jackson," *Mississippi Valley Historical Review* XIII (1927): 529–530.

32. James Marquis, *Andrew Jackson, Portrait of a President* (Indianapolis and New York: Bobbs-Merrill, 1937), 444.

33. Horace Greeley, *The American Conflict* (Greenwood, CT: Greenwood Press, 1969), 106.

34. James, *Andrew Jackson*, 235.

35. "Lewis F. Linn to Van Buren, 1836," Van Buren Letters, Library of Congress, Washington, D.C. The recipe was to combine 1 quart of hickory ashes, 1 teacup soot, and 1 gallon of boiling water and take 1 full glass four times a day.

36. "Lawrence Van Buren to Blair, Oct. 23, 1862," Blair-Lee Papers, Princeton University, Princeton, CA; *The New York Times*, July 25, 1862; *New York Evening Post*, July 25, 1862.

37. *Madisonian*, Mar. 6 and 9, 1841.

38. James D. Richardson, *Messages and Papers of the Presidents IV* (Washington, D.C.: Bureau of National Literature & Art, 1903), 22, 30, 31; Allan Nevins, ed., *The Diary of Philip Hone, 1828–1851, 2 Vols.* (New York: Dodd, Mead, 1927), 533–537; *National Intelligencer*, Mar. 31 and Apr. 5, 1841; and *Madisonian,* May 4, 1841.

39. *Richmond Enquirer*, July 15, 1841.

40. Charles A. McCoy, *Polk and the Presidency* (Austin: University of Texas Press, 1960), 155.

41. Richardson, *Messages and Papers of the Presidents*, 161.

42. James K. Polk, *The Diary of James K. Polk during His Presidency 1845 to 1849*, vol. 4, ed. Milo M. Ouaefe (Chicago: A. C. McClurg, 1910), 184, 375–376.

43. "Alexander H. Stephens to John J. Crittenden, Feb. 6, 1849," in *The Correspondence of Robert Toombs, Alexander H. Stephens and Howell Cobb, Annual Report of the American Historical Association for the Year 1911*, ed. Ulrich B. Phillips (Washington D.C.: Da Capo Press, 1913), 146.

44. *New York Tribune*, July 10, 1850.

45. Charles F. Faber and Richard B. Faber, *The American Presidents Ranked By Performance* (Jefferson, NC, and London: McFarland, 2000), 104–105.

46. Fillmore to Webster, Oct. 23, 1850, Buffalo Historical Society, Buffalo.

47. Ibid.

48. Ibid.

49. Horatio Bridge, *Personal Recollections of Nathaniel Hawthorne* (New York: Haskell House, 1968), 131; Charles Francis Adams, *Richard Henry Dana, a Biography* (Boston: Houghton Mifflin, 1890), 226.

50. Larry Gara, *The Presidency of Franklin Pierce* (Lawrence: University Press of Kansas, 1991), 47.

51. Richardson, *Messages and Papers of the Presidents V*, 197–203.

52. Gideon Welles, *Diary* (New York: W. W. Norton, 1960), Mar. 11, 1868.

53. Allen Nevins, *Ordeal of the Union, Vol. II* (New York: Scribner, 1944), 41–42.

54. Roy Franklin Nichols, *Franklin Pierce, Young Hickory of the Granite Hills* (Newtown, CT: American Political Biography Press, 1993).

55. Don E. Fehrenbacher, *Slavery, Law and Policies: The Dred Scott Case in Perspective* (New York: Oxford University Press, 1981), 168.

56. Abraham Lincoln, Acceptance Speech for Senate nomination, Dec. 1857. *The Living Words of Abraham Lincoln*, ed. Edward Lewis and Jack Belck (Kansas City, MO: Hallmark Editions, 1967), 44.

57. An Indiana man heard Lincoln say this at the White House. Benjamin P. Thomas, *Abraham Lincoln* (New York: Alfred A. Knopf, 1952).

58. Lincoln, Acceptance Speech.

59. Doris Kearns Goodwin, "My Whole Soul Is in It," *Smithsonian Magazine* 36.10 (2006): 48.

60. Ibid., 56.

61. Ibid., 56.

62. Abraham Lincoln, *Gettysburg Address.* November 19, 1863. *The Living Words of Abraham Lincoln*, 47–48.

63. Carl Sandburg, "The Incomparable Abraham Lincoln," Address to the United States Congress, Feb. 12, 1959.

64. Abraham Lincoln, Letter to a friend. Abraham Lincoln Papers, Library of Congress, Washington, D.C.

65. Ibid.

66. Mark Van Doren.

67. Abraham Lincoln to Secretary of Treasury, Hugh McCullock, Mar. 1865, Andrew Johnson Papers, Library of Congress, Washington, D.C.

68. "Parson" William Gannaway Brownlow to Chief Justice Chase. Mar. 1865. http//en.wikipedia.org.

69. Andrew Johnson, Speech at his Presidential Swearing-In, Apr. 15, 1865. Lately Thomas, *The First President Johnson, The Three Lives of the Seventeenth President of the United States of America* (New York: William Morrow, 1968), 318.

70. *New York Tribune*, June 13, 1868.

71. "Grant and The Israelites," *New York Times*, June 14, 1868. Ph. Van Bort, "General Grant and the Jews"(New York News Company, 1868).

72. *New York Tribune*, July 20, July 21, Aug. 1, and Aug. 27, 1868.

73. William B. Hesseltine, *Ulysses Grant, Politician* (New York: Dodd, Mead and Co., 1935).

74. Venila Lorina Shores, *The Hayes-Conkling Controversy* (Northampton, MA: Smith College Department of History, 1919), 228–231.

75. H. J. Eckenrode, *Rutherford B. Hayes, Statesman of Reunion* (New York: Dodd, Mead, 1930), 343.

76. Ibid., 344.

77. Invented by publicity man William C. Hudson.

78. From a speech by Reverend S. D. Burchard. Fifth Ave Hotel, New York, October 29, 1884. Allan Nevins Grover Cleveland, *A Study in Courage* (New York: Dodd, Mead, 1962) 145, 182, 187–88.

79. Lionel Sachville-West, British minister to the U. S., 1888, Letter of Charles A. Osgoodby to the Library of Congress. Feb. 13, 1931. Nevins, 429.

80. Cleveland's message to Congress, Dec. 1885. Nevins, 266–269.

81. Grover Cleveland Papers, Library of Congress, Washington, D.C.

82. Benjamin Harrison Papers, Collection of Benjamin Harrison Walker (privately held), Benjamin Harrison Home, Indianapolis; Benjamin Harrison, *This Country of Ours* (New York: Scribner's, 1887); Michael Medved, *The Shadow Presidents* (New York: Times Books, 1979), 88–91.

83. *New York Tribune*, May 1, 1889. Caroline Scott Harrison, "Diary," Apr. 30, 1889, Benjamin Harrison Papers, Collection of Benjamin Harrison (privately held), Benjamin Harrison Home, Indianapolis. Harry J. Sievers, *Benjamin Harrison, Hoosier Warrior*, Vol. 3 (New York: University Publishers, 1960), 75.

84. Sievers, *Benjamin Harrison,* Vol. 3, 117–128; Donald L. McMurry, "The Bureau of Pensions during the Administration of President Harrison," *Mississippi Valley Historical Review* 13(1926): 343–364; Benjamin Harrison to George F. Hoar, Sep. 12 and 23, 1889, George F. Hoar Papers, Massachusetts Historical Society, Boston; Richardson, *Messages and Papers of the Presidents IX*, 49–50.

85. Richardson, *Messages and Papers of the Presidents IX*, 49–50; Edward McPherson 1890, 125–127; Theda Skocpol, *Protecting Soldiers and Mothers* (Cambridge, MA: Harvard University Press, 1992), 128; Ben J. Wattenberg, ed., *The Statistical History of the United States: From Colonial Times to the Present* (New York: Basic Books, 1976), 1104, 1146.

86. *Speeches and Addresses of William McKinley* (New York: Doubleday and McClure, 1900), 2–15.

87. *New York Tribune*, Mar. 6 and 9, 1897; *Washington Post*, Mar. 6 and 9, 1897; *Chicago Evening Post*, Mar. 5, 1897.

88. *Washington Post*, 338; De Alva Stanwood Alexander, *History and Procedures of the House of Representatives* (New York: B. Franklin, 1970), 359.

89. Shelby M. Cullom, *Fifty Years of Public Service: Personal Recollections* (New York: Da Capo Press, 1969), 275–276; George F. Hoar, *Autobiography of Seventy Years* (New York: Scribner's, 1906), 46–47; Charles Sumner Olcott, *William McKinley*

(Boston and New York: Houghton Mifflin, 1916), 346; Leon Burr Richardson, *William E. Chandler, Republican* (New York: Dodd, Mead, 1940), 542.

90. Olcott, *William McKinley*. John D. Long, "Characteristics of President McKinley," *The Century Magazine* 63 (Nov. 1901): 144–146. John D. Long, *The New American Navy, Vol. 2* (New York: Oullook, 1903), 142ff 8.

91. N. B. Scott to A. B. White, March 1, 1897 White papers.

92. Woodrow Wilson, *Congressional Government* (New York: Houghton Mifflin. 1885). John Morton Blum, *The Progressive Presidents* (New York, London: W.W. Norton, 1980), 15.

93. Theodore Roosevelt, Ibid. 16.

94. Theodore Roosevelt to Henry Cabot Lodge. *The Letters of Theodore Roosevelt*, ed. E.E. Morrison. (Cambridge, MA: Harvard University Press, 1951–1954).

95. Theodore Roosevelt, *An Autobiography* (New York: Scribner's, 1920).

96. Theodore Roosevelt to an English friend (1908). Blum, 58.

97. William Howard Taft, in a speech at Bath, Maine, Sept. 5, 1906.

98. William Howard Taft, to various friends on various occasions.

99. William Howard Taft, in a speech at the Merchant's Association, Boston, Dec. 1907.

100. William Howard Taft, in an interview with Senator Murray Crane of Massachusetts, 1908.

101. After Taft's address on Memorial Day at Grant's Tomb.

102. Woodrow Wilson, to a friend early in his administration.

103. *New Republic* (1919). Blum, 67.

104. Blum, 69.

105. Harry Daugherty to Harding (Jan. 1919). Harding Papers, Ohio Historical Society, Columbus.

106. Ibid.

107. Daugherty denied that Secretary of the Interior Albert B. Fall had ever shouted any such remarks, although admitted that Fall had opposed the injunction in a vicious and pronounced way. Francis Russell, *The Shadow of Blooming Grove, Warren G. Harding in His Times* (New York and Toronto, McGraw-Hill, 1968), 547.

108. Ibid., 549.

109. Ibid., 637.

110. Harding to Charles Forbes in person in the White House.

111. Herbert Hoover, *The Memoirs of Herbert Hoover* (New York: Macmillan, 1952).

112. Calvin Coolidge, statement as governor of Massachusetts during the Boston police strike.

113. Calvin Coolidge, speech before the American Society Editors entitled "The Press Under a Free Government," Jan. 17, 1925. Peter Hannaford, *The Quotable Calvin Coolidge* (2001), 42. http www.whitehouse.gov/history/presidents/cc30html.

114. Claude M. Fuess, *Calvin Coolidge, The Man from Vermont* (1940), 383–384. http/www.whitehouse.gov/history/presidential/cc30html.

115. William Allen White, *A Puritan in Babylon: The Story of Calvin Coolidge* (New York: Capricorn Books, 1938).

116. David C. Whitney and Robin Vaughn Whitney, *The American Presidents* (Pleasantville, NY, and Montreal: Reader's Digest Association, 1996), 255.

117. Ibid.

118. Coolidge, "Government and Business."

119. Ibid.

120. Ibid.

121. William Allen White, *Colliers Weekly*.

122. Ibid.

123. Oswald Garrison Villard, "Calvin Coolidge Made by a Myth," *Nation*, Aug. 1, 1923.

124. Calvin Coolidge, "Credo," 1924. http/www.bookrags.com/biography/John-Calvin Coolidge.

125. Herbert Hoover, New Year's statement on January 1, 1926. War Library at Stanford University, Stanford, California.

126. William Allen White to David Henshaw, Dec. 1929. White Papers, Wichita State University, Wichita.

127. Richard Norton Smith, *An Uncommon Man; The Triumph of Herbert Hoover*. (New York: Simon & Schuster, 1984).

128. Ibid.

129. Ibid.

130. Ibid.

131. Earl Reeves, *This Man Hoover* (New York: A. L. Burt, 1928).

132. E. M. Sait, *American Parties and Elections* (New York and London: Century, 1927).

133. *Christian Science Monitor.*

134. Papers of Arch Shaw, Birch Tree, Missouri.

135. David Hinshaw, *Century Magazine*, 1930.

136. Ibid.

137. Franklin D. Roosevelt inaugural address, Mar. 4, 1933.

138. Ibid.; Campaign speech in 1936.

139. Margaret Truman, *Harry S. Truman* (New York: William Morrow, 1973), 351.

140. "Harry Truman, 33rd President, is dead: served in time of First A bomb, Marshall Plan, Nato and Korea," *The New York Times*, Dec. 27, 1972.

141. Harry Truman, *The New York Times*, Oct. 7, 1952.

142. Harry Truman, radio address to the nation, Apr. 8, 1952.

143. Harry Truman, radio address to the nation, quoted in Robert J. Dohovan, *Tumultuous Years: The Presidency of Harry S. Truman, 1949–1953* (New York: W. W. Norton, 1982), 156.

144. Ibid., 416. January 31, 1950.

145. Ibid., 416. Mimeographed handout (January 31, 1950).

146. Message to Congress, Sep. 6, 1945, in ibid., 286.

147. Civil rights message to Congress, Feb. 2, 1948, in ibid., 391–393.

148. "News Conference at Key West," March 30, 1950, Harry Truman Library & Museum, Independence, MO. Arthur M. Schlesinger Jr. and Roger Bruns, "Public Papers of the Presidents of the United States," in *Congress Investigates: A Documented History, 1792–1974* (New York: Chelsea House, 1983), 31–38, 80–83.

149. Arthur Krock, *New York Times*, Feb. 1950.

150. Truman, press conference on Mar. 30, 1950, quoted in Dohovan, *Tumultuous Years*, 429.

151. "News Conference at Key West"; Schlesinger, 31–38, 80–83.

152. Letter to Owen Lattimore's sister, quoted in ibid., 170.

153. Joseph McCarthy speech on the Senate floor, Feb. 1950; David McCullough, *Truman* (New York: Simon & Schuster, 1992).

154. "News Conference at Key West"; Schlesinger, 31–38, 80–83.

155. Ibid.

156. McCarthy speech, Feb. 1950.

157. Ibid.

158. Robert F. Burk, *Dwight Eisenhower, Hero and Politician* (Boston: Twayne Publishers, 1986).

159. Ibid.

160. Speechwriter overheard Eisenhower and McCarthy, October 2, 1952. Geoffrey Perret, *Eisenhower* (New York: Random House, 1999), 417.

161. Earl Warren, Supreme Court, 1954. The National Center for Policy Research, Washington D.C.

162. Ibid., 552, 657. Cable, Woodrow Wilson, Mann to Dwight David Eisenhower, Sept. 24, 1957.

163. John F. Kennedy, inaugural address, Washington, D.C., Jan. 20, 1961.

164. James Baldwin, *The New Yorker*, 1962.

165. Richard Reeves, *President Kennedy, Profile of Power* (New York: 1993).

166. White House Acting Press Secretary Malcolm Kildoff, http/www.arlington cemetary.net/mmkildoff,nhtm.

167. *Presidential Countdown: Mr. Kennedy: A Profile*, first broadcast 19 September 1960 by CBS.

168. "Physical Fitness: A Report of Progress," *Look Magazine*, Aug. 13, 1963.

169. To have been delivered at Dallas, TX, Nov. 22, 1963.

170. Tacoma, WA, Sep. 27, 1963.

171. Jefferson-Jackson Day Brunch, Middletown, OH, Oct. 17, 1960.

172. State of the Union Address to Congress, Washington, D.C., Jan. 14, 1963.

173. Great Falls, MT, Sep. 26, 1963.

174. Message to Congress, Washington, D.C., Mar. 1, 1962.

175. Television-Radio debate, Chicago, IL, Sep. 26, 1960.

176. Washington, D.C., June 22, 1962.

177. State of the Union Address to Congress, Washington, D.C., Jan. 11, 1962.

178. *After Two Years: A Conversation with the President*, first broadcast 22 October 1963 in Washington, D.C.

179. National Academy of Sciences, Washington, D.C., Oct. 22, 1963.

180. Television-Radio debate, Chicago, IL, Sep. 26, 1960.

181. Inauguration, Washington, D.C., Jan. 20, 1961.

182. Ibid.

183. Inaugural anniversary dinner, Washington, D.C., Jan. 20, 1962.

184. "John F. Kennedy 'Tells Youth How to Prepare for the Presidency,'" *Parade Magazine*, Sept. 23, 1962.

185. Dublin, Ireland, June 28, 1963.

186. "Our Commitment to Future Generations," *Country Beautiful Magazine*, Feb.–Mar. 1964.

187. Pinchot Institute for Conservation Studies, Milford, PA, Sep. 24, 1963.

188. Stewart L. Udall, "Introduction," in *The Quiet Crisis* (New York: Holt, Rinehart and Winston, 1963).

189. Ibid.

190. Pinchot Institute for Conservation Studies, Milford, PA, Sep. 24, 1963.

191. Tacoma, WA, Sept. 27, 1963.

192. Ibid.

193. State of the Union Address to Congress, Washington, D.C., Jan. 14, 1963.

194. Emancipation Day message, Washington, D.C., Sep. 22, 1962.

195. Washington, D.C., July 1963.

196. Television program, *Robert Frost: American Poet* (CBS), Feb. 26, 1961.

197. Opening of the new USIA transmitter complex at Greenville, NC, Feb. 8, 1963.

198. Blum, 168.

199. Ibid., 168, Summer, 1963.

200. Ibid., 168, Summer, 1963

201. Ibid., 172.

202. Ibid., Speech to Congress, Aug. 1965, Millet Center of Public Affairs, University of Virginia, Charlottesville.

203. Ibid.

204. Robert Dallek, *Lyndon B. Johnson, Portrait of a President* (New York: Oxford University Press, 2004).

205. Richard Milhous Nixon, *The Memoirs of Richard Nixon* (New York: Grosset and Dunlap, 1978), 337.

206. Ibid., 355.

207. Ibid., 341.

208. Ibid., 342.

209. Ibid., 342.

210. Stephen Hess, *First Impression: Presidents, Appointment and The Transition* (Washington D.C.: Brookings Press, 2000).

211. William Safire, *Before the Fall: An Inside View of the Pre–Watergate White House* (Garden City, NY: Doubleday, 1975), 108.

212. Nixon, *Memoirs*, 339.

213. Ibid.

214. Ibid.

215. www.whitehouse.gov/history/presidents/gf 38.html.

216. Jerald F. TerHorst, *Gerald Ford and the Future of the Presidency* (New York: Third Press, 1974). Ford misread the actual pardon period covered in the formal proclamation, saying, July 20, 1969, when he should have said January 20, 1969. Ibid., 231.

217. Ibid., 232.

218. Kenneth Quinn, "Ford's Best Legacy? Successful Indochinese Refugees," *Des Moines Register*, Jan. 8, 2007, p. 9A.

219. http://www.whitehouse.gov/ford.

220. Ibid.

221. Ibid.

222. James Pritched and James Woodward, "Going Home, Colleagues, Country Salutes Late Leader as Best of America," *The Des Moines Register*, Jan. 3, 2007, 1.

223. http://www.whitehouse.gov/ford.

224. Ibid.

225. James B. Simpson, *Simpson's Quotations* (Boston: Houghton Mifflin, 1988).

226. Ronald Reagan, *Ronald Reagan: An American Life* (New York: Pocket Books, 1990), 532.

227. Ronald Reagan Presidential Library, National Archives and Records Administration, Simi Valley, California.

228. Ibid., 532.

229. Dinesh D'Souza, *Ronald Reagan: How an Ordinary Man Became an Extraordinary Leader* (New York: Touchstone, 1999), 25–28.

230. Peter J. Wallison, *Ronald Reagan: The Power of Conviction and the Success of His Presidency* (Boulder, CO: Westview Press, 2003), 6.

231. Richard E. Neustadt, *Presidential Power and the Modern Presidents* (New York: Free Press, 1990).

232. Lou Cannon, *Ronald Reagan: The Role of a Lifetime* (New York: Public Affairs, 2000), 82.

233. Wallison, *Ronald Reagan*, 16.

234. Peggy Noonan, *When Character Was King: A Story of Ronald Reagan* (New York: Viking, 2001), 317.

235. George Bush Presidential Library, College Station, Texas.

236. Ibid.

237. Ibid.

238. Interview with George Bush, Mar. 7, 1996; *Congress and the Nation, Vol. 8* (Washington, D.C.: Congressional Quarterly Service), 743–752; Daniel Mitchell, Jr., "Bush's Rasputin," *National Review* (Dec. 28, 1992): 31; Michael Duffy and Dan Goodgame, *Marching in Place: The Status Quo Presidency of George Bush* (New York: Simon & Schuster, 1992), 79.

239. *Congress and the Nation, Vol. 8*, 780.

240. John F. Harris, *The Survivor: Bill Clinton in the White House* (New York: Random House, 2005), 263.

241. "Language: A Key Mechanism of Control," Go PAC: Newt Gingrich's political action committee.

2421. David Frum, *The Right Man: The Surprise Presidency of George W. Bush* (New York: Random House, 2003), 283–284.

243. Ibid., 284.

244. Ibid., 284.

245. "Bush budget favors tax cuts, security," *The Des Moines Register*, Feb. 6, 2006.

246. Cal Thomas, "Spending obscenities continue," *The Des Moines Register*, Mar. 21, 2006.

247. "War's High Price," *The Des Moines Register*, Jan. 24, 2006.

248. Seth Borenstein, "Fired FEMA Director says he was scapegoat," *The Des Moines Register*, Feb. 11, 2006.

249. Drew Brown, "UN report urges closure of Guantonamo Bay prison," *The Des Moines Register*, Feb. 17, 2006.

250. "A clear signal for Bush Congress must be consulted prior to use of secret wiretaps," *The Des Moines Register*, Feb. 9, 2006.

251. Pete Yost, "Many Gore Office E-Mails Not Stored," *The Des Moines Register*, Apr. 18, 2001.

Bibliography

Adams, Charles Francis. *Richard Henry Dana: A Biography*. Boston: Houghton, Mifflin, 1890.

Adams, Henry. *History of the United States of America during the Administration of Thomas Jefferson*. New York: McGraw-Hill, 1971.

Adams, John Quincy. *The Lives of James Madison and James Monroe*. Boston: Phillips, Sampson, 1850.

_____. *Memoirs of John Quincy Adams, Vol. IV*. New York: Praeger, 1970.

Adams, J. Q. "To Abigail and John Adams," St. Petersburg (June 30, 1811) Adams Papers, private collection.

After Two Years: A Conversation with the President, first broadcast 22 October 1963 in Washington, D.C.

Ammon, Harry. *James Monroe: The Quest for Identity*. New York: McGraw-Hill, 1971.

Baker, Jean H. *James Buchanan*. New York: Henry Holt, 2004.

Bassett, John Spencer, and David Maydole Matteson. *Correspondence of Andrew Jackson, Vol. V*. Washington, D.C.: Carnegie Institution of Washington, 1935.

Bemis, Samuel Flagg. *John Quincy Adams and the Union*. New York: Alfred A. Knopf, 1956.

Bernstein, R. B. *Thomas Jefferson*. New York: Oxford University Press, 2003.

Blum, John Morton. *The Progressive Presidents, Roosevelt, Wilson, Roosevelt, Johnson*. New York: W. W. Norton, 1980.

Blumberg, Rhoda. *What's the Deal? Jefferson, Napoleon, and the Louisiana Purchase*. Washington, D.C.: National Geographic Society, 1998.

Boorstin, Daniel J. *The Landmark History of the American People: Volume 1: From Plymouth to Appomattox*. New York: Random House, 1987.

Bourne, Peter G. *Jimmy Carter: A Comprehensive Biography from Plains to Post Presidency*. New York: Lisa Drew Books/Scribner, 1997.

Brandt, Irving. *The Fourth President: A Life of James Madison*. Indianapolis: Bobbs Merrill, 1930.

Bridge, Horatio. *Personal Recollections of Nathaniel Hawthorne*. New York: Haskell House, 1968.

Brinkley, Douglas. *The Unfinished Presidency: Jimmy Carter's Journey Beyond the White House*. New York and London: Viking Press, 1998.

Brownlow, "Parson" William Gannaway. *Parson to Chief Justice Chase* (Mar. 1865 letter). http//en.wikipedia. org.

Burk, Robert F. *Dwight D. Eisenhower, Hero and Politician*. Boston: Twayne Publishers, 1986.

Burns, James MacGregor, and Susan Dunn. *George Washington*. New York: Henry Holt, LLC, 2004.

Cannon, Lou. *Ronald Reagan: The Role*

of a Lifetime. New York: Public Affairs, 2000.

Carter, Jimmy. *Sharing Good Times*. New York and London: Simon and Schuster, 2004.

Chambers, William Nesbet. *Political Parties in a New Nation: The American Experience, 1776–1809*. New York: Oxford University Press, 1963.

Chidsey, Donald Barr. *Lewis and Clark: The Great Adventure*. New York: Crown Publishers, 1970.

Chitwood, Oliver Perry. *John Tyler, Champion of the Old South*. New York: Russell & Russell, 1964.

Clinton, Bill. *My Life*. New York and Toronto: Alfred A. Knopf, 2004.

Cresson, W. P. *James Monroe*. Chapel Hill: University of North Carolina Press, 1946.

Cullom, Shelby M. *Fifty Years of Public Service: Personal Recollections*. New York: Da Capo Press, 1969.

Dallek, Robert. *Lyndon B. Johnson: Portrait of a President*. New York: Oxford University Press, 2004.

Davis, Burke. *Old Hickory: A Life of Andrew Jackson*. New York: Dial Press, 1977.

Diggins, John Patrick. *John Adams*. New York: Henry Holt, 2003.

Dohovan, Robert J. *Tumultuous Years: The Presidency of Harry S. Truman, 1949–1953*. New York: W. W. Norton, 1982.

Donald, David Herbert. *Lincoln*. New York: Simon and Schuster, 1995.

D'Souza, Dinesh. *Ronald Reagan: How an Ordinary Man Became an Extraordinary Leader*. New York: Touchstone, 1999.

Duffy, Herbert S. *William Howard Taft*. Minton, Batch, 1930.

Duffy, Michael, and Dan Goodgame. *Marching in Place: The Status Quo Presidency of George Bush*. New York: Simon & Schuster, 1992.

Eckenrode, H. J. *Rutherford B. Hayes, Statesman of Reunion*. New York: Dodd, Mead, 1930.

Edwards, Lee. *Ronald Reagan: A Political Biography*. Houston: Nordland Publishing International, 1981.

Ellis, Joseph J. *Passionate Sage: The Character and Legacy of John Adams*. New York and London: W. W. Norton, 1993.

Eriksson, Eric M. "The Federal Civil Service under President Jackson." *Mississippi Valley Historical Review* XIII (1927): 529–530.

Faber, Charles F., and Richard B. Faber. *The American Presidents Ranked by Performance*. Jefferson, NC, and London: McFarland, 2000.

Fehrenbacher, Don E. *Slavery, Law and Policies: The Dred Scott Case in Perspective*. New York: Oxford University Press, 1981.

Ferling, John E. *The First of Men: A Life of George Washington*. Knoxville: University of Tennessee Press, 1988.

Fillmore to Webster. Buffalo, NY: Buffalo Historical Society (Oct. 23, 1850).

Flexner, James Thomas. *George Washington and the New Nation (1783–1793)*. Boston and Toronto: Little, Brown, 1969.

Ford, Paul Leicester, ed. *The Writings of Thomas Jefferson, Vol. 8*. New York: Putnam's, 1892.

Fritz, Jean. *The Great Little Madison*. New York: Putnam's, 1989.

Frost, Robert. *A Talk for Students*. New York: Fund for the Republic Publications, 1956.

Frum, David. *The Right Man: Surprise Presidency of George W. Bush*. New York: Random House, 2003.

Gara, Larry. *The Presidency of Franklin Pierce. American Presidency Series*. Lawrence: University Press of Kansas, 1963.

Goodwin, Doris Kearns. "My Whole Soul Is in It." *Smithsonian Magazine* 36.10 (2006): 48–55.

Greeley, Horace. *The American Conflict*. Greenwood, CT: Greenwood Press, 1969.

Harris, John F. *The Survivor: Bill Clinton in the White House*. New York: Random House, 2005.

Harrison, Benjamin. *This Country of Ours.* New York: Scribner's, 1887.

Hecht, Marie. *John Quincy Adams: A Personal History of an Independent Man.* New York: Macmillan, 1972.

Hess, Stephen. *First Impression: Presidents, Appointment and the Transition.* Washington, D.C.: Brookings Press, 2000.

Hesseltine, William B. *Ulysses S. Grant, Politician.* New York: Dodd, Mead, 1935.

Hoar, George F. *Autobiography of Seventy Years.* New York: Scribner's, 1906.

Hoover, Herbert. *The Memoirs of Herbert Hoover.* New York: Macmillan, 1952.

Hoyt, Edwin D. *James Buchanan.* Chicago: Reilly & Lee, 1966.

Ide, Arthur Frederick. *The Father's Son: George W. Bush, Jr.* Las Colinas, TX: Sepore, 1998.

James, Marquis. *Andrew Jackson: Portrait of a President.* Indianapolis and New York: Bobbs-Merrill, 1937.

Jeffers, H. Paul. *An Honest President: The Life and Presidencies of Glover Cleveland.* New York: Morrow, 2000.

Jenkins, Roy. *Franklin Delano Roosevelt.* New York: Henry Holt, 2003.

"John F. Kennedy 'Tells Youth How to Prepare for the Presidency.'" *Parade Magazine* (Sept. 23, 1962).

Kessel, John H. *The Domestic Presidency: Decision-making in the White House.* North Scituate, MA: Danbury Press, 1975.

"Lawrence Van Buren to Blair, Oct. 23, 1862," Blair-Lee Papers, Princeton University, Princeton, CA.

Leech, Margaret. *In the Days of McKinley.* New York: Harper, 1959.

"Lewis F. Linn to Van Buren, 1836," Van Buren Letters, Library of Congress, Washington, D.C.

Long, John D. "Characteristics of President McKinley." *The Century Magazine* 63 (Nov. 1901): 144–146.

_____. *The New American Navy, Vol. 2.* New York: Oullook, 1903.

Lorant, Stefan. *The Life and Times of Theodore Roosevelt.* Garden City, NY: Doubleday, 1964.

Lyons, Eugene. *Herbert Hoover: A Biography.* Garden City, NY: Doubleday, 1964.

Malone, Dumas. *Jefferson and His Time: Jefferson the President: First Term 1801–1805.* Boston: Little, Brown, 1970.

Mansfield, Stephen. *The Faith of George W. Bush.* New York: Tarchex/Penguin, 2003.

Mapp, Alf J., Jr. *Thomas Jefferson: Passionate Pilgrim.* Lanham, MD: Madison Books, 1981.

Marquis, James. *Andrew Jackson: Portrait of a President.* Indianapolis and New York: Bobbs-Merrill, 1937.

McCoy, Charles A. *Polk and the Presidency.* Austin: University of Texas Press, 1960.

McCullough, David. *Truman.* New York: Simon and Schuster, 1992.

McDonald, Forrest. *The American Presidency: An Intellectual History.* Lawrence: University Press of Kansas, 1994.

McElroy, Robert. *Grover Cleveland, the Man and the Statesman: An Authorized Biography.* 2 vol. New York: Harper & Brothers, 1923.

McMurry, Donald L. "The Bureau of Pensions during the Administration of President Harrison." *Mississippi Valley Historical Review* 13 (1926).

Medved, Michael. *The Shadow Presidents.* New York: Times Books, 1979.

Mee, Charles L., Jr. *The Ohio Gang: The World of Warren G. Harding.* New York: Henry Holt, 1983.

Meltzer, Milton. *Andrew Jackson and His America.* New York, London, and Toronto: Franklin Watts, 1993.

Mitchell, Daniel, Jr. "Bush's Rasputin." *National Review* (Dec. 28, 1992): 31.

Morgan, H. Wayne. *William McKinley and His America.* Syracuse: Syracuse University Press, 1963.

Morris, Edmund. *Theodore Rex.* New York: The Modern Library, 2001.

Morrison, E.E., ed. *The Letters of Theodore Roosevelt.* Cambridge, MA: Harvard University Press, 1951–1954.

Myers, Elisabeth P. *Benjamin Harrison.* Chicago: Reilly & Lee, 1969.

Neustadt, Richard E. *Presidential Power and the Modern Presidents.* New York: Free Press, 1990.

Nevins, Allan, ed. *The Diary of Philip Hone, 1828–1851, 2 Vols.* New York: Dodd, Mead, 1927.

_____. *Ordeal of the Union, Vol. II.* New York: Scribner's, 1944.

Nichols, Roy Franklin. *Franklin Pierce: Young Hickory of the Granite Hill.* Newtown, CT: American Biography Press, 1993.

Niven, John. *Martin Van Buren: The Romantic Age in American Politics.* New York: Oxford University Press, 1983.

Nixon, Richard Milhous. *The Memoirs of Richard Nixon.* New York: Grosset and Dunlap, 1978.

Noonan, Peggy. *When Character Was King: A Story of Ronald Reagan.* New York: Viking, 2001.

Nordham, George W. *The Age of Washington: George Washington's Presidency 1789–1797.* Chicago: Adams Press, 1989.

Olcott, Charles Sumner. *William McKinley.* Boston and New York: Houghton Mifflin, 1916.

Old, Wendie C. *Thomas Jefferson.* Springfield, NJ, and Aldershot, UK: Enslow Publishers, 1997.

Onuf, Peter S. *Jefferson's Empire: The Language of American Nationhood.* Charlottesville: University Press of Virginia, 2000.

"Our Commitment to Future Generations," *Country Beautiful Magazine,* Feb.-Mar. 1964.

Parmet, Herbert S. *George Bush: The Life of a Lone Star Yankee.* Scribner's, 1997.

Parton, John. *Life of Andrew Jackson,* 3 vols. New York: Mason Brothers, 1859–1860.

Perret, Geoffrey. *Jack: A Life Like No Other.* New York and Toronto: Random House, 2001.

Phelan, Mary Kay. *The Story of the Louisiana Purchase.* New York: Thomas Y. Crowell, 1979.

Phillips, Ulrich B., ed. *The Correspondence of Robert Toombs, Alexander H. Stephens and Howell Cobb, Annual Report of the American Historical Association for the Year 1911.* Washington D.C.: Da Capo Press, 1913.

Polk, James K., and Milo M. Ouaefe, ed. *The Dairy of James K. Polk during His Presidency, 1845 to 1849, Vol. 4.* Chicago: A. C. McClurg, 1910.

Presidential Countdown: Mr. Kennedy: A Profile, first broadcast 19 September 1960 by CBS.

Quinn, Kenneth. "Ford's Best Legacy? Successful Indochinese Refugees." *Des Moines Register,* Jan. 8, 2007, p. 9A.

Randolf, Sallis G. *Gerald R. Ford, President.* New York: Walker Publishing, 1987.

Rayback, Robert J. *Millard Fillmore.* Buffalo: Buffalo Historical Society, 1959.

Reagan, Ronald. *Ronald Reagan: An American Life.* New York: Pocket Books, 1990.

Reeves, Earl. *This Man Hoover.* New York: A. L. Burt, 1928.

Reeves, Richard. *President Nixon, Alone in the White House.* New York, London, Toronto, Sydney, and Singapore: Simon and Schuster, 2001.

Remini, Robert V. *John Quincy Adams.* New York: Henry Holt, 2002.

Richardson, James D. *Messages and Papers of the Presidents IV.* Washington, D.C.: Bureau of National Literature & Art, 1903.

Richardson, Leon Burr. *William E. Chandler, Republican.* New York: Dodd, Mead, 1940.

Robert Frost: American Poet, first broadcast 26 February 1961 by CBS.

Roosevelt, Theodore. *An Autobiography.* New York: Scribner's, 1920.

Rosenberger, Francis Coleman, ed. *Jefferson Reader: A Treasury of Writings about Thomas Jefferson.* New York: Dutton, 1953.

Russell, Francis. *The Shadow of Blooming Grove: Warren G. Harding in His Times.* New York: McGraw-Hill, 1968.

Rutland, Robert Allen. *James Madison: The Founding Father*. New York and London: Collier Macmillan, 1987.

Safire, William. *Before the Fall: An Inside View of the Pre-Watergate White House*. Garden City, NY: Doubleday, 1975.

Sait, E. M. *American Parties and Elections*. New York and London: Century, 1927.

Schlesinger, Arthur M., Jr. *The Age of Roosevelt: Vol. 2: The Coming of the New Deal*. Boston: Houghton Mifflin, 1959.

_____. *The Age of Roosevelt: Vol. 3: The Politics of Upheaval*. Boston: Houghton Mifflin, 1960.

_____, and Roger Bruns. *Congress Investigates: A Documented History, 1792–1974*. New York: Chelsea House Publishers, 1983.

Schuman, Michael A. *Harry S. Truman*. Springfield, NJ, and Aldershot, UK: Enslow Publishers, 1997.

Seager, Robert II. *And Tyler Too: A Biography of John and Julia Gardner Tyler*. New York: McGraw-Hill, 1963.

Shores, Venila Lorina. *The Hayes-Conkling Controversy*. Northampton, MA: Smith College Department of History, 1919.

Sidey, Hugh. *A Very Personal Presidency: Lyndon Johnson in the White House*. New York: Atheneum, 1968.

Sievers, Harry J., S.J. *Benjamin Harrison, Hoosier Warrior*. New York: University Publishers, 1960.

Simpson, James B. *Simpson's Quotations*. Boston: Houghton Mifflin, 1988.

Skocpol, Theda. *Protecting Soldiers and Mothers*. Cambridge, MA: Harvard University Press, 1992.

Slaughter, Thomas P. *Exploring Lewis and Clark: Reflections on Men and Wilderness*. New York and Toronto: Alfred A. Knopf, 2003.

Smith, Elbert B. *The Presidencies of Zachary Taylor and Millard Fillmore. The American Presidency Series*. Lawrence: The University Press of Kansas, 1988.

Smith, Page. *John Adams*. 2 Vols. Garden City, NY: Doubleday, 1962.

Smith, Richard Norton. *An Uncommon Man: The Triumph of Herbert Hoover*. New York: Simon and Schuster, 1984.

Sobel, Robert. *Coolidge: An American Enigma*. Washington, D.C.: Regnery, 1998.

Speeches and Addresses of William McKinley. New York: Doubleday and McClure, 1900.

Steinberg, Alfred. *John Adams*. New York: Putnam's, 1968.

TerHorst, Jerald F. *Gerald Ford and the Future of the Presidency*. New York: Third Press, 1974.

Thomas, Benjamin P. *Abraham Lincoln*. New York: Alfred A. Knopf, 1952.

Thomas, Lately. *The First President Johnson: The Three Lives of Andrew Johnson, the Seventeenth President of the United States of America*. New York: Morrow, 1968.

Truman, Margaret. *Harry S. Truman*. New York: William Morrow, 1973.

Tubbs, Stephanie Ambrose. *The Lewis and Clark Companion: An Encyclopedic Guide to the Voyage of Discovery*. New York: Henry Holt, 2003.

Tugwell, Rexford Guy. *Grover Cleveland*. New York: Macmillan, 1968.

Turner, Erin H. *It Happened on the Lewis and Clark Expedition*. New York: Twodot, 2003.

Udall, Stewart L. *The Quiet Crisis*. New York: Holt, Rinehart and Winston, 1963.

Villard, Oswald Garrison. "Calvin Coolidge Made by a Myth." *Nation*, Aug. 1, 1923.

Wallison, Peter J. *Ronald Reagan: The Power of Conservation and the Success of His Presidency*. Boulder, CO: Westview Press, 2003.

Wattenberg, Ben J., ed. *The Statistical History of the United States: From Colonial Times to the Present*. New York: Basic Books, 1976.

Welch, Richard E., Jr. *The Presidencies of Grover Cleveland. American Presidency Series*. Lawrence: The University Press of Kansas, 1988.

Welles, Gideon. *Diary*. New York: W. W. Norton, 1960.

Whitney, David C., and Robin Vaughn Whitney. *The American Presidents*. Pleasantville, NY, and Montreal: Reader's Digest Association 1996.

Wicker, Tom. *Dwight D. Eisenhower*. New York: Henry Holt, 2002.

_____. *George Herbert Walker Bush*. New York and London: Penguin Group, 2004.

Wilson, Woodrow. *Congressional Government*. New York: Houghton Mifflin, 1885.

Wood, James Playsted, and the editors of *Country Beautiful Magazine*. *The Life and Words of John F. Kennedy*. Elm Grove, WI: Country Beautiful Foundation, 1964.

Yost, Pete. "Many Gore Office E-Mails Not Stored." *The Des Moines Register*, Apr. 18, 2001.

Periodicals

Century Magazine
Christian Science Monitor
Colliers Weekly
The Des Moines Register
Madisonian
National Intelligencer
New Republic
New York Evening Post
The New York Times
New York Tribune
Richmond Enquirer
Washington Post

Index